INTRODUCING ANOVA
AND ANCOVA

ISM   Introducing Statistical Methods

Other titles in this series

INTRODUCING ANOVA AND ANCOVA

A GLM Approach

ANDREW RUTHERFORD

SAGE Publications
Los Angeles • London • New Delhi • Singapore
www.sagepublications.com

First published 2001. Reprinted 2007

SAGE Publications Ltd
1 Oliver's Yard
55 City Road
London EC1Y 1SP

SAGE Publications Inc
2455 Teller Road
Thousand Oaks
California 91320

SAGE Publications India Pvt. Ltd
B 1/I 1 Mohan Cooperative Industrial Area
Mathura Road, New Delhi 110 044
India

SAGE Publications Asia-Pacific Pte Ltd
33 Pekin Street #02-01
Far East Square
Singapore 048763

British Library Cataloguing in Publication Data

A catalogue record for this book is available from the British Library

ISBN-13 978-0-7619-5161-2 (pbk)
ISBN-13 978-0-7619-5160-5 (hbk)

Library of Congress Control Number Available

Typeset by Keytec Typesetting Ltd

To Patricia

CONTENTS

1 AN INTRODUCTION TO GENERAL LINEAR MODELS: REGRESSION, ANALYSIS OF VARIANCE AND ANALYSIS OF COVARIANCE

1.1 Regression, analysis of variance and analysis of covariance

Regression and analysis of variance are probably the most frequently applied of all statistical analyses. Regression and analysis of variance are used extensively in many areas of research, such as psychology, biology, medicine, education, sociology, anthropology, economics, political science, as well as in industry and commerce.

One reason for the frequency of regression and analysis of variance (ANOVA) applications is their suitability for many different types of study design. Although the analysis of data obtained from experiments is the focus of this text, both regression and ANOVA procedures are applicable to experimental, quasi-experimental and non-experimental data. Regression allows examination of the relationships between an unlimited number of predictor variables and a response or dependent variable, and enables values on one variable to be predicted from the values recorded on one or more other variables. Similarly, ANOVA places no restriction on the number of groups or conditions that may be compared, while factorial ANOVA allows examination of the influence of two or more independent variables or factors on a dependent variable. Another reason for the popularity of ANOVA is that it suits most effect conceptions by testing for differences between means.

Although the label analysis of covariance (ANCOVA) has been applied to a number of different statistical operations (Cox & McCullagh, 1982), it is most frequently used to refer to the statistical technique that combines regression and ANOVA. As the combination of these two techniques, ANCOVA calculations are more involved and time consuming than either technique alone. Therefore, it is unsurprising that greater availability of computers and statistical software is associated with an increase in ANCOVA applications. Although Fisher (1932; 1935) originally developed ANCOVA to increase the precision of experimental analysis, to date it is applied most frequently in quasi-experimental research. Unlike experimental research, the topics investigated with quasi-experimental methods are most likely to involve variables that, for practical or ethical reasons, cannot be controlled directly. In these situations, the statistical control provided by ANCOVA has particular value. Nevertheless, in line with Fisher's original conception, many experiments can benefit from the application of ANCOVA.

1.2   A pocket history of regression, ANOVA and ANCOVA

Historically, regression and ANOVA developed in different research areas and addressed different questions. Regression emerged in biology and psychology towards the end of the 19th century, as scientists studied the correlation between people's attributes and characteristics. While studying the height of parents and their adult children, Galton (1886; 1888) noticed that while short parents' children usually were shorter than average, nevertheless, they tended to be taller than their parents. Galton described this phenomenon as "regression to the mean". As well as identifying a basis for predicting the values on one variable from values recorded on another, Galton appreciated that some relationships between variables would be closer than others. However, it was three other scientists, Edgeworth (e.g. 1886), Pearson (e.g. 1896) and Yule (e.g. 1907), applying work carried out about a century earlier by Gauss (or Legendre, see Plackett, 1972), who provided the account of regression in precise mathematical terms. (Also see Stigler, 1986, for a detailed account.)

Publishing under the pseudonym "Student", W.S. Gosset (1908) described the *t*-test to compare the means of two experimental conditions. However, as soon as there are more than two conditions in an experiment, more than one *t*-test is needed to compare all of the conditions and when more than one *t*-test is applied there is an increase in Type 1 error. (A Type 1 error occurs when a true null hypothesis is rejected.) In contrast, ANOVA, conceived and described by Ronald A. Fisher (1924, 1932, 1935) to assist in the analysis of data obtained from agricultural experiments, is able to compare the means of any number of experimental conditions without any increase in Type 1 error. Fisher (1932) also described a form of ANCOVA that provided an approximate adjusted treatment sum of squares, before he described the exact adjusted treatment sum of squares (Fisher, 1935, and see Cox & McCullagh, 1982, for a brief history). In early recognition of his work, the *F*-distribution was named after him by G.W. Snedecor (1934).

In the subsequent years, the techniques of regression and ANOVA were developed and applied in parallel by different groups of researchers investigating different research topics, using different research methodologies. Regression was applied most often to data obtained from correlational or non-experimental research and only regression analysis was regarded as trying to describe and predict dependent variable scores on the basis of a model constructed from the relations between predictor and dependent variables. In contrast, ANOVA was applied to experimental data beyond that obtained from agricultural experiments (Lovie, 1991), but still it was considered as just a way of determining whether the average scores of groups differed significantly. For many areas of psychology, where the interest (and so tradition) is to assess the average effect of different experimental conditions on groups of subjects in terms of a particular dependent variable, ANOVA was the ideal statistical technique. Consequently, separate analysis traditions evolved and encouraged the mistaken belief that regression and ANOVA constituted fundamentally different types of statistical analysis. Although ANCOVA illustrates the compatability of regression and ANOVA, as a combination of two apparently discrete techniques employed by different researchers working on different topics, unsurprisingly, it remains a much less popular method that is frequently misunderstood (Huitema, 1980).

1.3 An outline of general linear models (GLMs)

Computers, initially mainframe but increasingly PCs, have had considerable consequence for statistical analysis, both in terms of conception and implementation. From the 1980s, some of these changes began to filter through to affect the way data is analysed in the behavioural sciences. Indeed currently, descriptions of regression, ANOVA and ANCOVA found in psychology texts are in a state of flux, as alternative characterizations based on the general linear model are presented by more and more authors (e.g. Cohen & Cohen, 1983; Hays, 1994; Judd & McClelland, 1989; Keppel & Zedeck, 1989; Kirk, 1982, 1995; Maxwell & Delaney, 1990; Pedhazur, 1997; Winer, Brown & Michels, 1991).

One advantage afforded by computer based analyses is the easy use of matrix algebra. Matrix algebra offers an elegant and succinct statistical notation. Unfortunately however, human matrix algebra calculations, particularly those involving larger matrices, are not only very hard work, but also tend to be error prone. In contrast, computer implementations of matrix algebra are not only error free, but also computationally efficient. Therefore, most computer based statistical analyses employ matrix algebra calculations, but the program output usually is designed to accord with the expectations set by traditional (scalar algebra–variance partitioning) calculations.

When regression, ANOVA and ANCOVA are expressed in matrix algebra terms, a commonality is evident. Indeed, the same matrix algebra equation is able to summarize all three of these analyses. As regression, ANOVA and ANCOVA can be described in an identical manner, clearly they follow a common pattern. This common pattern is the GLM conception. Unfortunately, the ability of the same matrix algebra equation to describe regression, ANOVA and ANCOVA has resulted in the inaccurate identification of the matrix algebra equation as the GLM. However, just as a particular language provides a means of expressing an idea, so matrix algebra provides only one notation for expressing the GLM.

The GLM conception is that data may be accommodated in terms of a model plus some error, as illustrated below:

$$\text{data} = \text{model} + \text{error}. \tag{1.1}$$

The model in this equation is a representation of our understanding or hypotheses about the data. The error component is an explicit recognition that there are other influences on the data. These influences are presumed to be unique for each subject in each experimental condition and include anything and everything not controlled in the experiment, such as chance fluctuations in behaviour. Moreover, the relative size of the model and error components is used to judge how well the model accommodates the data.

The model part of the GLM equation constitutes our understanding or hypotheses about the data and is expressed in terms of a set of variables recorded, like the data, as part of the study. As will be described, the tradition in data analysis is to use regression, ANOVA and ANCOVA GLMs to express different types of ideas about how data arises.

1.3.1 Regression analysis

Regression analysis attempts to explain data (the dependent variable scores) in terms of a set of independent variables or predictors (the model) and a residual component (error). Typically, a researcher who applies regression is interested in predicting a quantitative dependent variable from one or more quantitative independent variables, and in determining the relative contribution of each independent variable to the prediction: there is interest in what proportion of the variation in the dependent variable can be attributed to variation in the independent variable(s). Regression also may employ categorical (also known as nominal or qualitative) predictors: the use of independent variables such as sex, marital status and type of teaching method is common. Moreover, as regression is the elementary form of GLM, it is possible to construct regression GLMs equivalent to any ANOVA and ANCOVA GLMs by selecting and organizing quantitative variables to act as categorical variables (see Chapter 2). Nevertheless, the convention of referring to these particular quantitative variables as categorical variables will be maintained.

1.3.2 Analysis of variance

ANOVA also can be thought of in terms of a model plus error. Here, the dependent variable scores constitute the data, the experimental conditions constitute the model and the component of the data not accommodated by the model, again, is represented by the error term. Typically, the researcher applying ANOVA is interested in whether the mean dependent variable scores obtained in the experimental conditions differ significantly. This is achieved by determining how much variation in the dependent variable scores is attributable to differences between the scores obtained in the experimental conditions, and comparing this with the error term, which is attributable to variation in the dependent variable scores within each of the experimental conditions: there is interest in what proportion of variation in the dependent variable can be attributed to the manipulation of the experimental variable(s). Although the dependent variable in ANOVA is most likely to be measured on a quantitative scale, the statistical comparison is drawn between the groups of subjects receiving different experimental conditions and is categorical in nature, even when the experimental conditions differ along a quantitative scale. Therefore, ANOVA is a particular type of regression analysis that employs quantitative predictors to act as categorical predictors.

1.3.3 Analysis of covariance

As ANCOVA is the statistical technique that combines regression and ANOVA, it too can be described in terms of a model plus error. As in regression and ANOVA, the dependent variable scores constitute the data, but the model includes not only experimental conditions, but also one or more quantitative predictor variables. These quantitative predictors, known as covariates (also concomitant or control variables), represent sources of variance that are thought to influence the dependent variable, but have not been controlled by the experimental procedures. ANCOVA determines the covariation (correlation) between the covariate(s) and the dependent variable and then removes that variance associated with the covariate(s) from the dependent variable scores, prior to determining whether the differences between the experimental condition (dependent variable score) means are significant. As mentioned, this technique, in which the influence of the experimental conditions remains the major concern, but one or more quantitative variables that predict the dependent variable also are included in the GLM, is labelled ANCOVA most frequently, and in psychology is labelled ANCOVA exclusively (e.g. Cohen & Cohen, 1983; Pedhazur, 1997, cf. Cox & McCullagh, 1982). A very important, but seldom emphasized, aspect of the ANCOVA method is that the relationship between the covariate(s) and the dependent variable, upon which the adjustments depend, is determined empirically from the data.

1.4 The "general" in GLM

The term "general" in GLM simply refers to the ability to accommodate variables that represent both quantitative distinctions that represent continuous measures, as in regression analysis, and categorical distinctions that represent experimental conditions, as in ANOVA. This feature is emphasized in ANCOVA, where variables representing both quantitative and categorical distinctions are employed in the same GLM.

Traditionally, the label *linear modelling* was applied exclusively to regression analyses. However, as regression, ANOVA and ANCOVA are but particular instances of the GLM, it should be no surprise that consideration of the processes involved in applying these techniques reveals any differences to be more apparent than real.

Following Box and Jenkins (1976), McCullagh and Nelder (1989) distinguish

four processes in linear modelling: (1) model selection, (2) parameter estimation, (3) model checking and (4) the prediction of future values. (Box & Jenkins
refer to model identification rather than model selection, but McCullagh &
Nelder resist this terminology, believing it to imply that a correct model can be
known with certainty.) While such a framework is useful heuristically, McCullagh and Nelder acknowledge that in reality these four linear modelling
processes are not so distinct and that the whole, or parts, of the sequence may be
iterated before a model finally is selected and summarized.

Usually, prediction is understood as the forecast of new, or independent,
values with respect to a new data sample using the GLM already selected.
However, McCullagh and Nelder also include Lane and Nelder's (1982) account
of prediction, where it is employed to unify conceptions of ANCOVA and
different types of standardization. Lane and Nelder consider prediction in more
general terms and regard the values fitted by the GLM (graphically, the values
intersected by the GLM line or hyperplane) to be instances of prediction and
part of the GLM summary. As these fitted values are often called predicted
values, the distinction between the types of predicted value is not always
obvious, although there is greater standard error associated with the values
forecast on the basis of a new data sample (e.g. Cohen & Cohen, 1983; Neter,
Wasserman & Kutner, 1990; Pedhazur, 1997).

With the linear modelling process of prediction so defined, the four linear
modelling processes become even more recursive. For example, when selecting
a GLM, usually the aim is to provide a best fit to the data with the least number
of predictor variables (e.g. Draper & Smith, 1998; McCullagh & Nelder, 1989).
However, the model checking process that assesses best fit employs estimates of
parameters (and estimates of error), so the processes of parameter estimation
and prediction must be executed within the process of model checking.

The misconception that this description of general linear modelling refers
only to regression analysis is fostered by the effort invested in the model
selection process with correlational data obtained from non-experimental studies. Usually in non-experimental studies, many variables are recorded and the
aim is to identify the GLM which best predicts the dependent variable. In
principle, the only way to select the best GLM is to examine every possible
combination of predictors. As it takes relatively few potential predictors to
create an extremely large number of possible GLM selections, a number of
predictor variable selection procedures, such as all-possible-regressions, forward
stepping, backward stepping and ridge regression (Draper & Smith, 1998; Neter,
Wasserman & Kutner, 1990) have been developed to reduce the number of
GLMs that need to be considered.

Correlations between predictors, termed *multicollinearity* (but see p. 137,
Pedhazur, 1997; Neter, Wasserman & Kutner, 1990) creates three problems that
affect the processes of GLM selection and parameter estimation. The three
problems are the substantive interpretation of partial coefficients (if calculated
simultaneously, correlated predictors' partial coefficients are reduced), the sampling stability of partial coefficients (different data samples do not provide similar
estimates) and the accuracy of their calculation (Cohen & Cohen, 1983). The

reduction of partial coefficient estimates is due to correlated predictor variables accommodating similar parts of the dependent variable variance. Because correlated predictors share association with the same part of the dependent variable, but partial coefficients reflect only the unique association between predictors and the dependent variable, the shared association is excluded from the estimates of the partial coefficients. Moreover, when a correlated predictor is included in a GLM, all of the dependent variable variance common to the correlated predictors is accommodated by this first correlated predictor, making it appear that the remaining correlated predictors are of little importance.

When multicollinearity exists and there is interest in the contribution to the GLM of sets of predictors or individual predictors, a hierarchical regression analysis can be adopted (Cohen & Cohen, 1983). Essentially, this means that predictors (or sets of predictors) are entered into the GLM cumulatively in a principled order. After each predictor has entered the GLM, the new GLM may be compared with the previous GLM, with any changes attributable to the predictor just included. Although there is similarity between hierarchical regression and forward stepping procedures, they are distinguished by the, often theoretical, principles employed by hierarchical regression to determine the entry order of predictors into the GLM. Hierarchical regression analyses also concord with Nelder's (1977; McCullagh & Nelder, 1989) approach to ANOVA and ANCOVA, which attributes variance to factors in an ordered manner, accommodating the marginality of factors and their interactions (also see Bingham & Fienberg, 1982).

After selection, parameters must be estimated for each GLM and then model checking engaged. Again, due to the nature of non-experimental data, model checking is likely to detect more problems, which will require remedial measures. Finally, the nature of the issues addressed by non-experimental research make it much more likely that the GLMs selected will be used to forecast new values.

In contrast, a seemingly concise analysis of experimental data occurs. However, consideration reveals identical GLM processes underlying a typical analysis of experimental data. For experimental data, the GLM selected is an expression of the experimental design. Moreover, most experiments are designed so that the independent variables translate into independent (i.e. uncorrelated) predictors, so avoiding multicollinearity problems. The model checking process continues by assessing the predictive utility of the GLM components representing the experimental effects. Each significance test of an experimental effect requires an estimate of that experimental effect and an estimate of a pertinent error term. Therefore, the GLM process of parameter estimation is engaged to determine experimental effects, and as errors represent the mismatch between the predicted and the actual data values, the calculation of error terms also engages the linear modelling process of prediction. Consequently, all four GLM processes are involved in the typical analysis of experimental data. The impression of concise experimental analyses is a consequence of the experimental design acting to simplify the process of GLM selection and only attending to certain model checks.

1.5   The "Linear" in GLM

To explain the distinctions required to appreciate model linearity, it is necessary to describe a GLM in more detail. This will be done by outlining the application of a simple regression GLM to data from an experimental study. This example of a regression GLM also will be useful when least squares estimators and regression in the context of ANCOVA are considered.

Consider a situation where the relationship between study time and memory was examined. 24 subjects were divided equally between three study time groups and were asked to memorize a list of 45 words. Immediately after studying the words for 30, 60 or 180 s, subjects were given 2 min to write down on as many of the words they could remember. The results of this study are presented in a scatterplot in Figure 1.1. The scatterplot follows the convention that independent or predictor variables are plotted on the X-axis and dependent variables are plotted on the Y-axis.

Although it would be more usual for regression to be applied to a non-experimental situation, where the predictor variable could take any value and not just the three times defined by the experimental conditions, the nature of the regression analysis is unaffected. In geometric terms, the relationship between list study time and word recall can be described by the straight line drawn on the graph in Figure 1.1. This line is described by the equation,

$$\hat{Y}_i = \beta_0 + \beta_1 X_i \tag{1.2}$$

where the subscript i denotes values for the ith subject (ranging from $i = 1, 2, \ldots, N$), $\hat{Y}_i$ is the predicted dependent variable (free-recall) score for the ith subject, the parameter β_0 is a constant (the intercept on the Y-axis), the parameter β_1 is a regression coefficient (equal to the slope of the regression line) and X_i is the value of the independent variable (study time) recorded for the same ith subject. (β is called "beta".)

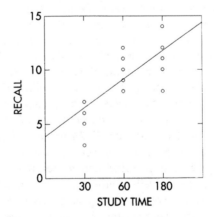

Figure 1.1   A plot of the number of words recalled as a function of word list study time

As the line describes the relationship between study time and recall, and equation (1.2) is an algebraic version of the line, equation (1.2) is also a description of the relationship between study time and recall. Indeed, the terms $(\beta_0 + \beta_1 X_1)$ constitute the *model* component of the regression GLM applicable to this data. However, the full GLM equation also includes an *error* component. The error represents the discrepancy between the scores predicted by the model, through which the regression line passes, and the actual data values. Therefore, the full regression GLM equation that describes the data is

$$Y_i = \beta_0 + \beta_1 X_i + \varepsilon_i \qquad (1.3)$$

where Y_i is the observed score for the ith subject and ε_i is a random variable denoting the error term for the same subject. (ε is called "epsilon".) Note that it is a trivial matter of moving the error term to right of equation (1.3) to obtain the formula that describes the predicted scores,

$$\hat{Y}_i = Y_i - \varepsilon_i = \beta_0 + \beta_1 X_i \qquad (1.4)$$

Now that some GLM parameters and variables have been specified, it makes sense to say that GLMs can be described as being linear with respect to both their parameters and predictor variables. Linear in the parameters means no parameter is mutiplied or divided by another, nor is any parameter above the first power. Linear in the predictor variables also means no variable is mutiplied or divided by another, nor is any above the first power. However, as shown below, there are ways around the variable requirement.

For example, equation (1.3) above is linear with respect to both parameters and variables. However, the equation

$$Y_i = \beta_0 + \beta_1^2 X_i + \varepsilon_i \qquad (1.5)$$

is linear with respect to the variables, but not to the parameters, as β_1 has been raised to the second power. Linearity with respect to the parameters also would be violated if any parameters were multiplied or divided by other parameters or appeared as exponents. In contrast, the equation

$$Y_i = \beta_0 + \beta_1 X_i^2 + \varepsilon_i \qquad (1.6)$$

is linear with respect to the parameters, but not with respect to the variables, as X_i^2 is X_i raised to the second power. However, it is very simple to define $Z_i = X_i^2$ and to substitute Z_i in place of X_i^2. Therefore, models such as described by equation (1.6) continue to be termed linear, whereas such as those described by equation (1.5) do not. In short, linearity is presumed to apply only to the parameters. Models which are not linear with respect to their parameters are described specifically as nonlinear. As a result, models can be assumed to be linear, unless specified otherwise, and frequently the term linear is omitted.

Nevertheless, the term "linear" in GLM often is misunderstood to mean that the relation between any data and any predictor variable must be described by a straight line. Although GLMs can describe straight line relationships, they are capable of much more. Through the use of transformations and polynomials,

GLMs can describe many complex curvilinear relations between the data and the predictor variables (Draper & Smith, 1998; Neter et al., 1990).

1.6   Least squares estimates

In statistics, parameters describe complete populations. However, it is rare for data from whole populations to be available. Much more available are samples of these populations. Consequently, parameters usually are estimated from sample data. A standard form of distinction is to use Greek letters, such as α (alpha) and β, to denote parameters and to place a hat on them, e.g. $\hat{\alpha}$, $\hat{\beta}$, when they denote parameter estimates. Alternatively, ordinary letters, such as a and b, may be used to represent parameter estimates.

By far the most frequently applied parameter estimation method is that of *least squares*. This method identifies parameter estimates that minimize the sum of the squared discrepancies between predicted and observed values. Given the GLM equation

$$Y_i = \beta_0 + \beta_1 X_i + \varepsilon_i \qquad (1.3, \text{rptd})$$

the sum of the squared deviations may be described as

$$\sum_{i=1}^{N} \varepsilon_i^2 = \sum_{i=1}^{N} (Y_i - \beta_0 - \beta_1 X_1)^2 \qquad (1.7)$$

The estimates of β_0 and β_1 are chosen to provide the smallest value of $\sum_{i=1}^{N} \varepsilon_i^2$. ($\Sigma$ is called sigma.) By differentiating equation (1.6) with respect to each parameter, two (simultaneous) normal equations are obtained. (More GLM parameters require more differentiations and produce more normal equations.) Solving the normal equations for each parameter provides the formulae for calculating their least squares estimates and in turn, all other GLM (least squares) estimates.

Least squares estimates have a number of useful properties. Employing an estimate of the parameter β_0 ensures that the residuals sum to zero. Given that the error terms are also uncorrelated, with constant variance, the least squares estimators are unbiased and have the minimum variance of all unbiased linear estimators. As a result they are termed the *best linear unbiased estimators* (BLUE). However, for conventional significance testing, it is also necessary to assume that the errors are distributed normally. Checks of these and other assumptions are considered in Chapter 7. (For further details of least squares estimates see Draper & Smith, 1998; Neter et al., 1990; Searle, 1987.)

1.7   Fixed, random and mixed effects analyses

Fixed effects, random effects and mixed effect analyses refer to different sampling situations. Fixed effects analyses employ only fixed variables in the

GLM model component, random effects analyses employ only random variables in the GLM model component, while mixed effect analyses employ both fixed and random variables in the GLM model component.

When a fixed effects analysis is applied to experimental data, it is assumed that all the experimental conditions of interest are included in the experiment. This assumption is made because the inferences made on the basis of a fixed effects analysis apply only to the specific experimental conditions and do not extend to any other conditions that might have been included. Therefore, the experimental conditions used in the original study are fixed in the sense that exactly the same conditions must be employed in any replication of the study. For most genuine experiments, this presents little problem: experimental conditions usually are chosen deliberately and with some care, so fixed effects analyses are appropriate for most experimental data (see Keppel, 1991 for a brief discussion). However, when ANOVA is applied to data obtained from non-experimental studies, care should be exercised in applying the appropriate form of analysis. However, excluding estimates of the magnitude of experimental effect, it is not until factorial designs are analysed that differences between fixed and random effect estimates are apparent.

Random effect anlyses consider those experimental conditions employed in the study to be only a random sample of a population of experimental conditions, and consequently inferences drawn from the study may be applied to the wider population of conditions and study replications need not be restricted to exactly the same experimental conditions. As inferences from random effects analyses are generalized more widely than fixed effects inferences, all else being equal, more conservative assessments are provided by random effects analyses.

In psychology, mixed effect analyses are encountered most frequently with respect to repeated measures (within subjects) designs. Due to the repeated measures on each subject, it is possible to identify effects uniquely attributable to subjects. This subject effect is represented by a random variable in the GLM model component, while the experimental conditions continue as fixed effects. (Although it is possible to mix randomly selected experimental conditions with fixed experimental conditions in a factorial design, with or without a random variable representing subjects, such designs tend to be rare in psychology.)

Statisticians have distinguished between regression analysis, which assumes fixed effects, and correlation analysis, which does not. Correlation analyses do not distinguish between predictor and dependent variables. Instead, they study the degree of relation between random variables and are based on bivariate–or multivariate–normal models. However, it is rare for this distinction to be maintained in practice. Regression is applied frequently to situations where the sampling of predictor variables is random and where replications employ predictors with values different to those used in the original study. Indeed, the term regression now tends to be interpreted simply as an analysis that predicts one variable on the basis of one or more other variables, irrespective of their fixed or random natures (Howell, 1997). In mitigation of this approach, it can be demonstrated that provided the other analysis assumptions are tenable, the least square parameter estimates and F-tests of significance continue to apply even with random predictor and dependent variables (Kmenta, 1971; Snedecor & Cochran, 1980; Wonnacott & Wonnacott, 1970).

All of the analyses described in this book treat experimental conditions as fixed. However, random effects are considered in the context of related measures designs.

1.8   The benefits of a GLM approach to ANOVA and ANCOVA

The pocket history of regression and ANOVA described their separate development and the subsequent appreciation and utilization of their communality, partly as a consequence of computer based data analysis that promoted the use of their common matrix algebra notation. However, the single fact that the GLM subsumes regression, ANOVA and ANCOVA seems an insufficient reason to abandon the traditional manner of carrying out these analyses and adopt a GLM approach. So what is the motivation for advocating the GLM approach?

The main reason for adopting a GLM approach to ANOVA and ANCOVA is that it provides conceptual and practical advantages over the traditional approach. Conceptually, a major advantage is the continuity the GLM reveals between regression, ANOVA and ANCOVA. Rather than having to learn about three apparently discrete techniques, it is possible to develop an understanding of a consistent modelling approach that can be applied to the different circumstances covered by regression, ANOVA and ANCOVA. A number of practical advantages also stem from the utility of the simply conceived and easily calculated error terms. The GLM conception divides data into model and error, and it follows that the better the model explains the data, the less the error. Therefore, the set of predictors constituting a GLM can be selected by their ability to reduce the error term. Comparing a GLM of the data that contains the predictor(s) under consideration with a GLM that does not, in terms of error reduction, provides a way of estimating effects that is both intuitively appreciable and consistent across regression, ANOVA and ANCOVA applications. Moreover, as most GLM assumptions concern the error terms, residuals, the error term estimates, provide a common means by which the assumptions underlying regression, ANOVA and ANCOVA can be assessed. This also opens the door for sophisticated statistical techniques, developed primarily to assist regression error analysis, to be applied to both ANOVA and ANCOVA. Finally, recognizing ANOVA and ANCOVA as instances of the GLM also provides connection to an extensive and useful literature on methods, analysis strategies and related techniques, such as structural equation modelling, which are pertinent to experimental and non-experimental analyses alike (e.g. Cohen & Cohen, 1983; Darlington, 1968; Draper & Smith, 1998; Gordon, 1968; Keppel & Zedeck, 1989; McCullagh & Nelder, 1989; Mosteller & Tukey, 1977; Nelder, 1977; Neter, et al., 1990; Pedhazur, 1997; Rao, 1965; Searle, 1979, 1987, 1997; Seber, 1977).

1.9 The GLM presentation

Several statistical texts have addressed the GLM and presented its application to ANOVA and ANCOVA. However, these texts differ in the kinds of GLM they employ to describe ANOVA and ANCOVA and how they present GLM calculations. ANOVA and ANCOVA have been expressed as experimental design GLMs (e.g. Maxwell & Delaney, 1990), cell mean GLMs (Searle, 1987) and regression GLMs (e.g. Cohen & Cohen, 1983; Judd & McClelland, 1989; Keppel & Zedeck, 1989; Pedhazur, 1997). Although each of these expressions has its merits, the main focus in this text will be on experimental design GLMs, which also may be known as structural models or effect models. (See Chapter 2 for further description and comparison of regression, cell mean and experimental design GLMs.)

Irrespective of the form of expression, GLMs may be described and calculated using scalar or matrix algebra. However, scalar algebra equations become increasingly unwieldy and opaque as the number of variables in an analysis increases. In contrast, matrix algebra equations remain relatively succinct and clear. Consequently, matrix algebra has been described as concise, powerful, even elegant, and as providing better appreciation of the detail of GLM operations than scalar algebra. These may seem peculiar assertions given the difficulties people experience doing matrix algebra calculations, but they make sense when a distinction between theory and practice is considered. You may know in theory how to add two numbers together, but this will not eliminate all errors if you have very many numbers to add. Similarly, matrix algebra can summarize succinctly and clearly matrix relations and manipulations, but the actual laborious matrix calculations are best left to a computer. Nevertheless, while there is much to recommend matrix algebra for expressing GLMs, unless you have some serious mathematical expertise, it is likely to be an unfamiliar notation. As this text is written to introduce GLMs and many readers will not be well versed in matrix algebra, for the most part, scalar algebra and verbal descriptions will be employed to facilitate comprehension.

1.10 Statistical packages for computers

Most commercially available statistical packages have the capability to implement regression, ANOVA and ANCOVA. The interfaces to regression and ANOVA programs reflect their separate historical developments. Regression programs require the specification of predictor variables, etc, while ANOVA requires the specification of experimental independent variables or factors, etc. ANCOVA interfaces tend to replicate the ANOVA approach, but with the additional requirement that one or more covariates are specified. More recently, satistical software packages offering GLM programs have become much more common (e.g. GENSTAT, MINITAB, SYSTAT), and indeed, SPSS now has replaced its factorial ANOVA program with a GLM program.

However, this text makes little reference to statistical packages. One reason is that, in addition to the often numerous and extensive manuals that accompany statistical software, there are already many excellent books written specifically to assist users in carrying out analyses with most, if not all, of the major statistical packages. Given the extent of this documentation (e.g. Pedhazur, 1997), there seems to be little point in adding to it. Another reason is that upgrades to statistical packages, as a consequence of statistical developments and the addition of new features, soon make any specific references to statistical software obsolete. Nevertheless, despite a lack of reference to specific statistical packages, some appreciation of ANOVA and ANCOVA implementation by statistical software should be provided by the use of the typical input and output formats used by the standard statistical packages.

2 TRADITIONAL AND GLM APPROACHES TO INDEPENDENT MEASURES SINGLE FACTOR ANOVA DESIGNS

2.1 Independent measures designs

The type of experimental design determines the particular form of ANOVA that should be applied. A wide variety of experimental designs and pertinent ANOVA procedures are available (e.g. Kirk, 1995). The simplest of these are independent measures designs. The defining feature of independent measures designs is that the dependent variable scores are assumed to be statistically independent or uncorrelated. In practice, this means that subjects are allocated to experimental conditions on a random basis and each subject provides only one dependent variable score.

Consider the independent measures design with three conditions presented in Table 2.1, where the subject numbers indicate their chronological allocation to conditions. Here, a sampling without replacement procedure has been implemented (Keppel, 1991). Subjects are allocated randomly with the proviso that one subject has been allocated to all conditions before a second subject is allocated to any condition. This procedure distributes any subject differences that vary over the course of the experiment randomly across conditions.

In order to analyse this data using t-tests, at least two would need to be carried out. The first might compare conditions A and B, while the second would compare conditions B and C. A third t-test would be necessary to compare conditions A and C. The problem with such a t-test analysis is that the probability of a type 1 error (i.e. rejecting the null hypothesis when it is true) increases with the number of significance tests carried out. Normally the

Table 2.1   Subject allocation for an independent measures design with three conditions

Condition A	Condition B	Condition C
subject 3	subject 2	subject 1
subject 5	subject 6	subject 4
subject 8	subject 9	subject 7
subject 12	subject 10	subject 11

likelihood of a type 1 error is equal to the significance level chosen (e.g. 0.05), but when two t-tests are applied, it rises to nearly double the tabled significance level, and when three t-tests are applied it rises to nearly three times the tabled significance level.

In contrast, ANOVA simultaneously examines for differences between any number of conditions while holding the type 1 error at the chosen significance level (usually 0.05). In fact, ANOVA may be considered as the t-test extension to more than two conditions that holds type 1 error constant. This may be seen if ANOVA is applied to compare two conditions. In such situations, the relationship between t- and F-values is

$$t^2_{(df)} = F_{(1,df)} \tag{2.1}$$

where df is the denominator degrees of freedom. Yet despite this apparently simple relationship, there is still room for confusion. For example, imagine data obtained from an experiment assessing a directional hypothesis, where a one-tailed t-test is applied. This might provide

$$t_{(20)} = 1.725, \qquad p = 0.05$$

However, if an ANOVA were applied to exactly the same data, in accord with equation (2.1) the F-value obtained would be

$$F_{(1,20)} = 2.976, \qquad p = 0.100$$

Given the conventional significance level of 0.05, the one-tailed t-value is significant, but the F-value is not. The reason for such differences is that the F-value probabilities reported by tables and computer output are always "two-tailed", in the sense that non-directional hypotheses always are tested. Kirk (1995, p. 96) provides a brief description of the F-test as providing "a one-tailed test of a non-directional null hypothesis because MSBG, which is expected to be greater than or approximately equal to MSWG, is always in the numerator of the F statistic." Although perfectly correct, this description may cause some confusion and obscure the reason for the apparently different t- and F-test results. As stated, the F-statistic in ANOVA is one-tailed because the MSBG, which reflects experimental effects, is always the numerator and should be larger than the MSWG, which reflects error variance. Consequently, the F-statistic produced should always be the larger of the two possibilities, and so only the right-hand tail of the F-distribution need be examined. Therefore, the F-test is one-tailed, but *not* because it tests a directional hypothesis. In fact, the reason a non-directional hypothesis is assessed by the F-test is to do with the nature of the F-test numerator, which, because it is derived from sums of squares, is inherently non-directional (differences between means are squared, so all numbers become positive and any directionality is lost). Nevertheless, perhaps such problems should never arise. As MacRae (1995) points out, one consequence of employing directional hypotheses is that any effect in the direction opposite to that predicted must be interpreted as a chance result, irrespective of the size of the effect. Very few researchers would be unable, or willing, to ignore a large and significant effect even though it was in the opposite direction to that predicted, but this is exactly what they should do if a directional hypothesis was tested. Therefore, to allow further analysis of such occurrences, logic dictates that non-directional hypotheses always should be tested. The topics of appropriate adjustments for type 1 error in the context of multiple comparisons (cf. more than one *t*-test) and tests of directional or non-directional hypotheses have generated considerable discussion. Some of these issues are considered in Chapter 9.

It should be noticed from the examples presented in Table 2.1 that equal numbers of subjects are allocated to experimental conditions. This is good design practice for at least three reasons. First, generalizing from the experiment is easier if the complication of unequal numbers of subjects in experimental conditions (also referred to as unbalanced data) is avoided. Second, the mathematical formulae for ANOVA with equal numbers of subjects in each experimental condition reduce, due to terms accommodating the different numbers per group cancelling out, and so are much simpler to follow, implement and interpret. Third, when there are equal numbers of subjects in each experimental condition, ANOVA is fairly robust with respect to certain assumption violations (i.e. distribution normality and variance homogeneity). Indeed, the benefits of balanced data are such that it is worth investing some effort to achieve. All of the analyses presented in this text employ balanced data and it would be wrong to presume that unbalanced data analysed in exactly the same way would provide the same results and allow the same interpretation. Detailed consideration of unbalanced designs may be found in the text by Searle (1987).

2.1.1 Factors and independent variables

The three experimental conditions above reflect three different periods of study time. Although these conditions are distinguished by quantitative differences in the amount of time available, it still makes sense to treat them categorically. A categorical analysis allows task performance to be compared across conditions, without the actual size of the time differences between conditions entering into the calculations. Irrespective of the type of analysis carried out, it is reasonable to label the independent variable as *study time*. Therefore, with categorical comparisons, it is up to the experimenter to keep the actual differences between conditions in mind. For example, condition A could be changed to one in which some auditory distraction is presented. Obviously, this would invalidate the independent variable label *study time*, but it would not invalidate exactly the same categorical comparisons of task performance under these three different conditions. The point here is to draw attention to the fact that the levels of a qualitative factor may involve multidimensional distinctions between conditions. While there should be some logical relation between the levels of any factor, they may not be linked in such a continuous fashion as is suggested by the term "independent variable". Therefore, from now on the label *factor* will be used.

2.2   Traditional ANOVA for single factor designs

In psychology, ANOVA is employed most frequently to address the question: are there significant differences between the mean scores obtained in different experimental conditions? Significant differences exceed those expected on the basis of chance. To determine significance, ANOVA procedures specify the calculation of an F-statistic. The size of the F-statistic reflects the extent to which differences between conditions diverge from that expected on the basis of chance. However, even when the null hypothesis is correct and no differences exist between the means of the experimental condition *populations*, due to chance sampling variation (sometimes called sampling error), it is possible to observe differences between the experimental condition means of the *samples*. The distributions of all F-statistics (i.e. whatever their dfs) when the null hypothesis is correct are known. Therefore, the probability that these or more extreme differences is due to chance sampling variation can be determined by comparing the distribution of the F-statistic with equivalent dfs under the null hypothesis with the F-statistic observed. If this probability is sufficiently low, it is reasonable to reject the possibility that the differences are due to such chance factors. The convention is that sufficiently low probabilities begin at 0.05 (i.e. 5/100).

In the traditional independent measures ANOVA, the total score variation is divided into between group and within group variance. The F-statistic is conceived as the ratio of between group variance to within group variance. If the scores in the different conditions are influenced by the experimental variables, then the scores should vary between conditions. Although scores within an experimental condition also vary, this variation is attributed to chance. Consequently, the variance of scores between groups has to be greater than the variance of scores within the experimental conditions, or the between groups variation also must be attributed to chance.

2.2.1   Variance

Variance, or equivalently, variation, is a vital concept in ANOVA and many other statistical techniques. Nevertheless, it can be a puzzling notion, particularly the concept of total variance. Variation measures how much the observed or calculated scores deviate from something. However, while between group variance reflects the deviation amongst condition means and within group variance reflects the deviation of scores from their condition means, it is less obvious what total variance reflects. In fact, total variance reflects the deviation of all the observed scores from the overall or grand mean.

Before this can be illustrated, some definitions are necessary. The most frequently employed measure of central tendency is the arithmetic average or mean ($\overline{Y}$). This is defined as

$$\overline{Y} = \frac{\sum_{i=1}^{N} Y_i}{N} \tag{2.2}$$

where Y_i is the ith subject's score, $\sum_{i=1}^{N} Y_i$ is the sum of all of the subjects' scores and N is the total number of subjects. The subscript i indexes the individual subjects and in this instance takes the values from 1 to N. The $\sum_{i=1}^{N}$ indicates that summation occurs over the subject scores, from 1 to N. In turn, the population variance (σ^2) is defined as

$$\sigma^2 = \frac{\sum_{i=1}^{N}(Y_i - \overline{Y})^2}{N} \tag{2.3}$$

Therefore, variance reflects the average of the squared deviations from the mean. In other words, the variance reflects the square of the average extent to which scores differ from the mean. However, for sample variance, this formula provides a biased estimate, in that it always underestimates this variance. An unbiased estimate of sample variance (s^2) is given by

$$s^2 = \frac{\sum_{i=1}^{N}(Y_i - \overline{Y})^2}{N - 1} \tag{2.4}$$

Nevertheless, while formulae (2.2) and (2.3) reveal the nature of variance quite well, they do not lend themselves to easy calculation. A more useful formula for calculating sample variance (s^2) is

$$s^2 = \frac{\sum_{i=1}^{N} Y_i^2 - [(\sum_{i=1}^{N} Y_i)^2/N]}{N - 1} \tag{2.5}$$

Another popular statistic is the standard deviation. This is simply the square root of the variance. Consequently, the population standard deviation (σ) is given by

$$\sigma = \sqrt{\frac{\sum_{i=1}^{N}(Y_i - \overline{Y})^2}{N}} \tag{2.6}$$

and the sample standard deviation (s) is given by

$$s = \sqrt{\frac{\sum_{i=1}^{N} Y_i^2 - [(\sum_{i=1}^{N} Y_i)^2/N]}{N - 1}} \tag{2.7}$$

2.2.2 EXAMPLE

The relation between total variation, between group variation and within group variation can be illustrated using some example experimental data. Figure 2.1 and Table 2.2 present data provided by 15 subjects over three experimental conditions. (Note: in Table 2.2 subjects are numbered consecutively per group merely for convenience and so subject number does not reflect the chronological assignment to groups as in Table 2.1.) Figure 2.1 presents the data from the memory experiment described in Chapter 1 on the relationship between word list study time and recall. Subjects' dependent variable (recall) scores are plotted against the experimental condition under which the scores were recorded. The means of conditions A (30 s study time), B (60 s study time) and C (180 s study

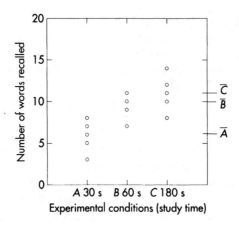

Figure 2.1   Dependent variable scores (words recalled) by experimental condition

Table 2.2   Experimental data and summary statistics

Subjects	Condition A	Subjects	Condition B	Subjects	Condition C
s1	7	s9	7	s17	8
s2	3	s10	11	s18	14
s3	6	s11	9	s19	10
s4	6	s12	11	s20	11
s5	5	s13	10	s21	12
s6	8	s14	10	s22	10
s7	6	s15	11	s23	11
s8	7	s16	11	s24	12
Total $\left(\sum\limits_{i=1}^{N} Y_i\right)$	48	$\sum Y_i$ 80		$\sum\limits_{i=1}^{N} Y_i$ 88	
$\sum Y_i^2$	304	$\sum Y_i^2$ 814		$\sum\limits_{i=1}^{N} Y_i^2$ 990	
Mean $(\overline{Y})$	6.00	$\overline{Y}$	10.00	$\overline{Y}$	11.00
Sample SD (s)	1.51	s	1.41	s	1.77
Sample variance (s^2)	2.29	s^2	1.99	s^2	3.13

time) are marked on the right Y-axis by, $\overline{A}$, $\overline{B}$ and $\overline{C}$. Table 2.2 lists and provides summary statistics for the same data.

The vertical spread of the scores in Figure 2.1 can provide some sense of between groups and within groups variance. Between groups variance reflects the differences between the means of the experimental conditions (see distances between $\overline{A}$, $\overline{B}$ and $\overline{C}$ on right axis of the graph). Within groups variance reflects the (average) spread of individual scores within each of the experimental conditions. Examination of Figure 2.1 suggests greatest within group variation is exhibited by experimental condition C, while condition A exhibits greater within group variation than condition B. These assessments are confirmed by the statistics presented in Table 2.2.

In most statistics texts, a numerical subscript is used to identify the experimental conditions. Typically, the subscript j indexes the experimental conditions, ranging from 1 to p, where $p =$ the number of experimental conditions. In this example, the p experimental conditions take the indicator values j, where $A = 1$, $B = 2$ and $C = 3$. For the sake of consistency, the numerical indexes are used in formulae, but for ease of exposition, the alphabetical indexes also may be employed to identify the experimental conditions.

The use of the N (or $N - 1$) denominator in formulae (2.2) to (2.5), reveals these variance estimates as reflecting the amount of deviation from the mean, averaged across all of the subjects' scores involved. In ANOVA, however, the initial calculations of variance do not employ averages. Such variance estimates are termed "sums of squares" (SS).

Total sum of square (SS) is conceived as the deviation of all the observed scores from the overall or grand mean. For this calculation, the only modification to formula (2.5) is to exclude the denominator that would provide the average.

$$SS_{total} = \frac{\sum_{i=1}^{N} Y_i^2 - (\sum_{i=1}^{N} Y_i)^2}{N} \tag{2.8}$$

$$= \frac{2108 - (216)^2}{24}$$

$$SS_{total} = 164.00$$

Within group variance is conceived in terms of the average of the separate spreads of scores from the mean in each of the experimental conditions. The separate experimental condition variance estimates averaged over all of the scores in the experimental condition are provided in Table 2.2. These estimates can be obtained by applying formula (2.5) separately to each of the experimental conditions.

The components of the *within group sum of squares* can be calculated using only the numerator of (2.9) below.

$$\frac{\sum_{i=1}^{N} Y_i^2 - (\sum_{i=1}^{N} Y)^2 / N_j}{N_j - 1} \tag{2.9}$$

For experimental condition A this gives

$$SS_{\text{experimental condition } A} = \sum_{i=1}^{N} Y_i^2 - \left(\sum_{i=1}^{N} Y \right)^2 \Big/ N_j \tag{2.10}$$

$$= 304 - (48)^2 / 8$$

$$= 16.00$$

Note that this value is simply

$$(N_j - 1)(s^2) = 7(2.29)$$

Similar calculations for experimental conditions B and C will provide the sum of squares estimates used below. The *within groups sum of squares* can be calculated by taking the sum of the separate experimental condition sum of squares estimates:

$$SS_{\text{within groups}} = SS_A + SS_B + SS_C,$$

$$= 16.00 + 14.00 + 22.00$$

$$SS_{\text{within groups}} = 52.00$$

Between groups variance is conceived in terms of the average of the differences amongst the means of the experimental conditions. However, the differences involved are not as simple as the mean of condition A minus the mean of condition B, etc. Instead, the variance attributable to the differences between the condition means and the grand mean are estimated. Although experimental condition means are obtained by averaging over all the subjects in the particular condition, each experimental condition mean is regarded as the score each subject in that experimental condition would record if error variation were eliminated. Consequently, in each experimental condition there would be N_j experimental condition mean scores.

$$\text{Between groups variance} = \sum_{j=1}^{p} N_j(\overline{Y}_j - \overline{Y}_G)^2 \qquad (2.11)$$

However, as before, the between groups sum of squares is calculated using only the numerator of (2.11):

Between groups sum of squares

$$= \sum_{j=1}^{p} N_j(\overline{Y}_j - \overline{Y}_G)^2$$

$$= 8(6 - 9)^2 + 8(10 - 9)^2 + 8(11 - 9)^2$$

$$SS_{\text{between groups}} = 112 \qquad (2.12)$$

The fact that

$$SS_{\text{total}} = SS_{\text{between groups}} + SS_{\text{within groups}} \qquad (2.13)$$

is easily verified by substituting any two of the estimates calculated for two of the terms above:

$$164.00 = 112.00 + 52.00$$

The sum of squares (SS) calculations represent the total variation attributable to between and within groups sources. The next step in traditional ANOVA calculation is to determine the average variance arising from between and within groups sources. This step requires SS denominators to provide the averages. The denominators are termed degrees of freedom, and the averages they provide are termed mean squares (MS).

Degrees of freedom (df) represent how many of the scores employed in constructing the estimate are able to take different values. For example, when sample variance is calculated using N as a denominator, underestimates of variance are obtained because in fact, there are not N dfs, but only $(N - 1)$ dfs. When the correct dfs are used as the denominator, an accurate estimate of sample variance is obtained.

The reason there are $(N - 1)$ and not N dfs is that one df is lost from the sample variance because a mean is used in the sample variance calculation. Once a mean is determined for a group of scores, it always is possible to state the value of the "last" score in that group. Internal consistency demands that this "last" score takes the value that provides the appropriate sum of scores, which, when divided by the number of scores, gives the previously calculated mean. For example, for the set of scores 4, 6, 4, 6 and 5, the mean is 25/5 $= 5$. If we know there are 5 scores, the mean is 25 and that four of the scores are 4, 6, 4 and 6 (which add to 20), then it stands to reason that the other score from the set must be 5. As variance estimate calculations also use the previously calculated mean and the individual scores, the "last" score is not free to vary – it must have the value that provides the previously calculated mean. Therefore, only $(N - 1)$ scores are really free to vary and so, there are $(N - 1)$ dfs.

For the between groups SS, although three experimental condition means are involved, it is their variation around a grand mean that is determined. As the grand mean is the average of the three experimental condition means (with balanced data), one df is lost. Consequently,

$$\text{Between groups df} = k - 1$$

$$= 3 - 1$$

$$= 2$$

The within groups SS comprises the variation of scores from the experimental condition mean, over the three different conditions. As a separate mean is employed in each condition, a df will be lost in each condition.

$$df_{\text{experimental condition A}} = (N - 1) = (8 - 1) = 7$$

$$df_{\text{experimental condition B}} = (N - 1) = (8 - 1) = 7$$

$$df_{\text{experimental condition C}} = (N - 1) = (8 - 1) = 7$$

$$\text{Within groups df} = 3(N - 1)$$

$$= 3(7)$$

$$= 21$$

Given sums of squares and dfs, mean squares (MS) can be calculated by dividing the former by the latter. The ratio of the between groups MS to the within groups MS provides the F-statistic. The last item provided in the ANOVA summary table (Table 2.3) is the probability of the calculated F-value being

Table 2.3   ANOVA summary table

Source	SS	df	MS	F	p
Between groups	112.000	2	56.000	22.615	<0.001
Within groups	52.000	21	2.476		
Total	164.000	23			

obtained by chance given the data analysed. As the probability associated with the between groups F-value is less than 0.05, the null hypothesis (H_0), which states there are no differences between experimental condition means, can be rejected and the alternate or experimental hypothesis (H_E), which states some experimental condition means differ, can be accepted. Further tests are required to identify exactly which experimental condition means differ.

2.3   GLM approaches to single factor ANOVA

2.3.1   Experimental design GLMs

GLM equations for ANOVA have become relatively common sights in statistical texts, even when a traditional approach to ANOVA is applied. However, when a GLM equation is provided in the context of traditional ANOVA, it is more common for the labels structural model, experimental effects model, or experimental design model to be employed. The equation,

$$Y_{ij} = \mu + \alpha_j + \varepsilon_{ij} \tag{2.14}$$

describes the GLM underlying the independent measures design ANOVA carried out on the data presented in Table 2.2. Y_{ij} is the ith subject's dependent variable score in the jth experimental condition, the parameter μ is a constant representing the dependent variable score free of the effect of any experimental condition, the parameter α_j is the effect of the jth experimental condition and the random variable, ε_{ij}, is the error term, which reflects variation due to any uncontrolled source. Therefore, equation (2.14) is actually a summary of a set, or system, of equations, where each equation describes a single dependent variable score.

Predicted scores are based on the *model* component of GLM equations. Therefore, inspection of equation (2.14) reveals predicted scores ($\hat{Y}_{ij}$) to be given by

$$\hat{Y}_{ij} = \mu + \alpha_j \tag{2.15}$$

As μ is a constant, the only variation in prediction can come from the effect of the j experimental conditions. Consequently, the experimental design GLM can predict only as many different scores as there are experimental conditions and every subject's score within an experimental condition is predicted to be the mean score for that experimental condition:

$$Y_{ij} = \mu_j \qquad\qquad (2.16)$$

Applied to the data in Table 2.2, the μ_j estimates are

$$6 = \mu_1$$

$$10 = \mu_2$$

$$11 = \mu_3$$

In the discussion of regression GLMs in Chapter 1, it was said that the regression line passes through all of the predicted scores and the same is true of experimental design GLMs. The line described by the experimental design GLM is presented in Figure 2.2. Here, as convention dictates, the dependent variable is plotted on the Y-axis and the levels of the independent variable are plotted on the X-axis, and the line passes through each of the predicted scores: the mean scores of each experimental condition. Note that the arbitary ordering of the levels of the categorical independent variable will determine the exact path of the experimental design GLM line, emphasizing the point that the term "linear" in "linear model" does not necessarily mean a *straight* line.

Equation (2.17) below defines the grand mean as

$$\mu = \frac{\sum_{j=1}^{P} \mu_j}{P} \qquad\qquad (2.17)$$

This reveals μ as the mean of the separate experimental condition means. Of course, with balanced data, this is also the mean of all dependent variable scores. Applying equation (2.17) to the data in Table 2.2 provides the estimate

$$\mu = (6 + 10 + 11)/3 = 9$$

which is identified by a dotted line in Figure 2.2. The effect of a particular experimental condition denoted by the term α_j is defined as

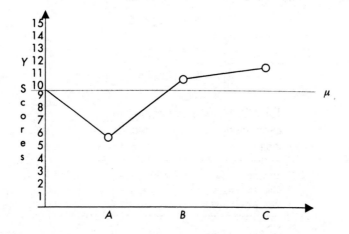

Figure 2.2   Dependent variable scores by experimental condition

$$\alpha_j = \mu_j - \mu \tag{2.18}$$

where μ_j is the population mean for experimental condition j. Equation (2.18) reveals the effect attributable to each experimental condition to be the difference between the mean of the particular experimental condition and the grand mean. Moreover, given equations (2.17), (2.18) and balanced data, it follows that

$$\sum_{j=1}^{p} \alpha_j = 0 \tag{2.18}$$

As can be seen in Table 2.4, applying equation (2.18) to the data in Table 2.2 and adding the estimates of the three experimental condition effects confirms equation (2.19).

When unbalanced data is analysed, the different numbers of subjects in the experimental conditions must be accommodated. Consequently, equation (2.19) becomes

$$\sum_{j=1}^{p} (N_i \alpha_j) = 0 \tag{2.20}$$

The fact that the experimental effects sum to zero is more than just a logical outcome of the calculations. In fact, it is a mathematical side condition required to allow unique estimation of the experimental design GLM parameters. The constraint is required because the experimental design GLM is overparameterized: it contains more parameters (μ, α_1, α_2 and α_3) than there are experimental condition means (A, B and C) from which to estimate them. Indeed, ANOVA may be defined as the special case of multiple regression which includes the side condition that experimental effects sum to zero.

Equation (2.15) summarizes a set of GLM equations which predict each subject's score. Bearing in mind that each subject in each experimental condition is predicted to obtain the same score (2.16), the predicted experimental condition means can be described by the GLM equations:

$$Y_{1,1} = 9 + (-3) = 6$$

$$Y_{1,2} = 9 + (1) = 10$$

$$Y_{1,3} = 9 + (2) = 6$$

Table 2.4   Estimates of the three experimental condition effects and their sum

estimate of a_1 =	6 − 9	=	−3
estimate of a_2 =	10 − 9	=	1
estimate of a_3 =	11 − 9	=	2
$\sum_{j=1}^{p} a_j$		=	0

In contrast to predicted scores, the ε_{ij} terms representing the discrepancy between actual and predicted scores may be different for each subject,

$$\varepsilon_{ij} = \mu_j - Y_{ij} \tag{2.21}$$

As the scores predicted by the experimental design GLM are the experimental condition means, it follows that

$$\text{MSe} = \frac{\sum_{i=1}^{N}(\varepsilon_{ij}^2)}{p(N_j - 1)} \tag{2.22}$$

where MSe is the ANOVA mean square error, N_j is the number of scores and/or subjects in each experimental condition, and p is the number of experimental conditions. The value provided by $p(N_j - 1)$ is the degrees of freedom of the ANOVA MSe. Table 2.5 illustrates the calculation of error terms and how they provide the error SS. Applying equation (2.22) provides the MSe.

$$52/3(8 - 1) = 52/21 = 2.476$$

It should be evident that the experimental design GLM can be used as the

Table 2.5 Calculation of error terms, their square and sums

ε_{ij}		$\mu_j - Y_{ij}$		ε_{ij}	$(\varepsilon_{ij})^2$
$\varepsilon_{1,1}$	=	$6 - 7$	=	-1	1
$\varepsilon_{2,1}$	=	$6 - 3$	=	3	9
$\varepsilon_{3,1}$	=	$6 - 6$	=	0	0
$\varepsilon_{4,1}$	=	$6 - 6$	=	0	0
$\varepsilon_{5,1}$	=	$6 - 5$	=	1	1
$\varepsilon_{6,1}$	=	$6 - 8$	=	-2	4
$\varepsilon_{7,1}$	=	$6 - 6$	=	0	0
$\varepsilon_{8,1}$	=	$6 - 7$	=	-1	1
$\varepsilon_{9,2}$	=	$10 - 7$	=	3	9
$\varepsilon_{10,2}$	=	$10 - 11$	=	-1	1
$\varepsilon_{11,2}$	=	$10 - 9$	=	1	1
$\varepsilon_{12,2}$	=	$10 - 11$	=	-1	1
$\varepsilon_{13,2}$	=	$10 - 10$	=	0	0
$\varepsilon_{14,2}$	=	$10 - 10$	=	0	0
$\varepsilon_{15,2}$	=	$10 - 11$	=	-1	1
$\varepsilon_{16,2}$	=	$10 - 11$	=	-1	1
$\varepsilon_{17,3}$	=	$11 - 8$	=	3	9
$\varepsilon_{18,3}$	=	$11 - 14$	=	-3	9
$\varepsilon_{19,3}$	=	$11 - 10$	=	1	1
$\varepsilon_{20,3}$	=	$11 - 11$	=	0	0
$\varepsilon_{21,3}$	=	$11 - 12$	=	-1	1
$\varepsilon_{22,3}$	=	$11 - 10$	=	1	1
$\varepsilon_{23,3}$	=	$11 - 11$	=	0	0
$\varepsilon_{24,3}$	=	$11 - 12$	=	-1	1
Σ				0	52

basis for partitioning variance in traditional ANOVA. Employing equations (2.16), (2.18) and (2.21) allows equation (2.14) to be rewritten as

$$Y_{ij} = \mu + (\mu_j - \mu) + (Y_{ij} - \mu_j) \tag{2.23}$$

Moving μ to the left side of equation (2.22) gives

$$(Y_{ij} - \mu) = (\mu_j - \mu) + (Y_{ij} - \mu_j) \tag{2.24}$$

Equation (2.24) defines the variation between the dependent variable scores (Y_{ij}) and the grand mean (μ) as comprising variation due to experimental conditions ($\mu_j - \mu$) and variation due to errors ($Y_{ij} - \mu_j$). However, to obtain accurate variance estimates based on all of the sample scores, the number of scores contributing to each estimate must be included. Although experimental condition means are obtained by averaging over all the subjects in the particular condition, each experimental condition mean is regarded as the score each subject in that experimental condition would record if error variation were eliminated. Consequently, in each experimental condition there would be N_j scores equal to the mean. Therefore, the SS partition is

$$\sum_{j=1}^{p} \sum_{i=1}^{N} (Y_{ij} - \mu)^2 = \sum_{j=1}^{p} N_j(\mu_j - \mu)^2 + \sum_{j=1}^{p} \sum_{i=1}^{n} (Y_{ij} - \mu_j)^2 \tag{2.25}$$

Equation (2.25) and the account of variation due to experimental conditions should seem familar, as exactly the same argument was applied to the estimation of the traditional ANOVA between groups SS. The variation due to experimental conditions for the data in Table 2.2 is calculated in Table 2.6.

$$\text{Experimental conditions SS} = \sum_{j=1}^{p} N_j(\mu_j - \mu)^2 \tag{2.26}$$

So,

$$\text{Experimental conditions SS} = 8(-3^2) + 8(1^2)8(2^2) = 8(14) = 112$$

The sum of squares due to experimental conditions calculated above is identical to that calculated for traditional ANOVA presented in Table 2.3. As degrees of freedom can be defined for the experimental design GLM as they were for traditional ANOVA, the mean square values also will be identical to those calculated for traditional ANOVA and presented in Table 2.3.

Table 2.6   Calculation of variation due to experimental conditions

		$(\mu_j - \mu)^2$		
Condition A	=	$(6 - 9)^2$	=	-3^2 =	9
Condition B	=	$(10 - 9)^2$	=	1^2 =	1
Condition C	=	$(11 - 9)^2$	=	2^2 =	4
Σ				=	14

$$\text{Experimental conditions MS} = \sum_{j=1}^{p} N_j (\mu_j - \mu)^2 / \text{df} \qquad (2.27)$$

$$= 112/2 = 56$$

With the error sum of squares and MSe calculated previously, it is clear that the components of equation (2.24), based on the experimental design GLM and the components of the traditional ANOVA equation (2.12), are equivalent:

$$\text{SS}_{\text{total}} = \text{SS}_{\text{between groups}} + \text{SS}_{\text{within groups}} \qquad (2.13, \text{rptd})$$

It is left to the reader to confirm that

$$\sum_{j=1}^{p} \sum_{i=1}^{N} (Y_{ij} - \mu)^2 = 112 + 52 = 164$$

2.3.2   Estimating effects by comparing full and reduced experimental design GLMs

The comparison of full and reduced GLMs to estimate experimental effects is more in the spirit of conventional linear modelling processes than any of the other methods of experimental effect estimation so far described. The comparison of full and reduced GLMs applies a distilled form of linear modelling processes to the analysis of experimental data.

In Chapter 1, the GLM conception was described as

$$\text{data} = \text{model} + \text{error} \qquad (1.1, \text{rptd})$$

Usually linear modelling processes attempt to identify the "best" GLM of the data by comparing different linear models. As in experimental analyses, these GLMs are assessed in terms of the relative proportions of data variance attributed to model and error components. Given a fixed data set and because the sum of the model and error components (the data variance) is a constant, clearly any increase in variance accommodated by the model component will result in an equivalent decrease in the error component.

Consider the experimental design GLM for the independent single factor experiment,

$$Y_{ij} = \mu + \alpha_j + \varepsilon_{ij} \qquad (2.14, \text{rptd})$$

This full model employs the grand mean, μ, and includes parameters α_j to accommodate any influence of the experimental conditions. Essentially, it presumes that subjects' dependent variable scores (data) are best described by the experimental condition means. The full GLM manifests the data description under a non-directional experimental hypothesis. This may be expressed more formally as

$$\alpha_j \neq 0 \text{ for some } j \qquad (2.28)$$

which states that the effects of all of the experimental conditions do not equal zero. An equivalent expression in terms of the experimental condition means is

$$\mu \neq \mu_j \text{ for some } j \tag{2.29}$$

which states that some of the experimental condition means do not equal the grand mean.

It is also possible to describe a reduced model that omits any effect of the experimental conditions. Here, the reduced GLM is described by the equation

$$Y_{ij} = \mu + \varepsilon_{ij} \tag{2.30}$$

which uses only the grand mean of scores (μ) to account for the data. This GLM presumes that subjects' dependent variable scores are best described by the grand mean of all scores. In other words, it presumes that the description of subjects' scores would not benefit from taking the effects of the experimental conditions (α_j) into account. The reduced GLM manifests the data description under the null hypothesis. By ignoring any influence of the experimental conditions, the reduced GLM assumes that the experimental conditions do not influence the data. This assumption may be expressed more formally as

$$\alpha_j = 0 \tag{2.31}$$

which states that the effect of all of the experimental conditions is zero. An equivalent expression in terms of the experimental condition means is

$$\mu = \mu_j \tag{2.32}$$

which states that the grand mean and the experimental condition means are equal.

Clearly, from what has been said above, the GLM providing the better data description should have the smaller error component. Moreover, any reduction in the size of the error component caused by including the effects of the experimental conditions will be matched by an equivalent increase in the size of the model component. Therefore, comparing the size of the error components before and after adding the effects of the experimental conditions to the model component provides a method of assessing the consequences of changing the model. Presenting the full and reduced GLM equations together should clarify this point.

$$\text{Reduced GLM:} \quad Y_{ij} = \mu + \varepsilon_{ij} \tag{2.30, rptd}$$

$$\text{Full GLM:} \quad Y_{ij} = \mu + \alpha_j + \varepsilon_{ij} \tag{2.14, rptd}$$

Any reduction in the error component of the full GLM can be attributed only to the inclusion of the experimental condition effects, as this is the only difference between the two GLMs.

The reduced GLM defines errors as,

$$\varepsilon_{ij} = Y_{ij} - \mu \tag{2.33}$$

Of course, as discussed, GLM errors sum to zero, so interest is in the sum of the squared errors (see Table 2.6). A convenient computational formula for the reduced GLM error term sum of squares (SS) is

$$\text{SSE}_{\text{RGLM}} = \sum_{i=1}^{N} Y_i^2 - \left(\sum Y_i \right)^2 \bigg/ N \tag{2.34}$$

Using the data from Table 2.3 provides

$$\text{SSE}_{\text{RGLM}} = 2108 - [(216)^2/24] = 164$$

Note that this is equivalent to the TOTAL SS, described by equation (2.8). The full GLM defines errors as

$$\varepsilon_{ij} = (\mu + \alpha_j) - Y_{ij} \tag{2.35}$$

$$\varepsilon_{ij} = \mu_j - Y_{ij} \tag{2.21, rptd}$$

A convenient computational formula for the full GLM error term SS is

$$\text{SSE}_{\text{FGLM}} = \sum_{i=1}^{N} Y_{ij}^2 - \left(\sum Y_{ij} \right)^2 \bigg/ N_j \tag{2.36}$$

Again using the data from Table 2.3 provides

$$\text{SSE}_{\text{FGLM}} = 304 - [(48)^2/8] + 814 - [(80)^2/8] + 990 - [(88)^2/8]$$

$$= 52$$

As this is equivalent to the within SS, described by (2.10), it should come as no surprise that

$$\text{SSE}_{\text{RGLM}} - \text{SSE}_{\text{FGLM}} = \text{Total SS} - \text{Within SS} = \text{Between SS}$$

$$= 164 - 52 = 112 \tag{2.37}$$

In other words, the reduction in the error component sum of squares, attributed to the inclusion of the experimental condition effects, is identical to the traditional ANOVA between groups sum of squares. Therefore, the reduction in the error component sum of squares, attributable to the effects of the experimental conditions, is given by

$$\text{SSE}_{\text{RGLM}} - \text{SSE}_{\text{FGLM}} = \sum_{j=1}^{P} N_j(\mu_j - \mu)^2 \tag{2.38}$$

which, of course, is equivalent to equation (2.26).

An F-test of the error component sum of squares, attributed to the inclusion of the experimental condition effects, is given by

$$F = \frac{(\text{SSE}_{\text{RGLM}} - \text{SSE}_{\text{FGLM}})/(df_{\text{RGLM}} - df_{\text{FGLM}})}{\text{SSE}_{\text{FGLM}}/df_{\text{FGLM}}} \tag{2.39}$$

Therefore,

$$F = \frac{164 - 52/23 - 21}{52/21} = F = \frac{56}{2.476}$$

$$F(2, 21) = 22.617.$$

A convenient alternative to solving equation (2.39) directly is to construct Table 2.7, an ANOVA summary table similar to Table 2.3.

2.3.3 Regression GLMs

The experimental design GLM equation (2.14) may be compared with an equivalent regression equation,

$$Y_i = \beta_0 + \beta_1 X_{i,1} + \beta_2 X_{i,2} + \varepsilon_i \tag{2.40}$$

where Y_i is the dependent variable score for the ith subject, β_0 is a constant, β_1 is the regression coefficient for the first predictor variable X_1, β_2 is the regression coefficient for the second predictor variable X_2 and the random variable ε_i represents error. Although frequently omitted, the subscript i on the predictor variables is included here to emphasize that while the regression coefficient parameters are common across subjects, each subject provides a value for each variable X. Equation (2.40) describes *multiple* regression, rather than *simple* regression, because $k = 2$ independent or predictor variables are employed, rather than one. Like the experimental design GLM, equation (2.40) is a summary of a set of equations, each describing the constitution of a single dependent variable score.

Schemes for coding experimental conditions

Certain coding schemes may be used to represent experimental conditions and other categories of data for GLM analysis. This is done by employing as predictors particular sets of quantitative variables that operate in established formulae to produce a "categorical" analysis. Variables used in this manner also may be termed indicator variables.

When a regression equation represents ANOVA, the predictor variables identify allocation to experimental conditions and a parameter is associated with each predictor variable. However, rather than requiring p predictor variables to

Table 2.7   ANOVA summary table

Source	SS	df	MS	F	p
Error reduction due to experimental conditions	112.000	2	56.000	22.615	< 0.001
FGLM error	52.000	21	2.476		
Total	164.000	23			

represent p experimental conditions, the ANOVA regression equation needs only $(p-1)$ predictor variables to represent all of the experimental conditions. This is why there are only two predictors in equation (2.40). Table 2.8 illustrates the example data from Table 2.2 using $p=3$ predictor variables, X_1, X_2 and X_3. Allocation to experimental condition A is denoted by 1s rather than 0s on variable X_1, allocation to experimental condition B is denoted by 1s rather than 0s on variable X_2 and allocation to experimental condition C is denoted by 1s rather than 0s on variable X_3. However, closer scrutiny of Table 2.8 reveals that three experimental conditions will be represented even if variable X_3 is eliminated. This is because allocation to experimental conditions A and B still is denoted by a 1 on variables X_1 and X_2, respectively, but now only condition C is denoted by a zero on X_1 *and* a zero on X_2. For the unique specification of experimental conditions A, B and C, variable X_3 is redundant. Indeed, not only is variable X_3 redundant, but it is necessary to exclude it when regression formulae employ the indicator variables in a quantitative fashion.

The reason why the particular $(p-1)$ predictor variables are used rather than p predictor variables has to do with linear dependence of predictors. For example, consider the matrix A below:

$$\mathbf{A} = \begin{bmatrix} 1 & 0 & 0 \\ 0 & 1 & 0 \\ 0 & 0 & 1 \end{bmatrix}$$

This matrix contains three rows, each corresponding to the coding for an experimental condition in Table 2.8. However, in every regression GLM, a variable representing the constant, β_0, also is used as a predictor. Moreover, every score is defined with respect to β_0, and so every row contains a 1 in this predictor column indicating the involvement of β_0 in defining every score. Therefore, the complete model matrix (Kempthorne, 1980) for the regression GLM is

Table 2.8   Dummy coding indicator variables representing subject allocation to experimental conditions

Conditions	Subjects	X_1	X_2	X_3	Y
A	s1	1	0	0	7
	...	...	...	...	...
	s8	1	0	0	7
B	s9	0	1	0	7
	...	...	...	...	...
	s16	0	1	0	11
C	s17	0	0	1	8
	...	...	...	...	...
	s24	0	0	1	12

$$\mathbf{B} = \begin{bmatrix} 1 & 1 & 0 & 0 \\ 1 & 0 & 1 & 0 \\ 1 & 0 & 0 & 1 \end{bmatrix}$$

The matrix **B** also can be considered as four (predictor variable) column vectors. Different scalars (s_n) can be associated with each column vector:

$$\begin{array}{cccc} X_0 & X_1 & X_2 & X_3 \\[4pt] s_0\begin{bmatrix} 1 \\ 1 \\ 1 \end{bmatrix} & s_1\begin{bmatrix} 1 \\ 0 \\ 0 \end{bmatrix} & s_2\begin{bmatrix} 0 \\ 1 \\ 0 \end{bmatrix} & s_3\begin{bmatrix} 0 \\ 0 \\ 1 \end{bmatrix} \end{array}$$

The column vectors are defined as linearly independent if the equation

$$s_0X_0 + s_1X_1 + s_2X_2 + s_3X_3 = 0$$

is satisfied only when *all* the scalars are zero. However, for matrix **B**, a set of scalars, some of which are not zero, can be found to satisfy this equation. For example, the value of the expression below is zero, but, as can be seen, all of the scalars in the set applied are non-zero:

$$\begin{array}{ccccc} X_0 & X_1 & X_2 & X_3 & 0 \\[4pt] 1\begin{bmatrix} 1 \\ 1 \\ 1 \end{bmatrix} + -1\begin{bmatrix} 1 \\ 0 \\ 0 \end{bmatrix} + -1\begin{bmatrix} 0 \\ 1 \\ 0 \end{bmatrix} + -1\begin{bmatrix} 0 \\ 0 \\ 1 \end{bmatrix} & = & \begin{bmatrix} 0 \\ 0 \\ 0 \end{bmatrix} \end{array}$$

Therefore, the X predictor column vectors are not linearly independent. This is because the redundant variable X_3 is included in the set of predictors. When X_3 is included, the predictor variable X_0 is a linear function of all the others ($X_0 = X_1 + X_2 + X_3$). Linear dependency amongst predictor variables prevents a unique solution to the system of normal simultaneous equations upon which GLM parameter estimation is based. However, simply eliminating the redundant X_3 results in linear independence amongst the remaining predictors (X_0, X_1 and X_2) and allows a unique solution to the system of normal simultaneous equations.

In summary, the dummy coding scheme uses only 1 and 0 values to denote allocation to experimental conditions. ($p - 1$) variables are used and one condition (most easily the last in sequence, e.g. C), is given 0s across all indicator variables. The other conditions (A and B) are denoted by 1s rather than 0s on variables X_1 and X_2, respectively.

Dummy coding sets the experimental condition coded by 0s on all predictors as a reference condition. The intercept β_0 reflects the mean of this reference condition. Moreover, the regression coefficient for each of the ($p - 1$) predictor variables reflects the difference between the mean of the reference condition (coded with 0s) and whichever experimental condition the predictor variable codes with 1s. Therefore, a test of the significance of the regression coefficient is equivalent to a test of the difference between these two means. All of these estimates are unaffected by unbalanced data. Dummy coding is ideal when all experimental conditions are to be compared with a (0 coded) control group.

As well as dummy coding, effect and orthogonal coding schemes can be used to denote experimental conditions. Effect coding operates very like dummy coding, but rather than the "last" experimental condition being denoted by all indicator variables taking 0 values, it is denoted by all indicator variables taking the value -1. Effect coding for the example data in Table 2.8 is presented in Table 2.9.

Like the experimental design GLM parameter μ, β_0 with effect coding reflects the mean of the experimental condition means (the unweighted mean). The regression coefficients reflect the difference between the mean of the condition coded with 1s and β_0, the mean of the experimental condition means. Therefore, the regression coefficient estimates equal the respective α_j parameter estimates in the experimental design GLM. This concordance gives effect coding its name and, together with the fact that it usually is employed in matrix algebra implementations of experimental design GLMs, probably explains why it is the most popular coding scheme.

The orthogonal coding scheme is quite different to dummy and effect coding schemes. The values taken by the predictor variables are the values of orthogonal coefficients (cf. multiple comparison test coefficients, e.g. Kirk, 1995) and their role is to implement particular orthogonal contrasts. While linear independence refers to non-redundant information, orthogonality refers to non-overlapping information. (Orthogonality is a special, more restricted, case of linear independence.) The information used in one orthogonal contrast is completely distinct from the information used in the other orthogonal contrasts. Two contrasts are defined mathematically as orthogonal if the sum of the products of the coefficients for their respective elements is zero. Given p groups, there are only ever $(p - 1)$ orthogonal contrasts available. With respect

Table 2.9   Effect coding to represent subject allocation to experimental conditions

Conditions	Subjects	X_1	X_2	Y
A	s1	1	0	7
	...	...	...	...
	s8	1	0	7
B	s9	0	1	7
	...	...	...	...
	s16	0	1	11
C	s17	-1	-1	8
	...	...	...	...
	s24	-1	-1	12

to experimental data in Table 2.2, it can be stated that there are $(3 - 1) = 2$ orthogonal contrasts. An orthogonal coding for the experimental conditions A, B and C is presented in Table 2.10.

contrast 1 (coded by variable X_1): $(1)A + (0)B + (-1)C$

contrast 2 (coded by variable X_2): $(1/2)A + (-1)B + (1/2)C$

Focusing on only the coefficients:

contrast 1: $(1) + (0) + (-1)$

contrast 2: $(1/2) + (-1) + (1/2)$

and so, (contrast 1) $\times$ (contrast 2):

$$(1)(1/2) + (0)(-1) + (-1)(1/2) = 1/2 + 0 - 1/2 = 1/2 - 1/2 = 0$$

Table 2.10 presented the full set of coefficient values taken by the ANOVA regression predictor variables to implement the orthogonal coding scheme just described. Notice that the particular contrasts amongst means are implemented by each predictor variable and the issue of whether the two sets of contrasts are orthogonal involves comparing X_1 with X_2:

Variable X_1 implements the contrast: $A - C$,

while variable X_2 implements the contrast: $[A + C]/2 - B$.

With orthogonal coding, irrespective of balanced or unbalanced data, the estimate of B_0 reflects the general mean of the dependent variable scores (i.e. the weighted mean), while the regression coefficients reflect the specific comparison coded on the predictor variable. Consequently, testing the significance of any predictor variable regression coefficient is equivalent to testing the significance of the contrast coded by that predictor variable. When only specific orthogonal contrasts are of interest, usually the preferred scheme is orthogonal coding.

Table 2.10 Orthogonal coding representing subject allocation to experimental conditions

Conditions	Subjects	X_1	X_2	Y
	s1	1	1/2	7
A	...	...	...	...
	s8	1	1/2	7
	s9	0	-1	7
B	...	...	...	...
	s16	0	-1	11
	s17	-1	1/2	8
C	...	...	...	...
	s24	-1	1/2	12

Examples of dummy and effect coding

As regression ANOVA GLMs are implemented most frequently using dummy and effect coding, only these schemes will be considered further. (Excellent accounts of orthogonal coding are provided by Cohen & Cohen, 1983 and Pedhazur, 1997.) As a single predictor variable can code a comparison between only two experimental conditions, whenever three or more conditions are involved, multiple, rather than simple regression analysis is required. As virtually all multiple regression analyses now are carried out using statistical software, the examples will consider the typical output from statistical software packages. Dummy or effect coded predictor variables are used by the multiple regression software just as any conventional (quantitative) predictor variable would be used.

Table 2.11 presents the ANOVA summary table output from statistical software when a regression ANOVA GLM is carried out on the data presented in Table 2.2 using dummy or effect (or orthogonal) coding schemes. The regression and residual sum of squares, dfs, mean squares, as well as the F-value obtained are equivalent to that obtained when an experimental design GLM is implemented (see Table 2.3). Most regression software provides the multiple correlation coefficient (R), its square and an adjusted R squared value. R squared estimates the proportion of the dependent variable variance that can be attributed to the predictors, but unfortunately this statistic exhibits an overestimate bias. The smaller adjusted R squared attempts to eliminate this bias (see Pedhazur, 1997). Irrespective of the coding scheme employed, the same values are obtained for all of these estimates.

Dummy coding

Table 2.12 provides the output pertinent to the multiple regression equation for dummy coding. The Constant is the estimate of β_0, the Y-axis intercept. The table also lists the estimate of the regression coefficient parameter (Coefficient), its standard error (Std error), the standardized regression coefficient (Std coef), and t-tests (sometimes F-tests) of the significance of including these terms in the GLM.

Predicted scores are given by

$$\hat{Y}_i = \beta_0 + \beta_1 X_{i,1} + \beta_2 X_{i,2} \tag{2.41}$$

Table 2.11   ANOVA summary table output from statistical software implementing a regression ANOVA GLM

R: 0.826,	R squared: 0.683,		Adjusted R squared: 0.653		
Source	SS	df	Mean square	F	p
Regression	112.000	2	56.000	22.615	<0.001
Residual	52.000	21	2.476		

Table 2.12   Output pertinent to multiple regression equation for dummy coding

Variable	Coefficient	Std error	Std coef	t	p (2 Tail)
Constant	11.000	0.556	0.0	19.772	< 0.001
X1	−5.000	0.787	−0.902	−6.355	< 0.001
X2	−1.000	0.787	−0.180	−1.271	0.218

Although equation (2.41) also summarizes a set of regression equations, only three experimental conditions are represented by the dummy coding scheme used. Therefore, like the experimental design GLM, there can be only three different predicted scores. These predicted scores are the means of the experimental conditions. Substituting the pertinent X predictor variable dummy codes and the parameter estimates from Table 2.12 into the system of equations summarized by (2.41) provides the following three separate predictions:

$$\text{Predicted } Y_A \text{ (i.e. } Y_1 \text{ to } Y_8) = 11 + (-5)(1) + (-1)(0) = 11 - 5 = 6$$

$$\text{Predicted } Y_B \text{ (i.e. } Y_7 \text{ to } Y_{16}) = 11 + (-5)(0) + (-1)(1) = 11 - 1 = 10$$

$$\text{Predicted } Y_C \text{ (i.e. } Y_{17} \text{ to } Y_{24}) = 11 + (-5)(0) + (-1)(0) = 11 - 0 = 11.$$

The mean of the condition coded 0 on both X_1 and X_2 variables (the "last" condition C) always is equal to the estimate of β_0, so the mean of condition $C = 11$. β_1 is the regression coefficient estimate for the predictor variable X_1, which dummy codes condition A, and β_2 is the regression coefficient estimate for the predictor variable X_2, which dummy codes condition B (see Table 2.8). Examination of the way in which predicted scores (condition means) are calculated reveals the β_1 and β_2 as representing deviations from the "last" condition, which here is C.

The t-values presented in Table 2.12 are given by

$$t = \text{coefficient/coefficient standard error}$$

where the dfs are equal to the residual term dfs.

The significance test of the Constant, β_0, has no corollary in ANOVA, but it may be considered as testing the hypothesis that the mean of condition C equals zero. Of much greater value are the significance tests of the β_1 and β_2 estimates. As the β_1 and β_2 estimates can be regarded as representing deviations from the "last" condition (i.e. condition C), tests of these regression coefficient estimates are equivalent to testing the difference between the means of the A and B conditions and condition C. As β_1 is the regression coefficient estimate for the predictor variable X_1, which dummy codes condition A, the test of β_1 is equivalent to testing the difference between the condition A and condition C means. Similarly, as β_2 is the regression coefficient estimate for the predictor variable X_2, which dummy codes condition B, the test of β_2 is equivalent to testing the difference between the condition B and condition C means.

Of course, any condition may be coded as the "last" and reference condition. Therefore, the same data can be recoded using condition A or B as the "last" and reference condition and reanalysed to provide the missing comparison between conditions A and B.

Effect coding

Table 2.13 provides the output pertinent to the multiple regression equation for effect coding. Effect coding takes its name from the concordance between the parameter estimates it provides and the experimental design GLM parameter estimates. Therefore, the Constant, β_0, represents the mean of the experimental condition means (μ).

As done above for dummy coding, substituting the pertinent X predictor variable effect codes and the parameter estimates from Table 2.13 into the system of equations summarized by (2.41) provides the following three separate predictions:

Predicted Y_A (i.e. Y_1 to Y_8) $= 9 + (-3)(1) + (1)(0) = 9 - 3 + 0 = 6$

Predicted Y_B (i.e. Y_9 to Y_{16}) $= 9 + (-3)(0) + (1)(1) = 9 + 0 + 1 = 10$

Predicted Y_C (i.e. Y_{17} to Y_{24}) $= 9 + (-3)(-1) + (1)(-1) = 9 + 3 - 1 = 11$.

Alternatively, the effect of the last experimental condition (C) can be found on the basis that

$$\sum_j a_j = 0 = a_A + a_B + a_C = 0, \quad \text{hence,} \quad a_C = -a_A - a_B$$

As β_1 and $\beta_2 = a_1$ and a_2, respectively, so, $a_C = -\beta_1 - \beta_2$. Therefore, $a_C = -(-3) - (1) = 3 - 1 = 2$. Consequently, the predicted Y_C (i.e. Y_{16} to Y_{24}) $= 9 + 2 = 11$.

As with dummy coding, a significance test of Constant, the μ parameter estimate, has no corollary in ANOVA, although it may be considered as a test of the hypothesis that μ equals zero. (The significance tests in Table 2.13 are calculated exactly as described for Table 2.12.) The regression coefficient parameter estimates obtained from effect coding also can be used to test differences between condition means, but the rationale and way in which it is done is a little more complicated because of the way in which the condition means are defined. For example, consider the calculation of the predicted score

Table 2.13   Output pertinent to multiple regression equation for effect coding

Variable	Coefficient	Std error	Std coef	t	p (2 Tail)
Constant	9.000	0.321	0.0	28.019	< 0.000
X1	−3.000	0.454	−0.937	−6.604	0.218
X2	1.000	0.454	0.312	2.201	0.039

(i.e. the mean) for condition A. Because the effect coding on variable X_2 is zero, this exerts no influence on the mean and can be omitted. Therefore,

$$Y_A = \mu + \beta_1 X_{i,1}$$

Moreover, as the actual code value is 1, which just indicates the presence of β_1, this also can be omitted, leaving

$$Y_A = \mu + \beta_1$$

Similarly,

$$Y_B = \mu + \beta_2$$

Therefore, the difference between the means of condition A and B can be written as

$$Y_A - Y_B = (\mu + \beta_1) - (\mu + \beta_2)$$

$$= \beta_1 - \beta_2$$

It follows that the difference between the means of condition A and C is

$$Y_A - Y_B = (\mu + \beta_1) - (\mu + [-\beta_1] - \beta_2)$$

$$= (\beta_1) - ([-\beta_1] - \beta_2)$$

$$= 2(\beta_1) + \beta_2$$

Substituting the regression coefficient parameter estimate values from Table 2.12 provides

$$Y_A - Y_C = 2(-3) + (1) = -6 + 1 = -5$$

To verify the accuracy of this approach, the actual mean of condition C may be subtracted from the mean of condition A,

$$Y_A - Y_C = 6 - 11 = -5$$

Testing differences between these regression coefficient parameter estimates requires the variance of estimate of the difference between the regression coefficients to be calculated (see Cohen & Cohen, 1983; Pedhazur, 1997). Therefore, using effect coding regression coefficient parameter estimates to test differences between condition means has little advantage over tests of the differences between the actual condition means.

Zero sum experimental effects and coding schemes

In Chapter 1, ANOVA was described as the special case of multiple regression which includes the side condition that the experimental effects sum to zero, that is

$$\sum_{j=1}^{P} (N_i a_j) = 0 \qquad\qquad (2.20, \text{rptd})$$

In fact, requiring experimental effects to sum to zero is equivalent to eliminating one of the parameters and redefining the condition previously specified by the eliminated parameter in terms of the other conditions. A more formal expression is

$$\text{because} \sum_{j=1}^{p}(N_j\alpha_j) = 0, \qquad \alpha_p = -\sum_{j=1}^{p}\alpha_j \qquad (2.42)$$

The use of only $p - 1$ predictors, where the "last" experimental condition is defined as the negative of the sum of the remaining conditions (so that experimental effects to sum to zero) is effect coding. Therefore, the implicit consequence of the side condition that effects sum to zero is made explicit in a regression ANOVA GLM using effect coding. Dummy coding does not result in experimental effects summing to zero, but redefines β_0 and the $(p - 1)$ experimental conditions in terms of p, the "last" experimental condition. Both of these techniques constitute reparameterization solutions to the overparameterization problem.

Omnibus F-tests and orthogonal contrasts

An infinite number of sets of orthogonal contrasts may be specified for any design, although each set contains only $p - 1$ orthogonal contrasts. The omnibus MS obtained from an orthogonally coded regression GLM is the average MS of the separate orthogonal contrasts, but all sets of orthogonal contrasts provide the same average MS: the omnibus MS provided by all forms of ANOVA implementation. Nevertheless, even when the average MS of a set of orthogonal contrasts is not significant, it is possible for individual orthogonal contrasts within the set to be significant. Moreover, orthogonal contrasts may identify a significant omnibus F-test as being due to differences between certain combinations of experimental condition means, such as represented by the X_2 variable in Table 2.10. This may seem to contradict the earlier description that a significant omnibus F-test indicates at least one of the experimental condition means differs from another experimental condition mean. However, as there are an infinite number of sets of orthogonal contrasts for any design, a significant omnibus F-test indicates that at least one of these sets will include a significant contrast between two distinct experimental condition means.

2.3.4   Cell mean GLMs

A relatively new solution to the overparameterization problem inherent with experimental design GLMs is to apply a cell mean GLM. Although this approach is increasingly popular with statisticians, so far it has made little impact in psychology.

Cell mean GLMs describe each dependent variable score as comprising the mean of the experimental condition plus error. The equation for this type of GLM is

$$Y_{ij} = \mu_j + \varepsilon_{ij} \qquad (2.43)$$

In contrast to the experimental design GLM, which expresses experimental effects in terms of deviation from the constant μ, the only structure imposed upon the data by the experimental design cell mean model is that of the experimental conditions. (This feature of the experimental design cell mean model becomes more prominent with factorial designs.) As cell mean GLMs do not employ the parameter μ, there are only as many experimental condition means as there are parameters to be estimated.

Apart from solving the problem of overparameterization, the cell mean GLM affords another advantage. When overparameterized experimental design GLMs are used, it is possible to obtain a unique solution to the problem of estimating parameters by reparameterization or estimable function techniques (Searle, 1987). These methods of circumventing the overparameterization problem work well with balanced data, but with unbalanced data, they can result in ambiguous hypothesis tests. In contrast, irrespective of balanced or unbalanced data, when cell mean GLMs are applied there is never any ambiguity about which hypothesis is tested.

2.3.5   Cell mean, regression and experimental design GLMs

Despite its attractions, the cell mean model is not quite the panacea it may appear. The major advantage afforded by cell mean GLMs is the elimination of ambiguity over hypothesis tests with unbalanced data. Nevertheless, good experimental design practice should ensure balanced data. Only single factor experiments have been considered so far, but neither cell mean nor regression ANOVA GLMs make explicit the terms in which multi-factor experiments are conceived and in which there is most interest – experimental main effects and interaction effects. Explicitly representing experimental effects in experimental design GLMs provides a clearer appreciation of experimental design issues (Collier & Hummel, 1977; Kirk, 1995). Indeed, the merit of experimental design GLMs is supported by the notations employed by the computer programs NAG GLIM, NAG GENSTAT (developed from Wilkinson & Rogers, 1973), SYSTAT, MINITAB, and SAS, as well as by numerous authors (e.g. Kirk, 1995; Howell, 1997; Maxwell & Delaney, 1990; McCullagh & Nelder, 1989; Searle, 1987; 1997; Winer et al., 1991). Accordingly, experimental design GLMs will be employed throughout the present text. However, regression implementations of experimental design GLMs via effect coding also will be described because carrying out ANOVA in such a manner using available statistical software packages immediately places ANOVA in the context of linear modelling. Readers interested in cell mean GLMs should consult Searle (1987).

3 GLM APPROACHES TO INDEPENDENT MEASURES FACTORIAL ANOVA DESIGNS

3.1 Factorial designs

Factorial designs are by far the most common type of design applied in psychological research. While single factor experiments manipulate a single variable, factorial experiments manipulate two or more variables, or factors, at the same time.

As naturally occurring circumstances usually involve the interplay of a multitude of variables acting together, there is an argument that factorial designs are closer approximations to reality and so more ecologically valid than single factor studies. Of course, the logical conclusion of this line of reasoning is that the most ecologically valid approach is just to observe reality. However, because reality is so complicated, understanding is impossible to obtain just by observation. Consequently, to allow understanding to develop, experiments aim to simplify by focusing on only a particular aspect of reality. The majority of factorial designs represent a biased compromise (unless an extremely large number of factors are involved) between these two extremes. Therefore, the experimental approach is reductionist, but this does not mean scientific theory must be reductionist (Rose, 1992).

Although the conditions under which performance is observed are defined by two or more variables, factorial designs allow the effects attributable to the separate factors to be estimated. The separate factor estimates are termed main effects and compare with the estimates of the effects of experimental conditions in single factor studies. Nevertheless, the unique feature of factorial designs is the ability to observe the way in which the manipulated factors combine to affect behaviour. The pattern of performance observed over the levels of a single factor may change substantially when combined with the levels of another factor. The influence of the combination of factors is called an interaction effect and reflects the variation in performance scores resulting specifically from the combination of factors. In other words, an interaction effect is in addition to any factor main effects. Indeed, in many factorial experiments the issue of whether there is an interaction may be of more interest than whether there are any main effects.

3.2 Factor main effects and factor interactions

The nature of main effects and factor interactions probably is explained best by way of an example. Consider an extension to the hypothetical experiment examining the influence of study time on recall. A researcher may be interested to know the consequences for recall of different encoding strategies when different periods of study time are available. To examine this issue, the same study time periods are crossed with two forms of encoding instruction. Subjects are instructed to "memorize the words", just as before, or they are instructed to use story and imagery mnemonics: construct a story from the stimulus words and imagine the story events in their mind's eye. As before, the recall period lasts for 2 min and begins immediately after the study period ends. The data obtained from this independent two factor (2 × 3) design is presented in Table 3.1, as are useful summary statistics.

Two conventions are relevant here. The first is that the factor with the fewest levels is labelled A and the factor with the next fewest levels is labelled B, etc. The second is that upper case (capital) letters are used to denote factors and lower case letters to denote factor levels. Therefore, Factor A represents the two levels of encoding, i.e. the two encoding conditions, with a_1 and a_2 representing the *memorize* and *story construction and imagery* conditions, respectively, while Factor B represents the study time conditions, with b_1, b_2 and b_3 representing 30, 60 and 180 s, respectively.

An alternative presentation of the six experimental conditions comprising the two factor design is provided by Table 3.2. Here, the mean memory performance observed in each of the experimental conditions is presented, as are marginal means (so termed because they appear in the table margins), which provide performance estimates under the levels of one factor, averaged over the influence of the other factor. (The mean in the bottom right corner is the average of all the averages.)

Table 3.1 Experimental data and summary statistics

Encoding instructions	a_1 Memorize			a_2 Story and Image		
Study time (s)	b_1 30	b_2 60	b_3 180	b_1 30	b_2 60	b_3 180
	7	7	8	16	16	24
	3	11	14	7	10	29
	6	9	10	11	13	10
	6	11	11	9	10	22
	5	10	12	10	10	25
	8	10	10	11	14	28
	6	11	11	8	11	22
	7	11	12	8	12	24
$\sum Y$	48	80	88	80	96	184
$(\sum Y)^2$	304	814	990	856	1186	4470
$\sum Y^2$	2304	6400	7744	6400	9216	33856

Table 3.2   Means and marginal means for the experimental data in Table 3.1

| | Study time (s) | | | |
| | b_1 | b_2 | b_3 | |
Encoding instructions	30	60	180	Marginal means
a_1 Memorize words	6	10	11	9
a_2 Story and imagery mnemonics	10	12	23	15
Marginal means	8	11	17	12

As seen, six experimental conditions result from crossing a two level independent factor with a three level independent factor. Indeed, the inclusion of all combinations of the factor levels is a defining feature of *factorial* designs, distinguishing them from other designs that may use more than one factor but not in a crossed fashion (e.g. see Kirk, 1995, on nested designs).

The equation

$$Y_{ijk} = \mu + \alpha_j + \beta_k + (\alpha\beta)_{jk} + \varepsilon_{ijk} \qquad (3.1)$$

describes the experimental design GLM for the independent measures, two factor ANOVA applicable to the data presented in Table 3.1. Y_{ijk} is the ith subject's dependent variable score in the experimental condition defined by the jth level of Factor A, where $j = 1, \ldots, p$, and the kth level of Factor B, where $k = 1, \ldots, q$. As in the single factor design, the parameter μ is a constant representing the dependent variable score free of the effect of any experimental condition. The parameter α_j is the effect of the j Factor A levels and the parameter β_k is the effect of the k Factor B levels. The effect of the interaction between Factors A and B over the j and k levels is represented by the parameter $(\alpha\beta)_{jk}$. Finally, the random variable, ε_{ijk}, is the error term, which reflects variation due to any uncontrolled source. Again equation (3.1) summarizes a set of equations, each of which describes the constitution of a single dependent variable score.

The parameter μ is defined as

$$\mu = \sum_{j=1}^{p} \sum_{k=1}^{q} \mu_{jk}/pq \qquad (3.2)$$

In other words, μ is the grand mean of the separate experimental condition means.

The parameters α_j are defined as

$$\alpha_j = \mu_j - \mu \qquad (3.3)$$

where μ_j is the marginal mean for Factor A, level j and μ is the grand mean as defined. Therefore, the effect of the j levels of Factor A is given by the difference between the j Factor A marginal means and the grand mean. The (marginal) mean for the jth level of Factor A is defined as

$$\mu_j = \sum_{k=1}^{q} \mu_{jk}/q \qquad (3.4)$$

where q is the number of levels of Factor B. Therefore,

$$\mu_1 = (6 + 10 + 11)/3 = 9$$

$$\mu_2 = (10 + 12 + 23)/3 = 15$$

For the current example,

$$\alpha_j = \mu_j - \mu \qquad (3.3, \text{rptd})$$

gives

$$\alpha_1 = 9 - 12 = -3$$

and

$$\alpha_2 = 15 - 12 = 3$$

Overall, the effect of the Factor A level 1 manipulation (the *memorize* instruction) is to reduce memory performance by three words, whereas the Factor A level 2 manipulation (the *story and imagery* mnemonics) is to increase memory performance by three words.

The parameters β_k are defined as

$$\beta_k = \mu_k - \mu \qquad (3.5)$$

where μ_k is the marginal mean for Factor B, level k. Therefore, the effect of the k levels of Factor B is given by the difference between the k Factor B marginal means and the grand mean. The (marginal) mean for the jth level of Factor B is defined as

$$\mu_k = \sum_{j=1}^{p} \mu_{jk}/p \qquad (3.6)$$

where p is the number of levels of Factor A. Therefore,

$$\mu_1 = (6 + 10)/2 = 8$$

$$\mu_2 = (10 + 12)/2 = 11$$

$$\mu_3 = (11 + 23)/2 = 17$$

For the current example,

$$\beta_k = \mu_k - \mu \qquad (3.5, \text{rptd})$$

gives

$$\beta_1 = 8 - 12 = -4$$

$$\beta_2 = 11 - 12 = -1$$

and

$$\beta_3 = 17 - 12 = 5.$$

Overall, the effect of the Factor B level 1 manipulation (30 s study time) is to reduce memory performance by four words, the Factor B level 2 manipulation (60 s) reduces memory performance by one word, while the Factor B level 3 manipulation (180 s) increases memory performance by five words.

Comparisons between marginal means compare with the effect of experimental conditions in single independent factor design presented earlier. However, while main effects in factorial designs bear comparison with experimental condition effects in single factor designs, subjects' performance is very unlikely to have been observed under identical circumstances. In single factor experiments there should be no systematic variation between experimental conditions other than the experimental manipulations defining the levels of the single factor. However, their factorial design counterparts, the marginal means, are estimated by averaging across any (systematic) influence of the other factor, and so they incorporate any influence of this factor. Therefore, factorial experiment marginal means are likely to differ from their single factor counterparts, the experimental condition means (e.g. compare the Factor B marginal means with the original "memorize the words" single factor condition means – level a_1 in Table 3.2). Nevertheless, because the factors are crossed, the three marginal means for Factor B average over exactly the same levels of Factor A. Therefore, after averaging over exactly the same levels of Factor A, the only difference between the scores summarized by the three marginal means for Factor B is in terms of the distinction between the Factor B levels (study time). Similarly, the two marginal means for Factor A are averaged over equivalent levels of Factor B, so the only difference between the scores summarized by the two marginal means for Factor A is in terms of the distinction between the Factor A levels (encoding instructions). Consequently, the averaging procedures result in orthogonal comparisons between the levels of Factor A and the levels of Factor B and the interaction between the Factor A and Factor B levels. Moreover, the ability to demonstrate the influence of a factor despite the changes defined by other factors is the basis for arguing that factorial designs are more ecologically valid than single factor studies.

The penultimate parameters $(\alpha\beta)_{jk}$ are defined as

$$(\alpha\beta)_{jk} = \mu_{jk} - (\mu + \alpha_j + \beta_k) \tag{3.7}$$

where μ_{jk} denotes the separate experimental condition means. Therefore, each interaction effect is the extent to which each separate experimental condition mean diverges from the additive pattern of main effects. Hopefully, this gives some substance to the earlier claim that the interaction effects were over and above any factor main effects. For the current example,

$$(\alpha\beta)_{11} = \mu_{11} - (\mu + \alpha_1 + \beta_1) = 6 - (12 - 3 - 4) = 1$$

$$(\alpha\beta)_{12} = \mu_{12} - (\mu + \alpha_1 + \beta_2) = 10 - (12 - 3 - 1) = 2$$

$$(\alpha\beta)_{13} = \mu_{13} - (\mu + \alpha_1 + \beta_3) = 11 - (12 - 3 + 5) = -3$$

$$(\alpha\beta)_{21} = \mu_{21} - (\mu + \alpha_2 + \beta_1) = 10 - (12 + 3 - 4) = -1$$

$$(\alpha\beta)_{22} = \mu_{22} - (\mu + \alpha_2 + \beta_2) = 12 - (12 + 3 - 1) = -2$$

$$(\alpha\beta)_{23} = \mu_{23} - (\mu + \alpha_2 + \beta_3) = 23 - (12 + 3 + 5) = 3$$

Overall, the effect of the interaction is to increase or decrease subjects' memory performance in each of the six experimental conditions by the number of words shown. For instance, in the experimental condition where subjects were instructed just to *memorize* the words and had 180s to do so (condition a_1b_3), memory performance was three words less than would be expected if Factors A and B had exerted only their main effects. This (non-zero) interaction effect indicates that this particular combination of these two factor levels affects memory performance in a manner different to the separate aggregate effects of the two factors.

Based on the *model* component of the two factor GLM equation, predicted scores are given by

$$\hat{Y}_{ijk} = \mu + \alpha_j + \beta_k + (\alpha\beta)_{jk} \tag{3.8}$$

and so the last parameters, the error terms, which represent the discrepancy between the actual scores observed and the scores predicted by the two factor GLM, are defined as

$$\varepsilon_{ijk} = Y_{ijk} - \hat{Y}_{ijk} \tag{3.9}$$

The two independent factors experimental design GLM has been described and its parameters defined. Attention now turns to how well the GLMs incorporating some or all of these parameters accommodate the experimental data. Two strategies for carrying out ANOVA by comparing GLMs will be considered. The first is a simple extension of the comparison between full and restricted GLMs for factorial experimental designs, while the second concords with hierarchical linear modelling.

At this point, one of the major benefits of an experimental approach for statistical analysis should be mentioned. In factorial designs, because factor levels are completely crossed, factor main and interaction effects are orthogonal. This means there is absolutely no overlap in information between the factors, and so any variance in the dependent variable attributed to one factor will be distinct from any dependent variable variance attributed to any other factor or interaction between factors. Therefore, no matter the order in which the sum of squares estimates for the factor main effects, interaction effects and error are calculated, the same values always are obtained. It may seem strange to think that different estimates for these effects could be calculated. After all, the statistical analysis is just working out what happened and what happened should not change depending on which effect you estimate first. However, this sort of perspective gives the statistical analysis far too much respect. Although the statistical analysis exhibits complete internal consistency, its meaning is dependent entirely upon the methodology that provides the numbers for analysis. For example, imagine if the two factors involved in the study were *study time* and *amount of effort expended trying to learn*. It would be likely that these two factors would be related: as the *amount of effort expended trying to learn* increased, so would *study time*. If the two factors are related, then it means they have something in common. Moreover, if this thing they have in common accounts for variation in subjects' memory scores, then through this common aspect, both of these factors will try to account for some of the same variation in subjects' memory scores. There are various consequences of this situation, depending on exactly how the calculations are done. For example, it could be that each factor is associated with 25% of the subjects' memory score variation, so 50% of the memory score variation should be accommodated by the two factors. But 50% will be an overestimate if each 25% includes a part shared with the other factor. Another possibility is that a factor is arbitrarily chosen and the variation in memory scores that can be attributed to it is calculated and removed from the memory scores. Consequently, when the variation attributable to the second factor is calculated, because variance that would have been associated with it has been removed already, the estimate of its effect on subjects' memory scores is reduced.

3.2.1   Estimating effects by comparing full and reduced experimental design GLMs

The major issue for a full and restricted GLM comparison approach is what are the pertinent GLMs to compare? The equation

$$Y_{ijk} = \mu + \alpha_j + \beta_k + (\alpha\beta)_{jk} + \varepsilon_{ijk} \qquad (3.1, \text{rptd})$$

describes the full experimental design GLM underlying the independent measures, two factor ANOVA. The hypotheses concerning the main effect of Factor A, the main effect of Factor B and the effect of the interaction between Factors A and B are assessed by constructing three reduced GLMs, which manifest data descriptions under the respective null hypotheses, and comparing their error components with that of the full model above.

This approach is simplified by virtue of all the main and interaction effects being orthogonal as a consequence of the factorial design. Orthogonality means that the effect estimates are completely distinct: there is absolutely no overlap.

The main effect of Factor A is assessed by constructing a reduced experimental design GLM that describes the data without accommodating any influence of Factor A. However, in order that only the effect of Factor A explains the difference between the reduced and full GLMs, the reduced GLM accommodates any influence of Factor B and any interaction between Factors A and B. Therefore, the reduced GLM for assessing the influence of Factor A is

$$Y_{ijk} = \mu + \beta_k + (\alpha\beta)_{jk} + \varepsilon_{ijk} \qquad (3.10)$$

This reduced GLM manifests the data description under the null hypothesis that the levels of Factor A do not influence the data. This assumption may be expressed more formally as

$$\alpha_j = 0 \qquad (3.11)$$

Applying the same rationale, the reduced GLM for assessing the effect of Factor B is

$$Y_{ijk} = \mu + \alpha_j + (\alpha\beta)_{jk} + \varepsilon_{ijk} \qquad (3.12)$$

This reduced GLM manifests the data description under the null hypothesis that the levels of Factor B do not influence the data. This assumption may be expressed more formally as

$$\beta_k = 0 \qquad (3.13)$$

Finally, the reduced GLM for assessing the effect of the interaction between Factors A and B is

$$Y_{ijk} = \mu + \alpha_j + \beta_k + \varepsilon_{ijk} \qquad (3.14)$$

This reduced GLM manifests the data description under the null hypothesis that the interaction between levels of Factors A and B do not influence the data. This assumption may be expressed more formally as

$$(\alpha\beta)_{jk} = 0 \qquad (3.15)$$

Note that the null hypotheses are expressed in terms of zero effects and not in terms of grand mean equivalence with marginal and experimental condition means. This is because the marginal and experimental condition means may vary from the grand mean as a consequence of one effect even though the effect being assessed is equal to zero.

Having established both full and reduced GLMs for the independent measures two factor ANOVA, it is time to illustrate the calculation of the error sums of squares for these models using the data from the memory experiment.

First, the difference between the full GLM and the Factor A reduced GLM error sum of squares will be calculated. For both reduced and full GLMs, the error SS can be defined as

$$\text{SSE} = \sum_{i=1}^{N}(\varepsilon_{ijk})^2 = \sum_{k=1}^{q}\sum_{j=1}^{p}\sum_{i=1}^{N}(Y_{ijk} - \hat{Y}_{ijk})^2 \qquad (3.16)$$

where $\hat{Y}_{ijk}$ is the predicted scores from either the full or the reduced GLM.

For the full GLM, the estimate of $\hat{Y}_{ijk}$ is $\overline{Y}_{jk}$ and so, for the Factor A reduced GLM, the equivalent estimate of $\hat{Y}_{ijk}$ is $\overline{Y}_{jk} - \alpha_j$. Therefore,

$$SSE_{ARGLM} = \sum_{k=1}^{q} \sum_{j=1}^{p} \sum_{i=1}^{N} (Y_{ijk} - \overline{Y}_{jk} - a_j)^2 \qquad (3.17)$$

Contained within the brackets of equation (3.17) are the full GLM error $(Y_{ijk} - \overline{Y}_{jk})$ and the effect of Factor A (a_j). The effect of Factor A has been defined as

$$a_j = \mu_j - \mu \qquad (3.3, \text{rptd})$$

and is estimated by

$$\hat{a}_j = \overline{Y}_j - \overline{Y}_G \qquad (3.18)$$

where $\overline{Y}_j$ represents the Factor A marginal means and $\overline{Y}_G$ is the grand mean. Substituting these terms and applying some algebra reveals

$$SSE_{ARGLM} = SSE_{FGLM} + N_{jk}q \sum_{j=1}^{p} (\overline{Y}_j - \overline{Y}_G)^2 \qquad (3.19)$$

where N_{jk} is the number of subjects in each experimental condition. It follows from equation (3.19) that

$$SSE_{ARGLM} - SSE_{FGLM} = N_{jk}q \sum_{j=1}^{p} (\overline{Y}_j - \overline{Y}_G)^2 \qquad (3.20)$$

Equation (3.20) specifies the reduction in the GLM error term when the effect of Factor A is accommodated in comparison to not accommodating only the Factor A effect in the reduced GLM, and is equal to the main effect sum of squares for Factor A (SS$_A$). A similar logic reveals the main effect sum of squares for Factor B (SS$_B$) as

$$SSE_{BRGLM} - SSE_{FGLM} = N_{jk}p \sum_{k=1}^{q} (\overline{Y}_k - \overline{Y}_G)^2 \qquad (3.21)$$

where $\overline{Y}_k$ represents the Factor B marginal means. Finally, the sum of squares for the interaction between the levels of Factors A and B (SS$_{AB}$) is given by

$$SSE_{ABRGLM} - SSE_{FGLM} = N_{jk} \sum_{j=1}^{p} \sum_{k=1}^{q} (\overline{Y}_{jk} - \overline{Y}_j - \overline{Y}_k + \overline{Y}_G)^2 \qquad (3.22)$$

Applying these sums of squares formulae to the example memory experiment data gives

$$SSE_{ARGLM} - SSE_{FGLM} = 8(3)[(9 - 12)^2 + (15 - 12)^2]$$

$$= 24[18]$$

$$= 432$$

$$SSE_{BRGLM} - SSE_{FGLM} = 8(2)[(8 - 12)^2 + (11 - 12)^2 + (17 - 12)^2]$$

$$= 16[42]$$

$$= 672$$

$$SSE_{ABRGLM} - SSE_{FGLM} = 8 \begin{bmatrix} (6 - 9 - 8 + 12)^2 + (10 - 9 - 11 + 12)^2 \\ + (11 - 9 - 17 + 12)^2 + (10 - 15 - 8 + 12)^2 \\ + (12 - 15 - 11 + 12)^2 + (23 - 15 - 17 + 12)^2 \end{bmatrix}$$

$$= 8[28]$$

$$= 224$$

In addition to the SS for main and interaction effects, the associated dfs are required. Previously dfs were described as the number of scores employed in constructing the estimate that genuinely were free to vary. Equivalently, the dfs may be defined in accord with the model comparison approach. The dfs for a GLM equals the number of scores minus the number of independent parameters employed in the model. And just as main and interactive effects are defined as the difference between reduced and full GLM errors, so the main and interactive effect dfs can be defined as the difference between the reduced and full GLM dfs.

The ANOVA solution to the overparameterization problem for experimental design GLMs is to constrain effects to sum to zero. (See the discussion of effect coding.) Therefore, μ constitutes one parameter, there are $(p - 1)$ parameters required to distinguish the levels of Factor A, $(q - 1)$ parameters are required for Factor B and $(p - 1)(q - 1)$ parameters for the interaction between Factors A and B. For the independent (2×3) factors experimental design GLM, a total of 6 independent parameters are employed. Consequently, for the (full) independent (2×3) factor experimental design GLM applied to the memory experiment data, there are

$$(N - 6) = (48 - 6) = 42 \text{ dfs}$$

For the Factor A reduced GLM, the $(p - 1)$ parameters distinguishing the Factor A levels are omitted, leaving $1 + (q - 1) + (p - 1)(q - 1) = 1 + (3 - 1) + (2 - 1)(3 - 1) = 5$. Therefore, for the Factor A reduced GLM there are

$$48 - 5 = 43 \text{ dfs}$$

As the Factor A reduced GLM has 43 dfs and the full independent (2×3) factor experimental design GLM has only 42 dfs, it follows that the main effect of Factor A has 1 df.

For the Factor B reduced GLM, the $(q - 1)$ parameters distinguishing the Factor B levels are omitted, leaving, $1 + (p - 1) + (p - 1)(q - 1) = 1 + (2 - 1) + (2 - 1)(3 - 1) = 4$. Therefore, for the Factor B reduced GLM there are

$$48 - 4 = 44 \text{ dfs}$$

As the Factor B reduced GLM has 44 dfs and the full experimental design GLM has 42 dfs, it follows that the main effect of Factor B has 2 dfs.

For the AB Factors interaction reduced GLM, the $(p - 1)(q - 1)$ parameters distinguishing the separate experimental conditions are omitted, leaving $1 + (p - 1) + (q - 1) = 1 + (2 - 1) + (3 - 1) = 4$. Therefore, for the AB Factors interaction reduced GLM there are

$$48 - 4 = 44 \text{ dfs}$$

As the AB Factors interaction reduced GLM has 44 dfs and the full experimental design GLM has 42 dfs, again it follows that the AB interaction effect has 2 dfs.

Armed with sums of squares and degrees of freedom for the two main effects and the interaction effect, the ANOVA summary table can be constructed (Table 3.3).

The last column in Table 3.3 provides the probability of the F-values being obtained by chance given the data analysed. As all of the probabilities are less than 0.05, all of the null hypotheses can be rejected and so, all of the GLMs manifesting the null hypotheses can be discarded in favour of the full GLM. Adopting the full GLM to describe the experimental data means that both Factors A and B and their interaction exert a significant effect on subjects' performance as measured by the dependent variable. As well as describing effects in terms of deviations from the grand mean, effects also can be considered as describing differences between marginal or condition means. Specifically, any effect may be interpreted as indicating that at least two of the means involved in defining the effect are not equal.

In the current example, interpreting the main effect of Factor A, encoding instructions, in terms of mean differences is quite simple. As there are only two levels of this factor, the (marginal) means of these two levels of Factor A are the only means that can be unequal. Therefore, all that remains to be done is to determine the direction of the effect by identifying the Factor A levels with the larger and smaller means. Plotting pertinent means on a graph is an extremely

Table 3.3   ANOVA summary table

Source	Sum of squares	df	Mean square	F	p
A Encoding Instructions	432.000	1	432.000	47.747	< 0.001
B Study Time	672.000	2	336.000	37.137	< 0.001
A × B Encode Inst × Study Time	224.000	2	112.000	12.379	< 0.001
Error	380.000	42	9.048		

useful tool in interpreting data from any experiment. The plot of the two Factor *A* marginal means presented in Figure 3.1 reveals the nature of this main effect.

Interpreting the main effect of Factor *B*, study time, in terms of mean differences is slightly more complicated. As there are three levels of this factor, the unequal (marginal) means may be any one or more of b_1 vs. b_2, b_2 vs b_3 and b_1 vs b_3. Further tests are required to identify exactly which (marginal) means differ (see Figure 3.2).

An interaction effect indicates that the effect of one factor is not consistent over all the levels of the other factor(s). This can be seen by the plot of the means of the six experimental conditions presented in Figure 3.3. Although there is no intrinsic continuity between the groups comprising the experimental conditions, and so strictly a line graph is inappropriate, it is used because it conveys the nature of the interaction most simply, avoiding any need to create the illusion of depth in order to lay out another row of columns. Clearly the pattern of effect over the levels of Factor *B* at a_1 differs from the pattern of effect over the levels of Factor *B* at a_2. If the effect of one factor were consistent over all the levels of the other factor, then two parallel lines would be observed.

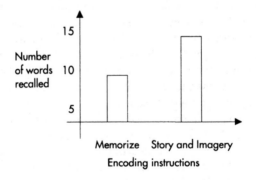

Figure 3.1   Number of words recalled as a function of encoding instructions

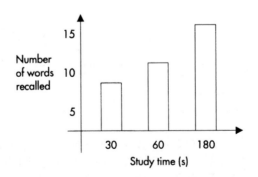

Figure 3.2   Number of words recalled as a function of study time

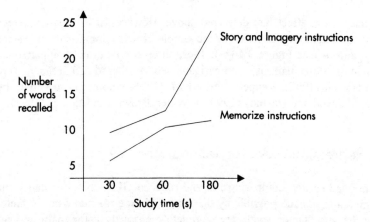

Figure 3.3   Number of words recalled as a function of encoding instructions and study time

The majority of statistical texts recommend that the particular interpretation of any interaction effect is investigated by assessing simple effects. For example, the memory experiment applied a two factor (2 × 3) design, which can be broken into assessments of simple effects as presented in Figure 3.4.

It should be evident that the simple effects comparisons of the three levels of Factor B at a_1 and also at a_2 (see Figure 3.4 (a)) correspond with the description

	b_1	b_2	b_3
a_1	6	10	11
a_2	10	12	23

	b_1	b_2	b_3
a_1	6	10	11

	b_1	b_2	b_3
a_2	10	12	23

(a) Comparison of simple effects of Factor B at a_1 and a_2

	b_1	b_2	b_3
a_1	6	10	11
a_2	10	12	23

	b_1
a_1	6
a_2	10

	b_2
a_1	10
a_2	12

	b_3
a_1	11
a_2	23

(b) Comparison of simple effects of Factor A at b_1, b_2 and b_3

Figure 3.4   Decomposition of 2 × 3 factor design into simple effects

of the interaction effect just delivered above. However, it is equally correct to describe the interaction in terms of the simple effects comparisons of Factor A at b_1, b_2 and b_3 (see Figure 3.4 (b)). These three simple effect comparisons are equivalent to three pairwise comparisons. For further detail, readers should consult Howell (1997), Keppel (1991), Kirk (1995, who refers to simple main effects), Maxwell and Delaney (1990) or Winer, Brown and Michels (1991).

3.3   Regression GLMs for factorial ANOVA

As mentioned earlier, comparing full and reduced GLMs is a distilled form of linear modelling, made possible by the nature of experimental data. In factorial designs, because factor levels are completely crossed, factor main and inter-action effects are orthogonal. This means there is absolutely no overlap in information between the factors, and so any variance in the dependent variable attributed to one factor will be distinct from any dependent variable variance attributed to any other factor or interaction between factors. Consequently, it makes no difference which term first enters the factorial ANOVA GLM. Irrespective of entry order, exactly the same results will be obtained.

The regression ANOVA GLM for the factorial (2×3) experimental design applied in the memory experiment is

$$Y_i = \beta_0 + \beta_1 X_1 + \beta_2 X_2 + \beta_3 X_3 + \beta_4 X_4 + \beta_5 X_5 + \varepsilon_i \qquad (3.23)$$

The effect coding required for the regression GLM to implement the factorial (2×3) ANOVA is presented in Table 3.4.

As only ($p - 1$) predictors are required to code p experimental conditions, the two levels of Factor A can be coded by the predictor variable X_1. Similarly, the three levels of Factor B can be coded by the predictor variables X_2 and X_3. Therefore, predictor X_1 represents the main effect of Factor A and predictors X_2 and X_3 represent the main effect of Factor B. The interaction between Factors A and B is coded by the variables X_4 and X_5. Variable X_4 is obtained by multiplying the codes of predictors X_1 and X_2, and variable X_5 is obtained by multiplying the codes of predictors X_1 and X_3. It is worth noting that the number of predictors required to code each main effect and the interaction effect ($A - X_1$, $B - X_2$ and X_3, $A \times B - X_4$ and X_5) equals the dfs for each effect ($A = 1$, $B = 2$ and $A \times B = 2$).

Table 3.5 presents the ANOVA summary table output from statistical software when the effect coded regression ANOVA GLM is applied to the data presented in Table 3.4.

The residual SS in Table 3.5 equals the error SS in Table 3.3. However, the regression SS in Table 3.5 is equivalent to the sum of the SS for Factors A, B and their interaction. For ANOVA, it is not the gross SS accommodated that is required, but rather the separate Factor and Factor interaction components of this sum. These components can be obtained in a variety of ways. Perhaps the simplest way is to carry out what corresponds to a hierarchical regression analysis (Cohen & Cohen, 1983).

Table 3.4   Effect coding for a two factor (2 × 3) experimental design

		X_1	X_2	X_3	X_4	X_5	Y
$A_1 B_1$	s1	1	1	0	1	0	7
	...						
	s8	1	1	0	1	0	7
$A_1 B_2$	s9	1	0	1	0	1	7
	...						
	s16	1	0	1	0	1	11
$A_1 B_3$	s17	1	−1	−1	−1	−1	8
	...						
	s24	1	−1	−1	−1	−1	12
$A_2 B_1$	s25	−1	1	0	−1	0	7
	...						
	s31	−1	1	0	−1	0	7
$A_2 B_2$	s32	−1	0	1	0	−1	7
	...						
	s40	−1	0	1	0	−1	7
$A_2 B_3$	s41	−1	−1	−1	1	1	7
	...						
	s48	−1	−1	−1	1	1	7

Table 3.5   ANOVA summary table output from statistical software implementing the regression ANOVA GLM described by equation (3.23) using effect coding

R: 0.882	R squared: 0.778		Adjusted R squared: 0.751		
Source	SS	df	Mean square	F	p
Regression	1328.000	5	265.000	29.356	< 0.001
Residual	380.000	42	9.048		
Total	1708.000	47			

3.3.1   Estimating main and interaction effects with regression GLMs

In step 1, Factor A, as represented by the predictor variable X_1, is entered into the regression GLM. This GLM is

$$Y_i = \beta_0 + \beta_1 X_1 + \varepsilon_i \tag{3.24}$$

Table 3.6 presents an ANOVA summary table for this regression, which reveals that the regression SS is identical to that for Factor A in Table 3.3. However, note that the residual SS at this step does not equal the ANOVA error SS.

In step 2, Factor B, represented by the predictor variables X_2 and X_3, is added to the regression. This GLM is

$$Y_i = \beta_0 + \beta_1 X_1 + \beta_2 X_2 + \beta_3 X_3 + \varepsilon_i \tag{3.25}$$

Table 3.7 presents an ANOVA summary table for this regression.

The increase in regression SS from step 1 to step 2, or the SS attributable to the inclusion of X_2 and X_3, is

$$1104.000 - 432.000 = 672.000$$

which is identical to the SS for Factor B in Table 3.3. Another way in which the SS attributable to predictors X_2 and X_3 could have been calculated is by determining the reduction of residual SS:

$$\text{step 1 residual} - \text{step 2 residual} = \text{residual reduction}$$

$$1276.000 - 604.000 = 672.000$$

Table 3.6　ANOVA summary of step 1

R: 0.503	R squared: 0.253		Adjusted R squared: 0.237		
Source	SS	df	Mean square	F	p
Regression	432.000	1	432.000	15.574	< 0.001
Residual	1276.000	46	27.739		
Total	1708.000	47	27.739		

Table 3.7　ANOVA summary of step 2

R: 0.804	R squared: 0.646		Adjusted R squared: 0.622		
Source	SS	df	Mean square	F	p
Regression	1104.000	3	368.000	26.808	< 0.001
Residual	604.000	44	13.727		
Total	1708.000	47	27.739		

In step 3, the interaction between factors A and B, represented by the predictor variables X_4 and X_5, is added to the regression. Of course, this is now the full regression ANOVA GLM described by equation (3.23) and summarized in Table 3.5.

4 GLM APPROACHES TO REPEATED MEASURES DESIGNS

4.1 Related measures designs

Repeated measures designs are particular instances of randomized block designs, which are members of the family of related measures designs. In contrast to independent measures designs, related measures designs accommodate relations between the dependent variable measures. The randomized block label refers specifically to designs that organize subjects into blocks. Subjects within each block are matched on one or more variables pertinent to the experiment, but between blocks, the subjects are dissimilar. For example, block 1 may contain ten subjects all matched on high IQ scores, while block 2 may contain ten subjects all matched on low IQ scores, with each block of subjects experiencing and providing data under all of the experimental conditions. This design is depicted in Table 4.1.

However, if there is only one subject per block, then the design is termed a repeated measures design, rather than a randomized block design. Table 4.2 depicts this design, where the same subjects provide data under more than one experimental condition, i.e. the same subjects are measured repeatedly.

Another related measures design which should be mentioned for completeness is the matched samples design. In the randomized block design, subjects within each block are matched on one or more variables pertinent to the

Table 4.1 A single factor randomized block design with 3 factor levels and 3 blocks

Condition A	Condition B	Condition C
Block 1	*Block 1*	*Block 1*
S1	S1	S1
. . .	. . .	. . .
S10	S10	S10
Block 2	*Block 2*	*Block 2*
S11	S11	S11
. . .	. . .	. . .
S20	S20	S20
Block 3	*Block 3*	*Block 3*
S21	S21	S21
. . .	. . .	. . .
S30	S30	S30

Table 4.2   A randomized block design
equivalent to a single factor repeated
measures design, as each block contains only
one subject

Condition A	Condition B	Condition C
Block 1	Block 1	Block 1
S1	S1	S1
Block 2	Block 2	Block 2
S2	S2	S2
Block 3	Block 3	Block 3
S3	S3	S3

experiment, but between blocks, the subjects are dissimilar. However, in matched samples designs, subjects matched on one or more variables pertinent to the experiment are allocated to different blocks. For example, in block 1, subject 1 may have a high IQ score. Another subject with a comparable IQ score would then be allocated to block 2, and if appropriate a third subject with a comparable IQ score would be allocated to block 3. Subjects with IQ scores comparable with that of subject 2 in block 1 would be allocated to blocks 2 and 3, and so on. The result is the opposite to the randomized block design. In Matched Samples designs subjects within each block may be dissimilar, but between blocks, the subjects are matched on one or more variables pertinent to the experiment. Nevertheless, the focus here is on Repeated Measures designs, as they are employed most frequently in psychological research. Other Related Measures designs and their analysis procedures are presented by Hays (1994), Howell (1997), Keppel (1991), Kirk (1995) and Winer et al. (1991).

4.2   Repeated measures designs

Like independent measures designs, the purpose of a repeated measures designs is to determine the effect of different experimental conditions on a dependent variable. Although repeated measures designs provide information about individual peformance over experimental conditions, description of individual subjects' performance is not an aim. Indeed, the use of a random factor to organize subject information emphasizes that the experiment aims to generalize to the population from which the subjects are drawn, rather than focus on the individual subjects providing the data. As if the labels, related measures designs and randomized block designs were insufficient, the typical definition of the experimental effect as a fixed effect and the definition of the subject effect as random also results in repeated measures designs being labelled as mixed designs. Although the mixed design term would be appropriate for single factor designs, usually it is applied only to factorial designs, where the levels of at least one factor are independent and the levels of at least one other factor are related.

In their discussion of overparameterized GLMs, Green, Marquis, Hershberger, Thompson and McCollam (1999) label GLMs applied to related designs as *general linear mixed models* (GLMMs). However, in common with all GLMs, experimental design GLMs employ additional terms to accommodate additional features of the experimental design. Therefore, Green et al.'s insertion of the term "mixed" into GLM is not only unnecessary, but also misleading, as it suggests something different about the nature of the linear modelling carried out.

An often quoted advantage of repeated measures designs is that subjects act as their own controls. However, as many experiments do not use a classic control condition, this statement can be rather obtuse. Perhaps a more accurate and more easily understood description is that subjects provide their own comparison: each subjects' performance can be compared across all conditions.

One of the advantages of repeated measures designs compared to equivalent independent measures designs is a reduction in the number of subjects required to provide the same amount of data. For example, the single factor repeated measures design with 3 conditions employing 3 subjects, illustrated in Table 4.2, provides as much data as nine subjects in the equivalent independent measures design. Another advantage is a reduction in error variance. It would be expected that the total amount of score variation will be less with three subjects each performing under 3 conditions, than with 9 subjects each performing under 1 condition. This reduction in variation is due to the greater similarity of the scores provided by the same subjects compared to those scores provided by different subjects. In other words, scores from the same subject are correlated. It is from correlations between scores that the benefits of related measures designs accrue. However, to make use of the correlation between the same subject's scores not only requires more complicated statistical analyses than independent measures designs, but also requires that additional statistical assumptions are tenable. (These assumptions are considered in Chapter 7.) It also should be appreciated that for some research issues repeatedly measuring subjects may not be an appropriate strategy. For example, measuring unintentional learning by a surprise memory test cannot be done repeatedly. Moreover, because of their nature, control procedures are more necessary when repeated measures designs are applied. Consider the design outlined in Table 4.2. If all subjects experience all experimental conditions, then each subject must experience conditions *A*, *B* and *C* in some order and the particular order experienced may affect the subjects' performance in each of the experimental conditions. For example, if all subjects experienced condition *A*, then condition *B*, then condition *C*, performance might increase from conditions *A* to *C* as a result of the practice the subject received as they performed the same experimental task under the different conditions. Alternatively, and particularly if the task were very demanding, subjects' performance might decrease from conditions *A* to *C* due to fatigue. Although these order effects (also termed sequence and carry-over effects) cannot be eliminated from subjects' performance, it is possible to exert some control. However, even when control is applied, a problem arises if the data reveals different effects of order. Differential order effects is the term for experimental condition effects that are attributable to particular experimental condition presentation orders. They are detected as an interaction between the experimental conditions and the presentation orders and indicate that subjects' experience in one experimental condition has particular consequence(s) for one or more of the other experimental conditions. For example, in a memory experiment comparing two encoding strategies, differences between conditions may be diminished because those subjects experiencing the semantic encoding strategy continue to apply it (intentionally or unintentionally) in the graphemic encoding strategy condition. However, the converse, applying the graphemic encoding strategy in the semantic encoding condition, may not occur, resulting in an interaction between the experimental conditions and the presentation orders. When differential order effects occur, the usual repeated measures analyses are invalid and it may be best to apply an independent measures design. Further discussion of differential order effects is provided by Keppel (1991) and Maxwell and Delaney (1990).

4.3 Order effect controls

4.3.1 Counterbalancing

Crossover designs

One way to control order effects is to determine how many different orders of conditions are possible in the experiment. In the current example, there are 3 conditions and so, $(3 \times 2 \times 1)$ 6 different order permutations possible – *ABC*, *ACB*, *BCA*, *BAC*, *CAB* and *CBA*. Allocating a subject to each experimental order does not eliminate the effect of any particular order, as each individual subject's performance continues to be influenced by the order of conditions they experience. Nevertheless, in a full crossover counterbalanced design, all orders are experienced by equal numbers of subjects and so, any performance benefit arising as a consequence of a particular order of conditions is counterbalanced by the effect of its counter-order (e.g. *ABC* and *CBA*). Moreover, including all orders in the experiment results in the orders being crossed with the other experimental factors. Provided more than one subject is allocated to each presentation order, it is possible to construct a factorial model of the data that explicitly represents the score variance due to the order effects and, if desired, the interaction between this factor and all the other factors in the experiment. However, differential order effects are indicated by any such significant inter-actions and conventional repeated measures analyses should not be applied when such effects are detected. Including and assessing interactions between experimental conditions and orders does provide a check that there are no significant differential order effects. Nevertheless, examination of the psycholo-gical literature reveals that GLMs applied to repeated measures designs frequently omit order terms. For this reason and due to restrictions on space, the GLMs described here for repeated measures designs also will omit these terms, even though the most efficient analyses are obtained when the study design is reflected fully in the linear model applied.

Latin square designs

With only 3 experimental conditions, it is quite feasible to allocate 2, 3 or more subjects to each experimental order. Even with 5 subjects per order, a total of only 30 subjects is required. However, as the number of experimental conditions increases, the number of order permutations increases exponentially. For example, 6 conditions provides ($6 \times 5 \times 4 \times 3 \times 2 \times 1$) 720 order permutations. Obviously, an experimenter will not want to run more than 720 subjects in a single experiment. However, there are alternatives to the fully counter-balanced crossover designs which may be applied even before the number of order permutations requires very large numbers of subjects. Rather than assign subjects to each of all possible orders, it is possible to determine a smaller set of orders, in which each experimental condition occurs once in each order position. This arrangement is termed a latin square design. An example of a latin square for the 4 experimental conditions *A*, *B*, *C* and *D* is provided in Table 4.3. As latin square designs employ a small set of orders to represent all of the order permutations, the selection of the orders constituting the latin square is an important consideration. The ideal is a digram-balanced latin square, as presented in Table 4.3. A digram-balanced latin square is obtained when each experimental condition both precedes and follows all others. The main disadvantage of digram-balanced latin squares is that they can be applied only when there are an even number of experimental conditions.

Two digram-balanced latin squares are needed when there are odd numbers of experimental conditions. Alternatively, when there are odd numbers of experimental conditions, a randomly permuted latin square may be applied. Of course, a randomly permuted latin square does not have the property that each experimental condition both precedes and follows all others, but they are a reasonable compromise (see Kirk, 1995; Maxwell & Delaney, 1990). In any event, the sort of latin square to avoid producing is a cyclic square. These latin squares arise when the same sequence of experimental conditions occurs in each order

Table 4.3   Latin square for single factor repeated measures design with 4 levels

| Order | Position in order | | | |
	P_1	P_2	P_3	P_4
1	A	B	C	D
2	C	A	D	B
3	B	D	A	C
4	D	C	B	A

employed, e.g. *ABCD*, *BCDA*, *CDAB* and *DABC*. Although each of the conditions occupy all positions once in the four orders, nevertheless, the same sequence *A* followed by *B* followed by *C* followed by *D* is maintained.

Kirk (1995) and Maxwell and Delaney (1990) present models for latin square designs that represent score variance due to order effects. However, unlike crossover designs, latin square designs employ only a particular set of the experimental condition orders and consequently, only order main effects can be estimated. Therefore, using order interaction effects to check the repeated measures assumption of constant order effects is precluded. Although Tukey's (1949; 1955) test for additivity (see Kirk, 1995) can provide some assurance that differential order effects are not present, a more simple and parsimonious assessment employing residuals is described in Chapter 7.

Although they may be conceived as single factor designs, all repeated measures designs are analysed as factorial designs. This is because an additional factor is employed to represent the influence on the data of each individual subject. Moreover, crossover and latin square counterbalance designs employ yet another factor to represent the order factor. Therefore, a "single factor" repeated measures design actually can involve three factors. However, rather than embark upon the description of such "multifactor" designs, the simplest single factor repeated measures design, where the order of experimental conditions experienced by subjects is randomized, is considered.

4.3.2 Randomization

The basic statistical theory underlying basic repeated measures designs assumes the order of experimental conditions experienced by subjects is randomly determined. Randomly generating and implementing an order for each subject means any order is equally likely to be generated and experienced by a subject. Therefore, it is extremely unlikely that there will be a sufficient accumulation of orders necessary to produce a systematic bias in the data. In the sense that randomization makes systematic data biases extremely unlikely, but does not specifically control for their influence, it provides an approximation to counterbalancing. Moreover, when the control procedure of randomizing condition order per subject is applied, the error term accommodates the score variance due to the orders experienced by the subjects. Therefore, compared with GLMs which remove this variance by accommodating it under additional GLM terms, randomized condition order GLMs will have lower analysis power.

4.4 The GLM approach to single factor repeated measures designs

Imagine the experiment described in Chapters 1 and 2 had been obtained from a single factor repeated measures design and not a single factor independent measures design. Rather than observing data from 24 different subjects spread equally across 3 conditions, the performance of the same 8 subjects would be observed under each of the 3 experimental conditions. Table 4.4 presents the data from Table 2.2 as if it had been obtained from a single factor repeated measures design.

The GLM underlying the single factor related/repeated measures design ANOVA is described by the equation

$$Y_{ij} = \mu + \pi_i + \alpha_j + (\pi\alpha)_{ij} + \varepsilon_{ij} \qquad (4.1)$$

where Y_{ij} is the ith subject's dependent variable score in the jth experimental condition, μ is the constant representing the dependent variable score free of the effect of any experimental condition, π_i is a parameter representing the random effect of the ith subject, α_j is the effect of the jth experimental condition, $(\pi\alpha)_{ij}$ is a parameter representing the interaction between the ith subject and the jth experimental condition and as always, the error term, ε_{ij}, reflects variation due to any uncontrolled source. As usual, equation (4.1) summarizes a system of equations, where each equation describes a single dependent variable score.

In comparison to the experimental design GLM for a single factor independent measures ANOVA, the only differences are the inclusion of the terms $[\pi_i]$ and $[(\pi\alpha)_{ij}]$. Therefore, the repeated measures experimental design GLM accommodates score variance attributable to different subjects. Specifically, the term $[\pi_i]$ represents the consistent effect on all of the scores across experimental conditions due to different subjects. In other words, it represents the average difference between the scores from different subjects. In contrast, the interaction term $[(\pi\alpha)_{ij}]$ represents the inconsistent effects on all of the scores across experimental conditions due to different subjects. As a major part of the single factor independent measures ANOVA error term is due to differences between subjects, specifically accommodating score variance attributable to different subjects with the $[\pi_i]$ term reduces the size of the repeated measures error variance considerably and is one of the reasons for the greater analysis power provided by repeated measures designs. However, the role played by the inter-

Table 4.4   Data from a single factor repeated measures design

Subjects	Condition A	Condition B	Condition C	Marginal means
s1	7	7	8	7.33
s2	3	11	14	9.33
s3	6	9	10	8.33
s4	6	11	11	9.33
s5	5	10	12	9.00
s6	8	10	10	9.33
s7	6	11	11	9.33
s8	7	11	12	10.00
Marginal means	6	10	11	9

Table 4.5 Data from a single factor repeated measures design with
subjects cast as a second factor

Experimental conditions	Subjects							
	b_1	b_2	b_3	b_4	b_5	b_6	b_7	b_8
a_1	7	3	6	6	5	8	6	7
a_2	7	11	9	11	10	10	11	11
a_3	8	14	10	11	12	10	11	12

action term $(\pi a)_{ij}$ in repeated measures experimental design GLMs is more
complicated.

Earlier it was said repeated measures designs are analyzed as factorial
designs. Table 4.5 presents the data from Table 4.4 cast in line with the two
factor conception.

Here, there are 3 levels of the experimental condition factor and 8 levels of
the subject factor, providing one score per experimental design cell (i.e. one
score per subject per experimental condition). However, usually factorial
ANOVA designs (see Chapter 3) contain several scores per cell. The mean of the
cell scores is taken as the best estimate of the cell score and is used to calculate
interaction effects, with the discrepancy between the mean and the actual score
providing the estimates of experimental error. Obviously, if there is only one
score per subject per experimental condition, then a mean and experimental
error cannot be calculated. Without these estimates, the experimental error (ε_{ij})
cannot be separated from the interaction effect $(\pi a)_{ij}$. Therefore, a more
accurate description of the single factor repeated measures experimental design
GLM applied most frequently is

$$Y_{ij} = \mu + \pi_i + a_j + [(\pi a)_{ij} + \varepsilon_{ij}] \tag{4.2}$$

Fortunately however, the lack of a specific error term does not prevent
assessment of the experimental conditions effect (a_j). When a single random
factor is included in a model with fixed effects and the fixed effects are to be
tested, limiting the interaction of the pertinent fixed factor and the random factor
to zero (i.e. setting it to zero) provides an appropriate error term. In repeated
measures designs, the fixed factor representing the influence of the experimental
conditions is to be tested, while the single random factor represents the influence
of the subjects. The interaction between these two factors can be set to zero
simply by omitting the interaction between these two factors from the GLM.
Consequently, the single factor repeated measures experimental design GLM for
ANOVA usually is described by the equation,

$$Y_{ij} = \mu + \pi_i + a_j + \varepsilon_{ij} \tag{4.3}$$

Equation (4.3) may be used for simplicity, but whenever an interaction between
experimental conditions and subjects exists, equation (4.2) describes the data

more accurately. Nevertheless, when such an interaction exists and the inter-action term is omitted, the expected mean square for the experimental condi-tions, like the expected mean square for error, includes variation attributable to the interaction between experimental conditions and subjects. Therefore, the F-test of the effect of experimental conditions involves the following expected mean squares:

$$F = \frac{E(MS_{\text{experimental conditions}})}{E(MS_{\text{error}})} = \frac{\sigma^2_{\text{experimental conditions}} + \sigma^2_{\text{experimental conditions} \times \text{subjects}} + \sigma^2_{\text{error}}}{\sigma^2_{\text{experimental conditions} \times \text{subjects}} + \sigma^2_{\text{error}}}$$

(4.4)

Therefore, setting the interaction between the fixed effect of experimental conditions and the random effect of subjects to zero, by omitting the interaction term from the single factor repeated measures GLM, provides an accurate F-test of the fixed effect of experimental conditions. However, an accurate F-test of the random effect of subjects is not provided (e.g. Maxwell & Delaney, 1990; Howell, 1997). Nevertheless, as the aim of repeated measures designs is to facilitate the test of the effect of the experimental conditions by removing variance attributable to subjects, the lack of a subject effects test is no real loss. Comparing the effect of the experimental conditions against the error-plus-interaction variation estimate also makes intuitive sense. The interaction repre-sents the extent to which the experimental condition effect is not consistent across the different subjects. The greater this inconsistency is in relation to the effect of the experimental conditions, the less likely it is that the experimental condition effect is reliable.

As always, the model component of the GLM equation describes the predicted scores

$$\hat{Y}_{ij} = \mu + \pi_i + \alpha_j$$

(4.5)

As μ is a constant, variation in prediction arises from the influence of the experimental conditions (α_j), but also from which subject provides the scores (π_i). Consequently, the repeated measures experimental design GLM can predict a different score for each subject in each experimental condition. However, as there is no interaction effect, the predicted scores for each experimental condition are equal to the mean of all subjects' scores per condition, as given by the marginal means at the bottom of Table 4.4.

The estimate of the single factor repeated measures experimental design GLM parameter μ is defined as the grand mean of the dependent variable scores:

$$\hat{\mu} = \frac{\sum_{i=1}^{n} \sum_{j=1}^{p} Y_{ij}}{np} = \overline{Y}_G$$

(4.6)

Applied to the data in Table 4.4 provides

$$\hat{\mu} = \overline{Y}_G = \frac{7 + 3 + \cdots + 11 + 12}{8(3)} = \frac{216}{24} = 9$$

With balanced designs, μ also may be defined as the mean of the experimental condition means:

$$\mu = \frac{\sum_{j=1}^{p} \mu_j}{p} \qquad (2.17, \text{rptd})$$

Applied to the data in Table 4.4, this provides

$$\hat{\mu} = \overline{Y}_G = \frac{6 + 10 + 11}{3} = 9$$

Given that $(\sum_{i=1}^{n} Y_{i,j}/n)$ are the experimental condition means $(\overline{Y}_j)$, the experimental effect estimates are defined by

$$\hat{\alpha}_j = \left(\frac{\sum_{i=1}^{n} Y_{ij}}{n}\right) - \overline{Y}_G \qquad (4.7)$$

Applying formula (4.7) to the data in Table 4.4 provides

$$\hat{\alpha}_1 = 6 - 9 = -3$$
$$\hat{\alpha}_2 = 10 - 9 = 1$$
$$\hat{\alpha}_3 = 11 - 9 = 2$$
$$\overline{\sum_{j=1}^{p} \hat{\alpha}_j = 0}$$

From these estimates of experimental effects, the experimental conditions SS can be calculated:

$$\text{experimental conditions SS} = \sum_{j=1}^{p} N_j(\mu_j - \mu)^2 \qquad (2.26, \text{rptd})$$

$$\text{experimental conditions SS} = \sum 8(-3^2) + 8(1^2) + 8(2^2)$$

$$= 72 + 8 + 32$$

$$= 112$$

Therefore, the estimate of the effect of experimental conditions in the single factor repeated measures design is identical to that obtained in the single factor independent measures design.

Given that $(\sum_{j=1}^{p} Y_{1j}/p)$ is the mean of the scores provided by each subject, the subject effect estimates are defined by

$$\hat{\pi}_i = \left(\frac{\sum_{j=1}^{p} Y_{1,j}}{p}\right) - \overline{Y}_G \qquad (4.8)$$

Applying formula (4.8) to the data in Table 4.4 provides

$$\hat{\pi}_1 = 7.333 - 9 = -1.667$$

$$\hat{\pi}_2 = 9.333 - 9 = 0.333$$

$$\hat{\pi}_3 = 8.333 - 9 = -0.667$$

$$\hat{\pi}_4 = 9.333 - 9 = 0.333$$

$$\hat{\pi}_5 = 9.000 - 9 = 0.000$$

$$\hat{\pi}_6 = 9.333 - 9 = 0.333$$

$$\hat{\pi}_7 = 9.333 - 9 = 0.333$$

$$\hat{\pi}_8 = 10.000 - 9 = 1.000$$

$$\sum_{i=1}^{N} \hat{\pi}_i = 0.000$$

As with the experimental effect estimates, it is possible to calculate the subjects SS:

$$\text{subjects SS} = \sum_{i=1}^{N} p(\mu_j - \mu)^2$$

$$= 3(-1.667^2) + 3(0.333^2) + 3(-0.667^2) + 3(0.333^2)$$

$$+ 3(0^2) + 3(0.333^2) + 3(0.333^2) + 3(1.000^2)$$

$$= 8.337 + 0.333 + 1.332 + 0.333 + 0 + 0.333 + 0.333 + 3.000$$

$$\text{subjects SS} = 14.000$$

Using each of the parameter estimates in equation (4.5) provides the predicted scores presented in Table 4.6.

Finally, the error estimate is provided by the discrepancy between each observed score (see Table 4.4) and each predicted score (see Table 4.6):

Table 4.6   Scores predicted by the single factor repeated measures experimental design GLM

Subjects	Condition A	Condition B	Condition C	Means
s1	4.333	8.333	9.333	7.333
s2	6.333	10.333	11.333	9.333
s3	5.333	9.333	10.333	8.333
s4	6.333	10.333	11.333	9.333
s5	6.000	10.000	11.000	9.000
s6	6.333	10.333	11.333	9.333
s7	6.333	10.333	11.333	9.333
s8	7.000	11.000	12.000	10.000
Means	6	10	11	9

$$\varepsilon_{ij} = Y_{ij} - \hat{Y}_{ij} \tag{4.9}$$

Table 4.7 presents the calculation of the errors and the sum of the squared errors. This is the estimate of the error sum of squares (SS_{error}) for the single factor repeated measures GLM described by equation (4.3).

Whereas the SS for the experimental conditions equalled that obtained with a single factor independent measures design, the single factor repeated measures design error SS is much smaller, with the difference between the two SS errors being that SS attributable to subjects (i.e. $52 - 38 = 14$).

Having calculated the sum of squares for both experimental conditions and error, the next step is to determine the degrees of freedom. The logic determining the experimental conditions dfs is identical to that for independent measures designs. Therefore,

$$df_{\text{Experimental Conditions}} = p - 1 = 3 - 1 = 2 \tag{4.10}$$

As for error dfs, a separate mean is employed in each experimental condition, so a df is lost from the N scores of each condition. However, a separate mean also is employed to describe every set of p scores a subject provides, so for every set of p scores a df is lost. Therefore,

$$df_{\text{error}} = (N_j - 1)(p - 1) = (8 - 1)(3 - 1) = 14 \tag{4.11}$$

All of this information can be placed in an ANOVA summary table, as in Table 4.8. However, the subject effect reported in Table 4.8 may not be presented, as generally it is of little interest and its significance cannot be tested.

Table 4.7   Calculation of the errors per experimental condition per subject and the sum of the squared errors

Subjects	Condition A	Condition B	Condition C
s1	$7 - 4.333 = 2.667$	$7 - 8.333 = -1.333$	$8 - 9.333 = -1.333$
s2	$3 - 6.333 = -3.333$	$11 - 10.333 = 0.667$	$14 - 11.333 = 2.667$
s3	$6 - 5.333 = 0.667$	$9 - 9.333 = -0.333$	$10 - 10.333 = -0.333$
s4	$6 - 6.333 = -0.333$	$11 - 10.333 = 0.667$	$11 - 11.333 = -0.333$
s5	$5 - 6.000 = -1.000$	$10 - 10.000 = 0.000$	$12 - 11.000 = 1.000$
s6	$8 - 6.333 = 1.667$	$10 - 10.333 = -0.333$	$10 - 11.333 = -1.333$
s7	$6 - 6.333 = -0.333$	$11 - 10.333 = 0.667$	$11 - 11.333 = -0.333$
s8	$7 - 7.000 = 0.000$	$11 - 11.000 = 0.000$	$12 - 12.000 = 0.000$
$\sum_{i=1}^{n} \varepsilon_{ij}^2$	$= 22.667$	$= 3.333$	$= 12.000$
$\sum_{i=1}^{N}\sum_{j=1}^{p} \varepsilon_{ij}^2$		38.000	

Table 4.8   Single factor repeated measures ANOVA summary table

Source	SS	df	MS	F	P
Subjects	14.000	7	2.000		
Expt conditions	112.000	2	56.000	20.634	<0.001
Error	38.000	14	2.714		
Total	164.000	23			

4.5   Estimating effects by comparing full and reduced single factor repeated measures design GLMs

The full single factor repeated measures experimental design GLM was described by equation (4.3), while the reduced GLM is similar but excludes experimental conditions. Therefore, the GLMs are

$$\text{reduced GLM: } Y_{ij} = \mu + \pi_i + \varepsilon_{ij} \qquad (4.12)$$

$$\text{full GLM: } Y_{ij} = \mu + \pi_i + a_j + \varepsilon_{ij} \qquad (4.3, \text{rptd})$$

The reduced GLM manifests the null hypothesis,

$$a_j = 0 \qquad (2.30, \text{rptd})$$

which states that the experimental condition effects equal zero, i.e. there is no effect of experimental conditions. The full GLM manifests the non-directional experimental hypothesis,

$$a_j \neq 0 \text{ for some } j \qquad (2.27, \text{rptd})$$

which states for some experimental conditions the effect is not zero, i.e. there is an effect of experimental conditions. A convenient formulae for the reduced GLM error SS is

$$\text{SSE}_{\text{RGLM}} = \sum_{i=1}^{N} \sum_{j=1}^{p} (Y_{ij} - \overline{Y}_j)^2 \qquad (4.13)$$

Applied to the data in Table 4.4, this provides the calculations presented in Table 4.9.

Similarly, a convenient formulae for the full GLM SS$_{\text{error}}$ is

$$\text{SSE}_{\text{FGLM}} = \sum_{i=1}^{N} \sum_{j=1}^{p} (Y_{ij} - \overline{Y}_j - \overline{Y}_i + \overline{Y}_G)^2 \qquad (4.14)$$

Applied to the data in Table 4.4, this provides the calculations presented in Table 4.10.

An F-test of the error component sum of squares, attributed to the inclusion of the experimental condition effects, is given by

Table 4.9   Calculation of the SS error for the reduced GLM

Subjects	Condition A	Condition B	Condition C
s1	$7 - 7.333 = -0.333$	$7 - 7.333 = -0.333$	$8 - 7.333 = 0.667$
s2	$3 - 9.333 = -6.333$	$11 - 9.333 = 1.667$	$14 - 9.333 = 4.667$
s3	$6 - 8.333 = -2.333$	$9 - 8.333 = 0.667$	$10 - 8.333 = 1.667$
s4	$6 - 9.333 = -3.333$	$11 - 9.333 = 1.667$	$11 - 9.333 = 1.667$
s5	$5 - 9.000 = -4.000$	$10 - 9.000 = 1.000$	$12 - 9.000 = 3.000$
s6	$8 - 9.333 = -1.333$	$10 - 9.333 = 0.667$	$10 - 9.333 = 0.667$
s7	$6 - 9.333 = -3.333$	$11 - 9.333 = 1.667$	$11 - 9.333 = 1.667$
s8	$7 - 10.000 = -3.000$	$11 - 10.000 = 1.000$	$12 - 10.000 = 2.000$

$$\sum_{i=1}^{N}\sum_{j=1}^{p}\varepsilon_{ij}^{2} \qquad\qquad 150.000$$

Table 4.10   Calculation of the SS error for the full GLM

Subjects	Condition A	Condition B	Condition C
s1	$7 - 4.333 = 2.667$	$7 - 8.333 = -1.333$	$8 - 9.333 = -1.333$
s2	$3 - 6.333 = -3.333$	$11 - 10.333 = 0.667$	$14 - 11.333 = 2.667$
s3	$6 - 5.333 = 0.667$	$9 - 9.333 = 0.333$	$10 - 10.333 = 0.333$
s4	$6 - 6.333 = -0.333$	$11 - 10.333 = 0.667$	$11 - 11.333 = -0.333$
s5	$5 - 6.000 = -1.000$	$10 - 10.000 = 0.000$	$12 - 11.000 = 1.000$
s6	$8 - 6.333 = 1.667$	$10 - 10.333 = -0.333$	$10 - 11.333 = -1.333$
s7	$6 - 6.333 = -0.333$	$11 - 10.333 = 0.667$	$11 - 11.333 = -0.333$
s8	$7 - 7.000 = 0.000$	$11 - 11.000 = 0.000$	$12 - 12.000 = 0.000$

$$\sum_{i=1}^{N}\sum_{j=1}^{p}\varepsilon_{ij}^{2} \qquad\qquad 38$$

$$F = \frac{(SSE_{RGLM} - SSE_{FGLM})/(df_{RGLM} - df_{FGLM})}{SSE_{FGLM}/df_{FGLM}} \qquad\text{(2.39, rptd)}$$

Therefore,

$$F = \frac{(150 - 38)/(23 - 14)}{38/14} = \frac{56}{2.714}$$

$$F(2, 14) = 20.634$$

However, it may be more convenient to carry out the calculations as an ANOVA summary table is constructed (Table 4.11).

Table 4.11   Single factor repeated measures ANOVA summary table

Source	SS	df	MS	F	P
Error reduction due to experimental conditions	112.000	2	56.000	20.634	< 0.001
FGLM error	38.000	14	2.714		
Total	164.000	23			

4.6   Regression GLMs for single factor repeated measures designs

The experimental design GLM equation (4.3) may be compared with the equivalent regression equation,

$$Y_i = \beta_0 + \beta_1 X_{i,1} + \beta_2 X_{i,2} + \beta_3 X_{i,3} + \beta_4 X_{i,4} + \beta_5 X_{i,5} + \beta_6 X_{i,6} + \beta_7 X_{i,7}$$
$$+ \beta_8 X_{i,8} + \beta_9 X_{i,9} + \varepsilon_i \tag{4.15}$$

where Y_i represents the ith dependent variable score (not the ith subject), β_0 is a constant, β_1 is the regression coefficient for the predictor variable X_1 and β_2 is the regression coefficient for the predictor variable X_2. However, in repeated measures design, the subjects providing the repeated measures also are represented. The N levels of the subject factor are represented by $(N - 1)$ variables. Therefore, the eight levels (i.e subjects) are represented by the first seven variables (X_1 to X_7). Similarly, the p levels of the experimental factor are represented by $(p - 1)$ variables. Therefore, the three experimental conditions are represented by the last two variables (X_8, X_9). Again, the random variable ε_i represents error.

Table 4.12 presents effect coding for the single factor repeated measures regression GLM. This coding scheme shows that scores associated with subjects 1 to 7 are identified by the presence of a 1 in the variable column representing the subject, while subject 8's scores are identified by $a - 1$ across all (X_1 to X_7) subject variables. As in GLM equation (4.3), terms representing the interaction between experimental conditions and subjects are omitted.

Applying a regression GLM to implement a single factor repeated measures ANOVA is a two stage procedure. For example, the first stage may employ a regression GLM using only those variables representing experimental conditions, while the second stage employs those variables representing both experimental conditions and subjects. A comparison of the first and second regressions provides all the information needed for the single factor repeated measures ANOVA. Moreover, as the variables representing experimental conditions are orthogonal to those representing subjects, which stage comes first does not matter, as identical results are obtained.

Table 4.12   Effect coding for the single factor repeated measures regression GLM

S	Y	X_1	X_2	X_3	X_4	X_5	X_6	X_7	X_8	X_9
s1	7	1	0	0	0	0	0	0	1	0
s2	3	0	1	0	0	0	0	0	1	0
s3	6	0	0	1	0	0	0	0	1	0
s4	6	0	0	0	1	0	0	0	1	0
s5	5	0	0	0	0	1	0	0	1	0
s6	8	0	0	0	0	0	1	0	1	0
s7	6	0	0	0	0	0	0	1	1	0
s8	7	−1	−1	−1	−1	−1	−1	−1	1	0
s1	7	1	0	0	0	0	0	0	0	1
s2	11	0	1	0	0	0	0	0	0	1
s3	9	0	0	1	0	0	0	0	0	1
s4	11	0	0	0	1	0	0	0	0	1
s5	10	0	0	0	0	1	0	0	0	1
s6	10	0	0	0	0	0	1	0	0	1
s7	11	0	0	0	0	0	0	1	0	1
s8	11	−1	−1	−1	−1	−1	−1	−1	0	1
s1	8	1	0	0	0	0	0	0	−1	0
s2	14	0	1	0	0	0	0	0	−1	0
s3	10	0	0	1	0	0	0	0	−1	0
s4	11	0	0	0	1	0	0	0	−1	0
s5	12	0	0	0	0	1	0	0	−1	0
s6	10	0	0	0	0	0	1	0	−1	0
s7	11	0	0	0	0	0	0	1	−1	0
s8	12	−1	−1	−1	−1	−1	−1	−1	−1	0

Consistent with estimating effects by comparing full and reduced GLMs, the first regression carried out here will be that for the full single factor repeated measures experimental design GLM, when all subject and experimental condition predictor variables are included (i.e. variables X_1 to X_9). The results of this analysis are presented in Tables 4.13 and 4.14.

Table 4.13 presents the predictor variable regression coefficients and standard deviations, the standardized regression coefficients, and significance tests (t- and p-values) of the regression coefficient. From the repeated measures ANOVA perspective, the information in this table is of little interest, although it is worth noting that the regression coefficient estimates are equivalent to the subject effect estimates calculated earlier.

Table 4.14 presents the ANOVA summary table for the regression GLM describing the complete single factor repeated measures ANOVA. As the residual SS is that obtained when both subject and experimental conditions are included in the regression, this is the error term obtained when the single factor repeated measures ANOVA GLM is applied.

In the second stage, the aim is to determine by how much the residual SS increases when the predictor variables representing the experimental conditions are omitted. To do this, a regression GLM corresponding with the reduced single

Table 4.13   Output pertinent to multiple regression equation for effect coding

Variable	Coefficient	Std error	Std coef	t	p (2 tail)
Constant	9	0.336	<0.001	26.762	<0.001
X_1	−1.667	1.654	−0.319	−1.008	0.329
X_2	0.333	1.654	0.064	0.202	0.843
X_3	−0.667	1.654	−0.128	−0.403	0.692
X_4	0.333	1.654	0.064	0.202	0.843
X_5	<0.001	1.654	<0.001	<0.001	1.000
X_6	0.333	1.654	0.064	0.202	0.843
X_7	0.333	1.654	0.064	0.202	0.843
X_8	−3.000	0.476	−0.937	−6.308	<0.001
X_9	1.000	0.476	0.312	2.103	0.054

Table 4.14   ANOVA summary table for subject and experimental condition effect regression

R: 0.877   R squared: 0.768   Adjusted R squared: 0.619

Source	SS	df	Mean square	F	p
Regression	126.000	9	14.000	5.158	0.003
Residual	38.000	14	2.714		

factor repeated measures experimental design GLM described by equation (4.12) is constructed. This regression GLM employs only those variables representing the subjects (variables X_1 to X_7) as predictors. As subject and experimental condition variables are orthogonal, the predictor variable regression coefficients, their standard deviations, the standardized regression coefficients, and the significance tests (t- and p-values) of the regression coefficients provided by this analysis are identical to those presented in Table 4.13. Therefore, the main interest is in the ANOVA summary table (Table 4.15). This presents the residual SS for the reduced single factor repeated measures experimental design GLM. (As the residual SS contains both SS for experimental conditions and SS error, the F-test is irrelevant.)

Table 4.15   ANOVA summary table for subject effect regression

R: 0.292   R squared: 0.085   Adjusted R squared: 0.000

Source	SS	df	Mean square	F	p
Regression	14.000	7	2.000	0.213	0.977
Residual	150.000	16	9.375		

The experimental condition effect now can be estimated by subtracting the full GLM residual from the reduced GLM residual:

SS error for reduced regression GLM	=	150.000
SS error for full regression GLM	=	38.000

SS error reduction due to experimental conditions   =   112.000

Putting this information and the corresponding dfs in Table 4.16 essentially recasts Table 4.14, but separates the regression SS and dfs into experimental condition SS and dfs, and subject SS and dfs.

Repeated measures ANOVA also may be implemented by a regression GLM which uses a single criterion scaled variable, rather than $(N - 1)$ variables, to accommodate the subject effect (e.g. Pedhazur, 1997). One advantage of this approach is the reduction in predictors required, especially with larger numbers of participants. This was particularly useful when statistical software was limited in the number of predictor variables that could be accommodated in a regression analysis. However, this is no longer a serious concern, as the capability of most statistical software now far exceeds the demands likely to be made by most repeated measures designs.

Table 4.16   ANOVA summary table for single factor repeated measures ANOVA

Source	SS	df	Mean square	F	p
Subjects	14.000	7	2.000		
Experimental conditions	112.000	2	56.000	20.634	< 0.001
Error	38.000	14	2.714		

5 GLM APPROACHES TO FACTORIAL REPEATED MEASURES DESIGNS

5.1 Factorial related measures designs

There are two sorts of factorial repeated measures designs. There are factorial designs where repeated measures fill the levels of all factors. In these fully related factorial designs, each subject provides scores in every condition defined by the factor combinations. The second sort of factorial repeated measures design includes one or more independent factors along with one or more repeated measures factors. In psychology, these may be termed mixed designs, as both independent and related factors are included, or split-plot designs. However, it is worth noting that in the statistical literature, the label "mixed design" refers to any design with a random factor and not just related factor designs. The name "split-plot design" reflects the design origins in agricultural research, where a plot of land was split into parts which received different treatments. Two factor fully related and mixed designs will be considered here. These designs are presented schematically in Table 5.1.

Table 5.1   Two factor fully related and mixed designs

Factor A		a_1			a_2	
Factor B	b_1	b_2	b_3	b_1	b_2	b_3
	s1	s1	s1	s1	s1	s1
	s2	s2	s2	s2	s2	s2
	...	...	...	...	...	...
	s8	s8	s8	s8	s8	s8

A two factor (2 × 3) fully related design

Factor A		a_1			a_2	
Factor B	b_1	b_2	b_3	b_1	b_2	b_3
	s1	s1	s1	s9	s9	s9
	s2	s2	s2	s10	s10	s10
	...	...	...	...	...	...
	s8	s8	s8	s16	s16	s16

A two factor (2 × 3) mixed design

Given the advantages of factorial and related measures designs, it is not surprising that related factors designs are popular in psychological research. However, the need to implement appropriate controls for order effects remains. In fully related factorial designs generally, where the subjects provide scores under all experimental conditions, there are a greater number of order permutations, so a more extensive implementation of order controls is required. Mixed designs are more popular, probably because they provide the efficiency of related designs, but do not require subjects to experience as many conditions as a fully related design. In turn, as subjects experience fewer experimental conditions, the potential for order effect problems is reduced and so is the effort required to control the order of experimental conditions. Mixed designs also lend themselves to the study of different groups of subjects over time (e.g. Hand & Crowder, 1996).

5.2   The fully related factorial design GLM

As with all factorial designs, there are a greater number of main and interaction effects in related factorial designs compared with related single factor designs. However, with fully related factorial designs, there is also an increase in the number of "error" terms. In fact, there is a separate "error" term for each fixed experimental factor and interaction between fixed experimental factors and as with single factor designs, each of these "error" terms actually comprises error plus the interaction between the subjects factor and the factor(s) assessed.

The GLM for a fully related two factor ANOVA is described by the equation,

$$Y_{ijk} = \mu + \pi_i + \alpha_j + \beta_k + (\pi\alpha)_{ij} + (\pi\beta)_{ik} + (\alpha\beta)_{jk} + \varepsilon_{ijk} \qquad (5.1)$$

where Y_{ijk} is the dependent variable score for the ith subject at the jth level of Factor A and the kth level of Factor B, μ is the constant representing the dependent variable score free of the effect of any experimental condition, π_i is a parameter representing the random effect of the ith subject, α_j is the effect of the jth level of Factor A, β_k is the effect of the kth level of Factor B, $(\pi\alpha)_{ij}$ is the effect of the interaction between the ith subject and the jth level of Factor A, $(\pi\beta)_{ik}$ is the effect of the interaction between the ith subject and the kth level of Factor B, $(\alpha\beta)_{jk}$ is the interaction effect of the jth level of Factor A and the kth level of Factor B, and as always, ε_{ijk} represents the random error associated with the ith subject in the jth level of Factor A and the kth level of Factor B.

As with single factor repeated measures designs, due to there being only one score per subject per experimental condition, the error term and the interaction between the two experimental factors and subjects cannot be separated, and so ε_{ijk} is written more accurately as $[(\pi\alpha\beta)_{ijk} + \varepsilon_{ijk}]$. In fully related factorial designs, the error term ε_{ijk} is used to assess only the effect of the interaction between the two fixed experimental factors. As described with respect to the single factor repeated measures design, when a single random factor is included in a model with fixed effects and the fixed effects are to be tested, limiting the interaction of the pertinent fixed factor(s) and the random factor to zero provides an appropriate error term. In this fully related factorial design, the term representing the interaction of the fixed factors A and B is to be tested, while the only random factor represents the influence of the subjects. Therefore, setting the $[(\pi\alpha\beta)_{ijk}]$ interaction to zero simply by omitting this term from the GLM provides an appropriate error term to assess the interaction between the two fixed experimental factors A and B.

This may seem to leave the main effects of Factors A and B without a denominator error term for the F-test. However, in the fully related factorial design, the variation associated with the interaction between Factor A and subjects $[(\pi\alpha)_{ij}]$ is used to assess the effect of the Factor A manipulation, while the variation associated with the interaction between Factor B and subjects $[(\pi\beta)_{ik}]$ is used to assess the effect of the Factor B manipulation (see Howell, 1997, for F-test numerator and denominator expected mean squares). As in the single factor repeated measures design, using these variation estimates to assess the main effects of Factors A and B also makes intuitive sense. In both instances, the interactions represent the extent to which the factor effect is not consistent across different subjects and the greater this inconsistency is in relation to the factor effect, the less likely is the factor effect to be reliable.

Consider the experiment presented in Chapter 3. Here, a fully related factorial design would not be appropriate. If subjects had to switch between "memorizing" the words and constructing stories from the words and imagining the story events, it is likely that the story construction/imagery strategy would be used in the "memorize" conditions, with the result that the distinction between these factor levels would diminish. Nevertheless, for the sake of illustrating the analysis of a fully related factorial design, imagine the data in Table 5.2 had been obtained from just 8 subjects participating in all conditions.

Table 5.2   Experimental data from a fully related two (2 × 3) factor design

| | Encoding instructions | | | | | | |
| | a_1 Memorize Study time (s) | | | a_2 Story and image Study time (s) | | | |
	b_1 30	b_2 60	b_3 180	b_1 30	b_2 60	b_3 180	Subject means
s1	7	7	8	16	16	24	13.000
s2	3	11	14	7	10	29	12.333
s3	6	9	10	11	13	10	9.833
s4	6	11	11	9	10	22	11.500
s5	5	10	12	10	10	25	12.000
s6	8	10	10	11	14	28	13.500
s7	6	11	11	8	11	22	11.500
s8	7	11	12	8	12	24	12.333
Expt condition means	6	10	11	10	12	23	12

As was described for the single factor repeated measures design, the manner of calculating experimental condition effects remains the same as in independent measures designs, emphasizing that repeated measures designs have consequence only for error estimates. Therefore, as the estimates of μ, and the α_j, β_k and $(\alpha\beta)_{jk}$ effects are defined just as for the independent measures factorial design, their definitions will not be repeated here.

The mean of the scores provided by each subject is

$$\hat{\mu}_i = \left(\frac{\sum_{j=1}^{p} \sum_{k=1}^{q} Y_{ij}}{pq} \right) \tag{5.2}$$

and so the subject effects are,

$$\hat{\pi}_i = \mu_i - \mu \tag{5.3}$$

Applying formula (5.3) to the data in Table 5.2 provides

$$\hat{\pi}_1 = 13.000 - 12 = 1.000$$

$$\hat{\pi}_2 = 12.333 - 12 = 0.333$$

$$\hat{\pi}_3 = 9.833 - 12 = -2.167$$

$$\hat{\pi}_4 = 11.500 - 12 = -0.500$$

$$\hat{\pi}_5 = 12.000 - 12 = 0.000$$

$$\hat{\pi}_6 = 13.500 - 12 = 1.500$$

$$\hat{\pi}_7 = 11.500 - 12 = -0.500$$

$$\hat{\pi}_8 = 12.333 - 12 = 0.333$$

$$\sum_{i=1}^{N} \hat{\pi}_i = 0.000$$

The subject SS is given by

$$SS_{subjects} = pq \sum_{i=1}^{N} (\mu_i - \mu)^2$$

$$= 6[(1.000^2) + (0.333^2) + (-2.167^2) + (-0.500^2)$$

$$+ (0^2) + (1.500^2) + (-0.500^2) + (0.333^2)]$$

$$SS_{subjects} = 52.008$$

The subject $\times$ Factor A interaction effects are defined by

$$(\pi\alpha)_{ij} = \mu_{ij} - (\mu + \pi_i + \alpha_j) \tag{5.4}$$

which reveals each interaction effect to be the extent to which each subject mean within each level of Factor A diverges from the additive pattern of subject and Factor A main effects. Applying formula (5.4) to the data in Table 5.2 provides

$$(\pi a)_{1,1} = 7.333 - (12.000 + 1.000 - 3) = -2.667$$
$$(\pi a)_{2,1} = 9.333 - (12.000 + 0.333 - 3) = 0.000$$
$$(\pi a)_{3,1} = 8.333 - (12.000 - 2.167 - 3) = 1.500$$
$$(\pi a)_{4,1} = 9.333 - (12.000 - 0.500 - 3) = 0.833$$
$$(\pi a)_{5,1} = 9.000 - (12.000 + 0.000 - 3) = 0.000$$
$$(\pi a)_{6,1} = 9.333 - (12.000 + 1.500 - 3) = -1.167$$
$$(\pi a)_{7,1} = 9.333 - (12.000 - 0.500 - 3) = 0.833$$
$$(\pi a)_{8,1} = 10.000 - (12.000 + 0.333 - 3) = 0.667$$

$$(\pi a)_{8,2} = 14.667 - (12.000 + 0.333 + 3) = -0.666$$
$$(\pi a)_{1,2} = 18.667 - (12.000 + 1.000 + 3) = 2.667$$
$$(\pi a)_{2,2} = 15.333 - (12.000 + 0.333 + 3) = 0.000$$
$$(\pi a)_{3,2} = 11.333 - (12.000 - 2.167 + 3) = -1.500$$
$$(\pi a)_{4,2} = 13.667 - (12.000 - 0.500 + 3) = -0.833$$
$$(\pi a)_{5,2} = 15.000 - (12.000 + 0.000 + 3) = 0.000$$
$$(\pi a)_{6,2} = 17.667 - (12.000 + 1.500 + 3) = 1.167$$
$$(\pi a)_{7,2} = 13.667 - (12.000 - 0.500 + 3) = -0.833$$
$$\sum_{i=1}^{N}(\pi a)_{ij} = 0.000$$

The subject $\times$ Factor A SS is given by

$$SS_{\text{subjects} \times \text{Factor } A} = q \sum_{i=1}^{N}[\mu_{ij} - (\mu + \pi_i + a_j)^2] \qquad (5.5)$$

or alternatively,

$$SS_{\text{subjects} \times \text{Factor} A} = q \sum_{i=1}^{N}(\pi a)_{ij}^2 \qquad (5.6)$$

Therefore,

$$SS_{\text{subjects} \times \text{Factor } A} = 3[(-2.667^2) + (0^2) + (1.500^2) + (0.833^2) + (0^2) + (-1.167^2)$$
$$+ (0.833^2) + (0.667^2) + (2.667^2) + (0^2) + (-1.500^2)$$
$$+ (-0.833^2) + (0^2) + (1.167^2) + (-0.833^2) + (-0.666^2)]$$

$$SS_{\text{subjects} \times \text{Factor } A} = 75.333$$

Similarly, the subject $\times$ Factor B interaction effects are defined by

$$(\pi\beta)_{ik} = \mu_{ik} - (\mu + \pi_i + \beta_k) \qquad (5.7)$$

which reveals each interaction effect to be the extent to which each subject mean within each level of Factor B diverges from the additive pattern of subject and Factor B main effects. Applying formula (5.5) to the data in Table 5.2 provides

$$(\pi\beta)_{1,1} = 11.500 - (12.000 + 1.000 - 4) = \quad 2.500$$
$$(\pi\beta)_{2,1} = \quad 5.000 - (12.000 + 0.333 - 4) = -3.333$$
$$(\pi\beta)_{3,1} = \quad 8.500 - (12.000 - 2.167 - 4) = \quad 2.667$$
$$(\pi\beta)_{4,1} = \quad 7.500 - (12.000 - 0.500 - 4) = \quad 0.000$$
$$(\pi\beta)_{5,1} = \quad 7.500 - (12.000 + 0.000 - 4) = -0.500$$
$$(\pi\beta)_{6,1} = \quad 8.500 - (12.000 + 1.500 - 4) = -1.000$$
$$(\pi\beta)_{7,1} = \quad 7.000 - (12.000 - 0.500 - 4) = -0.500$$
$$(\pi\beta)_{8,1} = \quad 7.500 - (12.000 + 0.333 - 4) = -0.833$$

$$(\pi\beta)_{1,2} = 11.500 - (12.000 + 1.000 - 1) = -0.500$$
$$(\pi\beta)_{2,2} = 10.500 - (12.000 + 0.333 - 1) = -0.833$$
$$(\pi\beta)_{3,2} = 11.000 - (12.000 - 2.167 - 1) = \quad 2.167$$
$$(\pi\beta)_{4,2} = 10.500 - (12.000 - 0.500 - 1) = \quad 0.000$$
$$(\pi\beta)_{5,2} = 10.000 - (12.000 + 0.000 - 1) = -1.000$$
$$(\pi\beta)_{6,2} = 12.000 - (12.000 + 1.500 - 1) = -0.500$$
$$(\pi\beta)_{7,2} = 11.000 - (12.000 - 0.500 - 1) = \quad 0.500$$
$$(\pi\beta)_{8,2} = 11.500 - (12.000 + 0.333 - 1) = \quad 0.167$$

$$(\pi\beta)_{1,3} = 16.000 - (12.000 + 1.000 + 5) = -2.000$$
$$(\pi\beta)_{2,3} = 21.500 - (12.000 + 0.333 + 5) = \quad 4.167$$
$$(\pi\beta)_{3,3} = 10.000 - (12.000 - 2.167 + 5) = -4.833$$
$$(\pi\beta)_{4,3} = 16.500 - (12.000 - 0.500 + 5) = \quad 0.000$$
$$(\pi\beta)_{5,3} = 18.500 - (12.000 + 0.000 + 5) = \quad 1.500$$
$$(\pi\beta)_{6,3} = 19.000 - (12.000 + 1.500 + 5) = \quad 0.500$$
$$(\pi\beta)_{7,3} = 16.500 - (12.000 - 0.500 + 5) = \quad 0.000$$
$$(\pi\beta)_{8,3} = 18.000 - (12.000 + 0.333 + 5) = \quad 0.667$$
$$\sum_{i=1}^{N}(\pi\beta)_{ik} \qquad\qquad = \quad 0.000$$

The subject $\times$ Factor B SS is given by

$$\text{SS}_{\text{subjects} \times \text{Factor } B} = p\sum_{i=1}^{N}[\mu_{ik} - (\mu + \pi_i + \beta_k)^2] \qquad (5.8)$$

or alternatively,

$$SS_{\text{subjects} \times \text{Factor } B} = p \sum_{i=1}^{N} (\pi\beta)_{ik}^2 \qquad (5.9)$$

$$
\begin{aligned}
SS_{\text{subjects} \times \text{Factor } B} = {} & 2[(2.500^2) + (-3.333^2) + (2.667^2) + (0^2) + (-0.500^2) \\
& + (-1.000^2) + (-0.500^2) + (-0.833^2) + (-0.500^2) \\
& + (-0.833^2) + (2.167^2) + (0^2) + (-1.000^2) + (-0.500^2) \\
& + (0.500^2) + (0.167^2) + (-2.000^2) + (4.167^2) + (-4.833^2) \\
& + (0^2) + (1.500^2) + (0.500^2) + (0^2) + (0.667^2)]
\end{aligned}
$$

$$SS_{\text{subjects} \times \text{Factor } B} = 161.000$$

Based on the *model* component of the fully related two factor experimental design GLM equation, predicted scores are given by

$$\hat{Y}_{ijk} = \mu + \pi_i + \alpha_j + \beta_k + (\pi\alpha)_{ij} + (\pi\beta)_{ik} + (\alpha\beta)_{jk} \qquad (5.10)$$

Using the parameter estimates in this formula provides the predicted scores per subject per experimental condition.

The final parameters for the fully related two factor experimental design GLM, the error terms, which represent the discrepancy between the actual scores observed (Table 5.2) and the scores predicted by the two factor GLM (Table 5.3), are defined as

$$\varepsilon_{ijk} = Y_{ijk} - \hat{Y}_{ijk} \qquad (5.11)$$

The error terms, obtained by subtracting the predicted scores in Table 5.3 from the observed scores in Table 5.2, are presented by subject and experimental condition in Table 5.4.

Degrees of freedom are required next. For the subject effect,

$$\text{dfs}_{\text{subject}} = N - 1$$

Table 5.3   Predicted scores for the fully related two (2 × 3) factor experiment

	a_1			a_2		
	b_1	b_2	b_3	b_1	b_2	b_3
s1	6.833	7.833	7.333	16.167	15.167	24.667
s2	3.000	9.500	15.500	7.000	11.500	27.500
s3	8.000	11.500	5.500	9.000	10.500	14.500
s4	6.333	10.333	11.333	8.667	10.667	21.667
s5	5.500	9.000	12.500	9.500	11.000	24.500
s6	6.333	9.833	11.833	12.667	14.167	26.167
s7	5.833	10.833	11.333	8.167	11.167	21.667
s8	6.167	11.167	12.667	8.833	11.833	23.333

Table 5.4   Error terms for the fully related two (2 × 3) factor experiment

| | a_1 | | | a_2 | | |
	b_1	b_2	b_3	b_1	b_2	b_3
s1	0.167	−0.833	0.667	−0.167	0.833	−0.667
s2	−0.000	1.500	−1.500	0.000	−1.500	1.500
s3	−2.000	−2.500	4.500	2.000	2.500	−4.500
s4	0.333	0.667	−0.333	0.333	−0.667	0.333
s5	−0.500	1.000	−0.500	0.500	−1.000	0.500
s6	1.667	0.167	−1.833	−1.667	−0.167	1.833
s7	0.167	0.167	−0.333	−0.167	−0.167	0.333
s8	0.833	−0.167	−0.667	−0.833	0.167	0.667
$\sum_{i=1}^{N} \varepsilon_{ijk}^2$	7.889	10.722	27.223	7.889	10.723	27.222
$\sum_{i=1}^{N}\sum_{j=1}^{p}\sum_{k=1}^{q} \varepsilon_{ijk}^2$			91.668			

This reflects how the subject effect is calculated from the deviation of N means from μ, which is the mean of these N means. Therefore, as described before, only $(N - 1)$ of the component means are free to vary. As the subject factor has N levels, clearly the subject × Factor A interaction effect,

$$df_{\text{subject} \times \text{Factor } A} = (N - 1)(p - 1)$$

and the subject × Factor B interaction effect,

$$df_{\text{subject} \times \text{Factor } B} = (N - 1)(q - 1)$$

follow the same rationale as for any interaction dfs. For error dfs, a separate mean is employed in each experimental condition, so a df is lost from the N scores of each condition. However, a separate mean is employed to describe every set of p scores a subject provides, so for every set of p scores a df is lost, and similarly, a separate mean is employed to describe every set of q scores a subject provides, so for every set of q scores a df is lost. Therefore,

$$df_{\text{error}} = (N - 1)(p - 1)(q - 1)$$

Placing each of the SS estimates just calculated, along with the SS for the experimental Factors A and B calculated in Chapter 3 and the dfs, into an ANOVA summary table gives Table 5.5.

5.3 Estimating effects by comparing full and reduced fully related factorial experimental design GLMs

The full experimental design GLM for the fully related two factor ANOVA was described by equation (5.1). As with the independent factors ANOVA estimated

Table 5.5   Fully related two factor ANOVA summary table

Source	Sum of squares	df	Mean square	F	p
Subjects (S)	52.000	7	7.429		
A (Encoding Instructions)	432.000	1	432.000	40.141	< 0.001
S × A	75.333	7	10.762		
B (Study time)	672.000	2	336.000	29.217	< 0.001
S × B	161.00	14	11.500		
A × B (Encode inst × study time)	224.000	2	112.000	17.105	< 0.001
Error	91.668	14	6.548		

by comparing full and reduced experimental design GLMs, the hypotheses concerning the main effect of Factor A, the main effect of Factor B and the effect of the interaction between Factors A and B may be assessed by constructing three reduced GLMs, which manifest data descriptions under the respective null hypotheses, and comparing their error components with the full model. Again this approach is simplified by virtue of all the subject, experimental factors and their interactions being orthogonal. As the effect estimates are completely distinct, omitting or including any particular effect has no consequence for the estimates of the other effects.

The main effect of Factor A is assessed by constructing the reduced experimental design GLM,

$$Y_{ijk} = \mu + \pi_i + \beta_k + (\pi\alpha)_{ij} + (\pi\beta)_{ik} + (\alpha\beta)_{jk} + \varepsilon_{ijk} \qquad (5.12)$$

This model manifests the null hypothesis that the p levels of Factor A do not influence the data. More formally this is expressed as

$$\alpha_j = 0 \qquad (5.13)$$

The main effect of Factor B is assessed by constructing the reduced experimental design GLM:

$$Y_{ijk} = \mu + \pi_i + \alpha_j + (\pi\alpha)_{ij} + (\pi\beta)_{ik} + (\alpha\beta)_{jk} + \varepsilon_{ijk} \qquad (5.14)$$

This model manifests the null hypothesis that the q levels of Factor B do not influence the data. Expressed more formally this is

$$\beta_k = 0 \qquad (5.15)$$

Finally, the reduced GLM for assessing the effect of the interaction between Factors A and B is

$$Y_{ijk} = \mu + \pi_i + \alpha_j + \beta_k + (\pi\alpha)_{ij} + (\pi\beta)_{ik} + \varepsilon_{ijk} \qquad (5.16)$$

This reduced GLM manifests the data description under the null hypothesis that the interaction between levels of Factors A and B do not influence the data and is expressed more formally as

$$(\alpha\beta)_{jk} = 0 \qquad (5.17)$$

Nevertheless, when fully related two factor ANOVAs are carried out by hand, the strategy of comparing different experimental design GLM residuals is very laborious, as there are so many reduced experimental design GLMs. In addition to the full experimental design GLM error term, reduced experimental design GLM error terms have to be calculated for each of the effects (A, B and AB), and then further reduced experimental design GLMs must be constructed to obtain the error terms for the main effect of Factor A ($S \times A$), the main effect of Factor B ($S \times B$) and the interaction effect (the error term which also reflects $S \times A \times B$). Therefore, when hand calculations are employed, instead of calculating the error SS associated with each of these reduced experimental design GLMs and comparing them with the full experimental design GLM, it is more efficient to calculate directly the SS for each of the effects and errors. Formulae for calculating all of the fully related two factor ANOVA effects directly, which are more convenient than those used to define and illustrate the SS calculation, are provided in Table 5.6. However, the strategy of estimating fully related ANOVA effects by comparing different GLM residuals is relatively easy to achieve using regression GLMs.

Table 5.6   Formulae for the (balanced) fully related two factor ANOVA effects

Effect	Formulae
Subject	$pq \sum\limits_{i=1}^{N}(\bar{Y}_i - \bar{Y}_G)^2$
A	$qN \sum\limits_{j=1}^{p}(\bar{Y}_j - \bar{Y}_G)^2$
$S \times A$	$q \sum\limits_{i=1}^{N}\sum\limits_{j=1}^{p}(\bar{Y}_{ij} - \bar{Y}_i - \bar{Y}_j + \bar{Y}_G)^2$
B	$pN \sum\limits_{k=1}^{q}(\bar{Y}_k - \bar{Y}_G)^2$
$S \times B$	$p \sum\limits_{i=1}^{N}\sum\limits_{k=1}^{q}(\bar{Y}_{ik} - \bar{Y}_i - \bar{Y}_j + \bar{Y}_G)^2$
$A \times B$	$N \sum\limits_{j=1}^{p}\sum\limits_{k=1}^{q}(\bar{Y}_{jk} - \bar{Y}_j - \bar{Y}_k + \bar{Y}_G)^2$
Error	$\sum\limits_{i=1}^{N}\sum\limits_{j=1}^{p}\sum\limits_{k=1}^{q}(Y_{ijk} - \bar{Y}_{ij} - \bar{Y}_{ik} - \bar{Y}_{jk} + \bar{Y}_i + \bar{Y}_j + \bar{Y}_k - \bar{Y}_G)^2$

5.4   Regression GLMs for the fully related factorial ANOVA

The fully related (2×3) factor experimental design GLM equation (5.1) may be compared with the equivalent regression equation,

$$Y_i = \beta_0 + \beta_1 X_{i,1} + \beta_2 X_{i,2} + \beta_3 X_{i,3} + \beta_4 X_{i,4} + \beta_5 X_{i,5} + \beta_6 X_{i,6} + \beta_7 X_{i,7}$$

$$+ \beta_8 X_{i,8} + \beta_9 X_{i,9} + \beta_{10} X_{i,10} + \beta_{11} X_{i,11} + \beta_{12} X_{i,12} + \beta_{13} X_{i,13} + \beta_{14} X_{i,14}$$

$$+ \beta_{15} X_{i,15} + \beta_{16} X_{i,16} + \beta_{17} X_{i,17} + \beta_{18} X_{i,18} + \beta_{19} X_{i,19} + \beta_{20} X_{i,20} + \beta_{21} X_{i,21}$$

$$+ \beta_{22} X_{i,22} + \beta_{23} X_{i,23} + \beta_{24} X_{i,24} + \beta_{25} X_{i,25} + \beta_{26} X_{i,26} + \beta_{27} X_{i,27} + \beta_{28} X_{i,28}$$

$$+ \beta_{29} X_{i,29} + \beta_{30} X_{i,30} + \beta_{31} X_{i,31} + \beta_{32} X_{i,32} + \beta_{33} X_{i,33} + \varepsilon_i \qquad (5.18)$$

where Y_i represents the ith dependent variable score (not the ith subject), β_0 is a constant, β_1 is the regression coefficient for the predictor variable X_1 and β_2 is the regression coefficient for the predictor variable X_2, etc. As with the single factor repeated measures regression GLM, there are 7 variables which represent scores from individual subjects (X_1 to X_7), 3 variables which represent experimental factors (X_8 to X_{10}) and 21 variables which represent interactions between the subjects and the experimental factors (X_{11} to X_{31}) and finally, 2 variables which represent the interaction between the experimental factors (X_{32}, X_{33}).

Clearly, equation (5.18) is unwieldy and the earlier mention of the proliferation of predictor variables required for repeated measures designs can be appreciated. Nevertheless, once the effect coding scheme has been established in a computer data file, it is relatively simple to carry out the fully related factorial ANOVA. Effect coding applied to the data in Table 5.2 is presented in Table 5.7.

Applying a regression GLM to implement a fully related factors ANOVA may be done in a manner consistent with estimating effects by comparing full and reduced GLMs. As all of the variables representing effects are orthogonal in a balanced design, the order in which SSs are calculated is of no consequence. The first regression carried out is that for the full fully related factorial experimental design GLM, when all subject and experimental condition predictor variables are included (i.e. variables X_1 to X_{33}). Although information about each of the predictor variables will be provided by linear regression software, as most of the experimental design effects are represented by two or more regression predictor variables, information about the individual predictor coefficients, etc. generally is of little interest. Of much more interest is the ANOVA summary presented in Table 5.8, which provides the full GLM residual SS. This may be compared with the fully related factorial experimental design GLM error term in Table 5.5.

Having obtained the full GLM residual SS, the next stages involve the implementation of the various reduced GLMs to obtain their estimates of residual SS. The reduced GLM for the effect of the subjects factor is obtained

Table 5.7 Effect coding for a fully related two factor (2 × 3) experimental design

s	Y	S							A	B		S × A								S × B													A × B	
		X_1	X_2	X_3	X_4	X_5	X_6	X_7	X_8	X_9	X_{10}	X_{11}	X_{12}	X_{13}	X_{14}	X_{15}	X_{16}	X_{17}	X_{18}	X_{19}	X_{20}	X_{21}	X_{22}	X_{23}	X_{24}	X_{25}	X_{26}	X_{27}	X_{28}	X_{29}	X_{30}	X_{31}	X_{32}	X_{33}
s1	7	1	0	0	0	0	0	0	1	-1	0	1	0	0	0	0	0	0	-1	0	0	0	0	0	0	0	0	0	0	0	0	0	-1	0
s2	3	0	1	0	0	0	0	0	1	-1	0	0	1	0	0	0	0	0	0	-1	0	0	0	0	0	0	0	0	0	0	0	0	-1	0
s3	6	0	0	1	0	0	0	0	1	-1	0	0	0	1	0	0	0	0	0	0	-1	0	0	0	0	0	0	0	0	0	0	0	-1	0
s4	6	0	0	0	1	0	0	0	1	-1	0	0	0	0	1	0	0	0	0	0	0	-1	0	0	0	0	0	0	0	0	0	0	-1	0
s5	5	0	0	0	0	1	0	0	1	-1	0	0	0	0	0	1	0	0	0	0	0	0	-1	0	0	0	0	0	0	0	0	0	-1	0
s6	8	0	0	0	0	0	1	0	1	-1	0	0	0	0	0	0	1	0	0	0	0	0	0	-1	0	0	0	0	0	0	0	0	-1	0
s7	6	0	0	0	0	0	0	1	1	-1	0	0	0	0	0	0	0	1	0	0	0	0	0	0	-1	0	0	0	0	0	0	0	-1	0
s8	7	-1	-1	-1	-1	-1	-1	-1	1	-1	-1	-1	-1	-1	-1	-1	-1	-1	1	1	1	1	1	1	1	0	0	0	0	0	0	0	-1	0
s1	7	1	0	0	0	0	0	0	1	0	-1	-1	0	0	0	0	0	0	0	0	0	0	0	0	0	-1	0	0	0	0	0	0	0	-1
s2	11	0	1	0	0	0	0	0	1	0	-1	0	-1	0	0	0	0	0	0	0	0	0	0	0	0	0	-1	0	0	0	0	0	0	-1
s3	9	0	0	1	0	0	0	0	1	0	-1	0	0	-1	0	0	0	0	0	0	0	0	0	0	0	0	0	-1	0	0	0	0	0	-1
s4	11	0	0	0	1	0	0	0	1	0	-1	0	0	0	-1	0	0	0	0	0	0	0	0	0	0	0	0	0	-1	0	0	0	0	-1
s5	10	0	0	0	0	1	0	0	1	0	-1	0	0	0	0	-1	0	0	0	0	0	0	0	0	0	0	0	0	0	-1	0	0	0	-1
s6	10	0	0	0	0	0	1	0	1	0	-1	0	0	0	0	0	-1	0	0	0	0	0	0	0	0	0	0	0	0	0	-1	0	0	-1
s7	11	0	0	0	0	0	0	1	1	0	-1	0	0	0	0	0	0	-1	0	0	0	0	0	0	0	0	0	0	0	0	0	-1	0	-1
s8	8	-1	-1	-1	-1	-1	-1	-1	1	0	-1	1	1	1	1	1	1	1	-1	0	0	0	0	0	0	-1	-1	-1	-1	-1	-1	-1	0	-1
s1	14	1	0	0	0	0	0	0	1	1	1	-1	0	0	0	0	0	0	0	0	0	0	0	0	0	-1	0	0	0	0	0	0	1	1
s2	10	0	1	0	0	0	0	0	1	1	1	0	-1	0	0	0	0	0	0	0	0	0	0	0	0	0	-1	0	0	0	0	0	1	1
s3	11	0	0	1	0	0	0	0	1	1	1	0	0	-1	0	0	0	0	0	0	0	0	0	0	0	0	0	-1	0	0	0	0	1	1
s4	11	0	0	0	1	0	0	0	1	1	1	0	0	0	-1	0	0	0	0	0	0	0	0	0	0	0	0	0	-1	0	0	0	1	1
s5	12	0	0	0	0	1	0	0	1	1	1	0	0	0	0	-1	0	0	0	0	0	0	0	0	0	0	0	0	0	-1	0	0	1	1
s6	10	0	0	0	0	0	1	0	1	1	1	0	0	0	0	0	-1	0	0	0	0	0	0	0	0	0	0	0	0	0	-1	0	1	1
s7	11	0	0	0	0	0	0	1	1	1	1	0	0	0	0	0	0	-1	-1	0	0	0	0	0	0	0	0	0	0	0	0	-1	1	1
s8	12	-1	-1	-1	-1	-1	-1	-1	1	1	1	1	1	1	1	1	1	1	-1	-1	-1	-1	-1	-1	-1	-1	-1	-1	-1	-1	-1	-1	1	1
s1	16	1	0	0	0	0	0	0	-1	0	0	0	0	0	0	0	0	0	-1	-1	-1	-1	-1	-1	-1	0	0	0	0	0	0	0	0	0

continued overleaf

Table 5.7 (continued)

s	Y	S							A	B		S×A							S×B														A×B	
		X_1	X_2	X_3	X_4	X_5	X_6	X_7	X_8	X_9	X_{10}	X_{11}	X_{12}	X_{13}	X_{14}	X_{15}	X_{16}	X_{17}	X_{18}	X_{19}	X_{20}	X_{21}	X_{22}	X_{23}	X_{24}	X_{25}	X_{26}	X_{27}	X_{28}	X_{29}	X_{30}	X_{31}	X_{32}	X_{33}
s2	7	0	1	0	0	0	0	0	−1	1	0	0	−1	0	0	0	0	0	0	1	0	0	0	0	0	0	0	0	0	0	0	0	−1	0
s3	11	0	0	1	0	0	0	0	−1	1	0	0	0	−1	0	0	0	0	0	0	1	0	0	0	0	0	0	0	0	0	0	0	−1	0
s4	9	0	0	0	1	0	0	0	−1	1	0	0	0	0	−1	0	0	0	0	0	0	1	0	0	0	0	0	0	0	0	0	0	−1	0
s5	10	0	0	0	0	1	0	0	−1	1	0	0	0	0	0	−1	0	0	0	0	0	0	1	0	0	0	0	0	0	0	0	0	−1	0
s6	11	0	0	0	0	0	1	0	−1	1	0	0	0	0	0	0	−1	0	0	0	0	0	0	1	0	0	0	0	0	0	0	0	−1	0
s7	8	0	0	0	0	0	0	1	−1	1	0	0	0	0	0	0	0	−1	0	0	0	0	0	0	1	0	0	0	0	0	0	0	−1	0
s8	8	−1	−1	−1	−1	−1	−1	−1	−1	1	0	1	1	1	1	1	1	1	−1	−1	−1	−1	−1	−1	−1	0	0	0	0	0	0	0	−1	0
s1	16	1	0	0	0	0	0	0	−1	0	1	−1	0	0	0	0	0	0	0	0	0	0	0	0	0	1	0	0	0	0	0	0	0	−1
s2	10	0	1	0	0	0	0	0	−1	0	1	0	−1	0	0	0	0	0	0	0	0	0	0	0	0	0	1	0	0	0	0	0	0	−1
s3	13	0	0	1	0	0	0	0	−1	0	1	0	0	−1	0	0	0	0	0	0	0	0	0	0	0	0	0	1	0	0	0	0	0	−1
s4	10	0	0	0	1	0	0	0	−1	0	1	0	0	0	−1	0	0	0	0	0	0	0	0	0	0	0	0	0	1	0	0	0	0	−1
s5	10	0	0	0	0	1	0	0	−1	0	1	0	0	0	0	−1	0	0	0	0	0	0	0	0	0	0	0	0	0	1	0	0	0	−1
s6	14	0	0	0	0	0	1	0	−1	0	1	0	0	0	0	0	−1	0	0	0	0	0	0	0	0	0	0	0	0	0	1	0	0	−1
s7	11	0	0	0	0	0	0	1	−1	0	1	0	0	0	0	0	0	−1	0	0	0	0	0	0	0	0	0	0	0	0	0	1	0	−1
s8	12	−1	−1	−1	−1	−1	−1	−1	−1	0	1	1	1	1	1	1	1	1	0	0	0	0	0	0	0	−1	−1	−1	−1	−1	−1	−1	0	−1
s1	24	1	0	0	0	0	0	0	−1	−1	−1	−1	0	0	0	0	0	0	−1	0	0	0	0	0	0	−1	0	0	0	0	0	0	1	1
s2	29	0	1	0	0	0	0	0	−1	−1	−1	0	−1	0	0	0	0	0	0	−1	0	0	0	0	0	0	−1	0	0	0	0	0	1	1
s3	10	0	0	1	0	0	0	0	−1	−1	−1	0	0	−1	0	0	0	0	0	0	−1	0	0	0	0	0	0	−1	0	0	0	0	1	1
s4	22	0	0	0	1	0	0	0	−1	−1	−1	0	0	0	−1	0	0	0	0	0	0	−1	0	0	0	0	0	0	−1	0	0	0	1	1
s5	25	0	0	0	0	1	0	0	−1	−1	−1	0	0	0	0	−1	0	0	0	0	0	0	−1	0	0	0	0	0	0	−1	0	0	1	1
s6	28	0	0	0	0	0	1	0	−1	−1	−1	0	0	0	0	0	−1	0	0	0	0	0	0	−1	0	0	0	0	0	0	−1	0	1	1
s7	22	0	0	0	0	0	0	1	−1	−1	−1	0	0	0	0	0	0	−1	0	0	0	0	0	0	−1	0	0	0	0	0	0	−1	1	1
s8	24	−1	−1	−1	−1	−1	−1	−1	−1	−1	−1	1	1	1	1	1	1	1	1	1	1	1	1	1	1	1	1	1	1	1	1	1	1	1

Table 5.8   ANOVA summary table for the full fully related factorial experimental design GLM (subjects and experimental condition effects regression)

	R: 0.973	R squared: 0.946	Adjusted R squared: 0.820		
Source	SS	df	Mean square	F	p
Regression	1616.333	33	48.980	7.481	< 0.001
Residual	91.667	14	6.548		

by carrying out the regression analysis again but omitting the predictors representing the subjects – variables X_1 to X_7. The summary of this ANOVA, presented in Table 5.9, provides the subjects reduced GLM residual SS. Therefore,

			dfs
Subjects factor reduced GLM residual SS	=	143.667	21
Full GLM residual SS	=	91.667	14
SS attributable to subjects factor	=	52.000	7

Next, the Reduced GLM for the effect of Factor A is applied by omitting only the predictor representing the Factor A experimental conditions – variable X_8. The summary of this ANOVA, presented in Table 5.10, provides the Factor A reduced GLM residual SS.

Table 5.9   ANOVA summary table for the reduced GLM which omits the subjects factor

	R: 0.957	R squared: 0.916	Adjusted R squared: 0.812		
Source	SS	df	Mean Square	F	p
Regression	1564.333	26	60.167	8.795	
Residual	143.667	21	6.841		

Table 5.10   ANOVA summary table for the reduced GLM which omits the Factor A experimental conditions

	R: 0.833	R squared: 0.693	Adjusted R squared: 0.039		
Source	SS	df	Mean square	F	p
Regression	1184.333	32	37.010	1.060	0.470
Residual	523.667	15	34.911		

Therefore,

			dfs
Factor A reduced GLM residual SS	=	523.667	15
Full GLM residual SS	=	91.667	14
SS attributable to Factor A	=	432.000	1

Next, the subjects $\times$ Factor A Reduced GLM is applied by omitting only the predictors representing the subjects $\times$ Factor A interaction – variables X_{11} to X_{17}. The summary of this ANOVA, presented in Table 5.11, provides the subject $\times$ Factor A reduced GLM residual SS. Therefore,

			dfs
Subject $\times$ Factor A interaction reduced GLM residual SS	=	167.000	21
Full GLM residual SS	=	91.667	14
SS attributable to subject $\times$ Factor A interaction	=	75.333	7

Next, the Factor B reduced GLM is applied by omitting only the predictors representing the Factor B experimental conditions – variables X_9 and X_{10}. The summary of this ANOVA, presented in Table 5.12, provides the Factor B reduced GLM residual SS. Therefore,

Table 5.11   ANOVA summary table for the reduced GLM which omits the subject $\times$ Factor A interaction

R: 0.950	R squared: 0.902		Adjusted R squared: 0.781		
Source	SS	df	Mean square	F	p
Regression	1541.000	26	59.269	7.453	< 0.001
Residual	167.000	21	7.952		

Table 5.12   ANOVA summary table for the reduced GLM which omits the Factor B experimental conditions

R: 0.744	R squared: 0. 553		Adjusted R squared: 0.000		
Source	SS	df	Mean square	F	p
Regression	944.333	31	30.462	0.638	0.862
Residual	763.667	16	47.729		

		dfs
Factor B reduced GLM residual SS	= 763.667	1
Full GLM residual SS	= 91.667	14

SS attributable to Factor B	= 672.000	2

Next, the subjects $\times$ Factor B reduced GLM is applied by omitting only the predictors representing the subjects $\times$ Factor B interaction – variables X_{18} to X_{31}. The summary of this ANOVA, presented in Table 5.13, provides the subject $\times$ Factor B reduced GLM residual SS. Therefore,

		dfs
Subject $\times$ Factor B interaction reduced GLM residual SS	= 252.667	28
Full GLM residual SS	= 91.667	14

SS attributable to subject $\times$ Factor B interaction	= 161.000	14

Next, the Factor $A \times$ Factor B interaction reduced GLM is applied by omitting only the predictors representing the Factor $A \times$ Factor B interaction – variables X_{32} and X_{33}. The summary of this ANOVA, presented in Table 5.14, provides the Factor $A \times$ Factor B reduced GLM residual SS. Therefore,

		dfs
Factors $A \times B$ interaction reduced GLM residual SS	= 315.667	16
Full GLM residual SS	= 91.667	14

SS attributable to Factor $A \times$ Factor B interaction	= 224.000	2

Table 5.13 ANOVA summary table for the reduced GLM which omits the subject $\times$ Factor B interaction

R: 0.925   R squared: 0.852   Adjusted R squared: 0.752

Source	SS	df	Mean square	F	p
Regression	1455.333	19	76.596	8.488	<0.001
Residual	252.667	28	9.024		

Table 5.14 ANOVA summary table for the reduced GLM which omits the Factor $A \times$ Factor B interaction

R: 0.903   R squared: 0.815   Adjusted R squared: 0.457

Source	SS	df	Mean square	F	p
Regression	1392.333	31	44.914	2.277	0.042
Residual	315.667	16	19.729		

Using the SS and dfs calculated for each effect by comparing full and reduced GLMs, the ANOVA summary table (Table 5.5) can be reconstructed.

5.5 Mixed factorial ANOVA

Consider again the experiment presented in Chapter 3. Here, a mixed factorial design, with an independent experimental factor and a related experimental factor, would be a good choice of design. By having different groups of subjects receive "memorize" and "story/image" instructions, the problem of subjects in "memorize" conditions employing a "story/image" strategy is minimized. Table 5.15 presents the data from the two factor experiment described in Chapter 3 cast as if it had been obtained with a two factor mixed design.

The GLM for the mixed two factor ANOVA is described by the equation

$$Y_{ijk} = \mu + \pi_{i(j)} + \alpha_j + \beta_k + (\alpha\beta)_{jk} + \varepsilon_{ijk} \tag{5.19}$$

where Y_{ijk} is the dependent variable score for the ith subject at the jth level of Factor A and the kth level of Factor B, μ is the constant representing the dependent variable score free of the effect of any experimental condition, $\pi_{i(j)}$ is a parameter representing the random effect of the ith subject in the jth level of Factor A, α_j is the effect of the jth level of Factor A, β_k is the effect of the kth level of Factor B, $(\alpha\beta)_{jk}$ is the interaction effect of the jth level of Factor A and the kth level of Factor B, and as always, ε_{ijk} represents the random error associated with the ith subject in the jth level of Factor A and the kth level of Factor B. The use of brackets around the subscript j indicates that these effects

Table 5.15   Experimental data from a mixed two (2 × 3) factor design

	\multicolumn{9}{c}{Encoding instructions}								
	\multicolumn{4}{c}{a_1 Memorize}				\multicolumn{4}{c}{a_2 Story and image}			

	\multicolumn{3}{c}{Study time (s)}			\multicolumn{3}{c}{Study time (s)}	
	b_1 30	b_2 60	b_3 180	Subject means		b_1 30	b_2 60	b_3 180	Subject means
s1	7	7	8	7.333	s9	16	16	24	18.667
s2	3	11	14	9.333	s10	7	10	29	15.333
s3	6	9	10	8.333	s11	11	13	10	11.333
s4	6	11	11	9.333	s12	9	10	22	13.667
s5	5	10	12	9.000	s13	10	10	25	15.000
s6	8	10	10	9.333	s14	11	14	28	17.667
s7	6	11	11	9.333	s15	8	11	22	13.667
s8	7	11	12	10.000	s16	8	12	24	14.667
Expt condition means	6	10	11	9	Expt condition means	10	12	23	15

involve the scores of subjects nested within the j levels of Factor A (i.e. separate groups of subjects are employed in each of the p levels of Factor A). Although the subjects factor is crossed with the levels of Factor B: all subjects receive all levels of Factor B, the subjects factor is nested under the levels of Factor A, so a different group of subjects receive each level of Factor A.

Experimental effects in mixed factorial designs are assessed using fewer error terms than their equivalent fully related factorial designs, but more than are employed in equivalent independent measures factorial designs. Mixed designs may be conceived as separate related designs nested within each of the levels of the independent factors. In the example presented in Table 5.15, the two independent factor levels, a_1 and a_2, each contain a single factor repeated measures design. As each subject again provides only one score in each level of the related factor, it is not possible to separate the error from the subject and related factor interaction. Therefore, the ε_{ijk} term is written more accurately as $[\varepsilon_{ijk} + (\pi\beta)_{ik(j)}]$, where $(\pi\beta)_{ik(j)}$ is the interaction effect of the ith subject and the kth level of Factor B in the jth level of Factor A. However, conceived as two single factor repeated measures designs, it can be appreciated that this problem and its solution are analogous to that discussed with respect to both single factor repeated measures (and also fully related factorial) designs. Indeed, the error term based on ε_{ijk} is a weighted average of the two single factor repeated measures error terms, each weighted by $(N_j - 1)$, so in balanced designs ε_{ijk} is just the average of the two single factor repeated measures error terms. In mixed designs therefore, the pertinent error term for the related factor main effect is ε_{ijk}. Moreover, because subjects are nested within, not crossed with, the independent factor levels, there is no term representing the interaction between the subjects factor and the two experimental factors (A and B). However, as the experimental factors interaction involves comparison of the nested related factor (B) effects across the independent factor levels, and the effect of nesting (i.e score variance due to different groups of subjects) is accommodated by the independent factors error term $\pi_{i(j)}$, so the experimental factors interaction is limited to comparisons of the related Factor B effects, making $(\pi\beta)_{ik(j)}$ the pertinent basis for the independent and related factors interaction effect.

As before, the estimates of μ, and the α_j, β_k and $(\alpha\beta)_{jk}$ effects are defined just as for the independent measures factorial design and so their definitions will not be repeated here. This leaves only the two error terms to be calculated. The simplest of these is the error term used to assess the independent experimental Factor A. This is obtained by taking the average of the scores provided by each subject. Essentially, this eliminates the related experimental Factor B and, with each subject providing a single (average) score and different subjects in each level of the independent factor, produces an independent measures ANOVA.

The mean of the scores provided by each subject is

$$\mu_{i(j)} = \left(\frac{\sum_{k=1}^{q} Y_{i(j)}}{q}\right) \tag{5.20}$$

Therefore, the effect due to the different subjects nested within the levels of the independent factor is

$$\hat{\pi}_{i(j)} = \mu_{i(j)} - \mu_j \qquad (5.21)$$

Applying formula (5.21) to the data in Table 5.15 provides

$$
\begin{array}{llll}
\hat{\pi}_1 = & 7.333 - 9 = -1.667 & \hat{\pi}_1 = 18.667 - 15 = & 3.667 \\
\hat{\pi}_2 = & 9.333 - 9 = & 0.333 & \hat{\pi}_2 = 15.333 - 15 = & 0.333 \\
\hat{\pi}_3 = & 8.333 - 9 = -0.667 & \hat{\pi}_3 = 11.333 - 15 = -3.667 \\
\hat{\pi}_4 = & 9.333 - 9 = & 0.333 & \hat{\pi}_4 = 13.667 - 15 = -1.333 \\
\hat{\pi}_5 = & 9.000 - 9 = & 0.000 & \hat{\pi}_5 = 15.000 - 15 = & 0.000 \\
\hat{\pi}_6 = & 9.333 - 9 = & 0.333 & \hat{\pi}_6 = 17.667 - 15 = & 2.667 \\
\hat{\pi}_7 = & 9.333 - 9 = & 0.333 & \hat{\pi}_7 = 13.667 - 15 = -1.333 \\
\hat{\pi}_8 = & 10.000 - 9 = & 1.000 & \hat{\pi}_8 = 14.667 - 15 = -0.333
\end{array}
$$

$$\sum_{i=1}^{N} \pi_{i(j)} = 0.000 \qquad \sum_{i=1}^{N} \pi_{i(j)} = 0.000$$

$$\sum_{i=1}^{N} \pi_{i(j)}^2 = 4.667 \qquad \sum_{i=1}^{N} \pi_{i(j)}^2 = 37.782$$

$$\sum_{j=1}^{P} \sum_{i=1}^{N} \pi_{i(j)}^2 = 42.449$$

The error SS due to the different subjects nested within the levels of the independent factor is

$$\text{subject error SS} = q \sum_{j=1}^{P} \sum_{i=1}^{N} \pi_{i(j)}^2 = 3(42.449) = 127.347 \qquad (5.22)$$

The last error term required is that based on the subject × Factor B inter-action. Based on the *model* component of the fully related two factor experi-mental design GLM equation, predicted scores are given by

$$\hat{Y}_{ijk} = \mu + \pi_{i(j)} + \alpha_j + \beta_k + (\alpha\beta)_{jk} \qquad (5.23)$$

Inserting the parameter estimates determined earlier into this formula provides the predicted scores per subject per experimental condition.

The final parameters for the fully related two factor experimental design GLM, the error terms, which represent the discrepancy between the actual scores observed (Table 5.15) and the scores predicted by the two factor GLM (Table 5.16), are defined as

$$\varepsilon_{ijk} = Y_{ijk} - \hat{Y}_{ijk} \qquad (5.24)$$

The error terms (observed scores in Table 5.15 minus the predicted scores in Table 5.16) are presented by subject and experimental condition in Table 5.17.

Table 5.16 Predicted scores for the mixed two (2 × 3) factor experiment

	a_1					a_2		
	b_1	b_2	b_3			b_1	b_2	b_3
s1	4.333	8.333	9.333		s9	13.667	15.667	26.667
s2	6.333	10.333	11.333		s10	10.333	12.333	23.333
s3	5.333	9.333	10.333		s11	6.333	8.333	19.333
s4	6.333	10.333	11.333		s12	8.667	10.667	21.667
s5	6.000	10.000	11.000		s13	10.000	12.000	23.000
s6	6.333	10.333	11.333		s14	12.667	14.667	25.667
s7	6.333	10.333	11.333		s15	8.667	10.667	21.667
s8	7.000	11.000	12.000		s16	9.667	11.667	22.667

Table 5.17 Error terms for the mixed two (2 × 3) factor experiment

	b_1	b_2	b_3			b_1	b_2	b_3
s1	2.667	−1.333	−1.333		s9	2.333	0.333	−2.667
s2	−3.333	0.667	2.667		s10	−3.333	−2.333	5.667
s3	0.667	−0.333	−0.333		s11	4.667	4.667	−9.333
s4	−0.333	0.667	−0.333		s12	0.333	−0.667	0.333
s5	−1.000	0.000	1.000		s13	0.000	−2.000	2.000
s6	1.667	−0.333	−1.333		s14	−1.667	−0.667	2.333
s7	−0.333	0.667	−0.333		s15	−0.667	0.333	0.333
s8	0.000	0.000	0.000		s16	−1.667	0.333	1.333
$\sum_{i=1}^{N}\varepsilon_{ijk}^2$	22.667	3.333	11.999			44.446	32.446	137.663
$\sum_{j=1}^{p}\sum_{k=1}^{q}\sum_{i=1}^{N}\varepsilon_{ijk}^2$				252.554				

Degrees of freedom are required next. For the error SS due to the different subjects nested within the levels of the independent factor,

$$df = (N - p) = (16 - 2) = 14$$

and for the error term based on ε_{ijk},

$$df = (N - p)(q - 1) = (16 - 2)(3 - 1) = 14(2) = 28$$

Placing these SS and dfs and the SS and dfs for the experimental effects obtained previously in an ANOVA summary table provides Table 5.18.

Table 5.18　Mixed two factor ANOVA summary table

Source	Sum of squares	df	Mean square	F	p
A (Encoding instructions)	432.000	1	432.000	47.493	< 0.001
S(A) (Error of subjects nested within encoding instructions)	127.347	14	9.096		
B (Study time)	672.000	2	336.000	37.251	< 0.001
A × B (Encode inst × study time)	224.000	2	112.000	12.417	< 0.001
Error	252.554	28	9.020		

5.6　Estimating effects by comparing full and reduced experimental design GLMs

The full experimental design GLM for the mixed two factor ANOVA was described by equation (5.19). As with all the previous factorial ANOVAs calculated by comparing full and reduced experimental design GLMs, the hypotheses concerning the main effect of Factor A, the main effect of Factor B and the effect of the interaction between Factors A and B are assessed by constructing three reduced GLMs, which manifest data descriptions under the respective null hypotheses, and comparing their error components with the full model. Again this approach is simplified by virtue of all the subject, experimental factors and their interactions being orthogonal. As all of the effect estimates are completely distinct, omitting or including any particular effect has no consequence for the effect estimates.

The main effect of Factor A is assessed by constructing the reduced experimental design GLM,

$$Y_{ijk} = \mu + \pi_{i(j)} + \beta_k + (\alpha\beta)_{jk} + \varepsilon_{ijk} \tag{5.25}$$

This model manifests the data description under the null hypothesis,

$$\alpha_j = 0 \tag{5.26}$$

The main effect of Factor B is assessed by constructing the reduced experimental design GLM,

$$Y_{ijk} = \mu + \pi_{i(j)} + \alpha_j + (\alpha\beta)_{jk} + \varepsilon_{ijk} \tag{5.27}$$

This model manifests the data description under the null hypothesis,

$$\beta_k = 0 \tag{5.28}$$

Finally, the reduced GLM for assessing the effect of the interaction between Factors A and B is

$$Y_{ijk} = \mu + \pi_{i(j)} + \alpha_j + \beta_k + \varepsilon_{ijk} \tag{5.29}$$

This reduced GLM manifests the data description under the null hypothesis,

$$(\alpha\beta)_{jk} = 0 \tag{5.30}$$

Although fewer error terms need be calculated for mixed ANOVAs, when hand calculations are employed, instead of calculating the error SS associated with each of these Reduced experimental design GLMs and comparing them with the full experimental design GLM, it may be more efficient to calculate directly the SS for each of the effects and errors. Formulae for calculating all of the mixed two factor ANOVA effects directly, which are more convenient than those used to define and illustrate the SS calculation, are provided in Table 5.19. However, again the strategy of estimating mixed ANOVA effects by comparing different GLM residuals is relatively easy to achieve using regression GLMs.

5.7 Regression GLMs for the mixed factorial ANOVA

The mixed (2×3) factor experimental design GLM equation (5.19) may be compared with the equivalent regression equation,

$$Y_i = \beta_0 + \beta_1 X_{i,1} + \beta_2 X_{i,2} + \beta_3 X_{i,3} + \beta_4 X_{i,4} + \beta_5 X_{i,5} + \beta_6 X_{i,6} + \beta_7 X_{i,7}$$
$$+ \beta_8 X_{i,8} + \beta_9 X_{i,9} + \beta_{10} X_{i,10} + \beta_{11} X_{i,11} + \beta_{12} X_{i,12} + \beta_{13} X_{i,13} + \beta_{14} X_{i,14}$$
$$+ \beta_{15} X_{i,15} + \beta_{16} X_{i,16} + \beta_{17} X_{i,17} + \beta_{18} X_{i,18} + \beta_{19} X_{i,19} + \varepsilon_i \tag{5.31}$$

Table 5.19 Formulae for the (balanced) fully related two factor ANOVA effects

Effect	Formulae
A	$qN \sum\limits_{j=1}^{p} (\overline{Y}_j - \overline{Y}_G)^2$
S(A)	$q \sum\limits_{i=1}^{N} \sum\limits_{j=1}^{p} (\overline{Y}_{ij} - \overline{Y}_j)^2$
B	$pN \sum\limits_{k=1}^{q} (\overline{Y}_k - \overline{Y}_G)^2$
A × B	$N \sum\limits_{j=1}^{p} \sum\limits_{k=1}^{q} (\overline{Y}_{jk} - \overline{Y}_j - \overline{Y}_k + \overline{Y}_G)^2$
Error	$\sum\limits_{i=1}^{N} \sum\limits_{j=1}^{p} \sum\limits_{k=1}^{q} (Y_{ijk} - \overline{Y}_{ij} - \overline{Y}_{ik} + \overline{Y}_i)^2$

where Y_i represents the ith dependent variable score, β_0 is a constant, β_1 is the regression coefficient for the predictor variable X_1 and β_2 is the regression coefficient for the predictor variable X_2, etc.

As with the fully related factorial design, there are X variables which represent experimental factors and their interactions (X_1 to X_5), while 14 variables (X_6 to X_{19}) identify the subjects providing the scores. The first seven subject variables (X_6 to X_{12}) identify those subjects providing scores in the condition labelled as Factor A level one (*memorize*), while the second set of seven subject variables identify those subjects providing scores in the condition labelled as Factor A level two (*story and imagery*).

Equation (5.31) is only sightly more wieldy than equation (5.18), but as before, once the effect coding scheme has been established in a computer data file, it is relatively simple to carry out the mixed factorial ANOVA. Table 5.20 presents effect coding applied to the data in Table 5.17.

Applying a regression GLM to implement a mixed factors ANOVA also may be done in a manner consistent with estimating effects by comparing full and reduced GLMs. In such balanced designs, the predictor variables representing experimental factors and those identifying subjects' scores again are orthogonal, and so the order in which SSs are calculated is of no consequence.

The first regression carried out is that for the full mixed factorial experimental design GLM, when all experimental condition and subject predictor variables are included (i.e. variables X_1 to X_{19}). Of interest is the ANOVA summary presented in Table 5.21, which provides the full GLM residual SS. This may be compared with the mixed factorial experimental design GLM error term in Table 5.18.

Having obtained the full GLM residual SS, the next stages involve implementing the various reduced GLMs to obtain their estimates of residual SS. First, the reduced GLM for the effect of the subjects nested within Factor A is obtained by carrying out the regression analysis again but omitting the predictors identifying the subjects providing the scores (X_6 to X_{19}). The summary of this ANOVA, presented in Table 5.22, provides the subjects nested within Factor A reduced GLM residual SS. Therefore,

			dfs
Subjects (Factor A) reduced GLM residual SS	=	380.000	42
Full GLM residual SS	=	252.667	28
SS attributable to subjects nested within Factor A	=	127.333	14

Next, the reduced GLM for the effect of Factor A is applied by omitting only the predictor variable representing the Factor A experimental conditions (X_1). The summary of this ANOVA presented in Table 5.23 provides the Factor A reduced GLM residual SS. Therefore,

Table 5.20 Effect coding for the mixed (2 × 3) factorial ANOVA

Sbj	Y	A	B		A×B		A = 1 subjects							A = −1 subjects						
		X_1	X_2	X_3	X_4	X_5	X_6	X_7	X_8	X_9	X_{10}	X_{11}	X_{12}	X_{13}	X_{14}	X_{15}	X_{16}	X_{17}	X_{18}	X_{19}
1	7	1	1	0	1	0	1	0	0	0	0	0	0	0	0	0	0	0	0	0
2	3	1	1	0	1	0	0	1	0	0	0	0	0	0	0	0	0	0	0	0
3	6	1	1	0	1	0	0	0	1	0	0	0	0	0	0	0	0	0	0	0
4	6	1	1	0	1	0	0	0	0	1	0	0	0	0	0	0	0	0	0	0
5	5	1	1	0	1	0	0	0	0	0	1	0	0	0	0	0	0	0	0	0
6	8	1	1	0	1	0	0	0	0	0	0	1	0	0	0	0	0	0	0	0
7	6	1	1	0	1	0	0	0	0	0	0	0	1	0	0	0	0	0	0	0
8	7	1	1	0	1	0	−1	−1	−1	−1	−1	−1	−1	0	0	0	0	0	0	0
1	7	1	0	1	0	1	1	0	0	0	0	0	0	0	0	0	0	0	0	0
2	11	1	0	1	0	1	0	1	0	0	0	0	0	0	0	0	0	0	0	0
3	9	1	0	1	0	1	0	0	1	0	0	0	0	0	0	0	0	0	0	0
4	11	1	0	1	0	1	0	0	0	1	0	0	0	0	0	0	0	0	0	0
5	10	1	0	1	0	1	0	0	0	0	1	0	0	0	0	0	0	0	0	0
6	10	1	0	1	0	1	0	0	0	0	0	1	0	0	0	0	0	0	0	0
7	11	1	0	1	0	1	0	0	0	0	0	0	1	0	0	0	0	0	0	0
8	11	1	0	1	0	1	−1	−1	−1	−1	−1	−1	−1	0	0	0	0	0	0	0
1	8	1	−1	−1	−1	−1	1	0	0	0	0	0	0	0	0	0	0	0	0	0
2	14	1	−1	−1	−1	−1	0	1	0	0	0	0	0	0	0	0	0	0	0	0
3	10	1	−1	−1	−1	−1	0	0	1	0	0	0	0	0	0	0	0	0	0	0
4	11	1	−1	−1	−1	−1	0	0	0	1	0	0	0	0	0	0	0	0	0	0
5	12	1	−1	−1	−1	−1	0	0	0	0	1	0	0	0	0	0	0	0	0	0
6	10	1	−1	−1	−1	−1	0	0	0	0	0	1	0	0	0	0	0	0	0	0
7	11	1	−1	−1	−1	−1	0	0	0	0	0	0	1	0	0	0	0	0	0	0

continued overleaf

Table 5.20 (continued)

Sbj	Y	A	B		A×B		A = 1 subjects							A = −1 subjects						
		X_1	X_2	X_3	X_4	X_5	X_6	X_7	X_8	X_9	X_{10}	X_{11}	X_{12}	X_{13}	X_{14}	X_{15}	X_{16}	X_{17}	X_{18}	X_{19}
8	12	1	−1	−1	−1	−1	−1	−1	−1	−1	−1	−1	−1	0	0	0	0	0	0	0
1	16	−1	1	0	−1	0	0	0	0	0	0	0	0	1	0	0	0	0	0	0
2	7	−1	1	0	−1	0	0	0	0	0	0	0	0	0	1	0	0	0	0	0
3	11	−1	1	0	−1	0	0	0	0	0	0	0	0	0	0	1	0	0	0	0
4	9	−1	1	0	−1	0	0	0	0	0	0	0	0	0	0	0	1	0	0	0
5	10	−1	1	0	−1	0	0	0	0	0	0	0	0	0	0	0	0	1	0	0
6	11	−1	1	0	−1	0	0	0	0	0	0	0	0	0	0	0	0	0	1	0
7	8	−1	1	0	−1	0	0	0	0	0	0	0	0	0	0	0	0	0	0	1
8	8	−1	1	0	−1	0	0	0	0	0	0	0	0	−1	−1	−1	−1	−1	−1	−1
1	16	−1	0	1	0	−1	0	0	0	0	0	0	0	1	0	0	0	0	0	0
2	10	−1	0	1	0	−1	0	0	0	0	0	0	0	0	1	0	0	0	0	0
3	13	−1	0	1	0	−1	0	0	0	0	0	0	0	0	0	1	0	0	0	0
4	10	−1	0	1	0	−1	0	0	0	0	0	0	0	0	0	0	1	0	0	0
5	14	−1	0	1	0	−1	0	0	0	0	0	0	0	0	0	0	0	1	0	0
6	11	−1	0	1	0	−1	0	0	0	0	0	0	0	0	0	0	0	0	1	0
7	12	−1	0	1	0	−1	0	0	0	0	0	0	0	0	0	0	0	0	0	1
8	12	−1	0	1	0	−1	0	0	0	0	0	0	0	−1	−1	−1	−1	−1	−1	−1
1	24	−1	−1	−1	1	1	0	0	0	0	0	0	0	1	0	0	0	0	0	0
2	29	−1	−1	−1	1	1	0	0	0	0	0	0	0	0	1	0	0	0	0	0
3	10	−1	−1	−1	1	1	0	0	0	0	0	0	0	0	0	1	0	0	0	0
4	22	−1	−1	−1	1	1	0	0	0	0	0	0	0	0	0	0	1	0	0	0
5	25	−1	−1	−1	1	1	0	0	0	0	0	0	0	0	0	0	0	1	0	0
6	28	−1	−1	−1	1	1	0	0	0	0	0	0	0	0	0	0	0	0	1	0
7	22	−1	−1	−1	1	1	0	0	0	0	0	0	0	0	0	0	0	0	0	1
8	24	−1	−1	−1	1	1	0	0	0	0	0	0	0	−1	−1	−1	−1	−1	−1	−1

Table 5.21 ANOVA summary table for the full mixed factorial experimental design GLM (experimental condition and subjects effects regression)

R: 0.923   R squared: 0.852   Adjusted R squared: 0.752

Source	SS	df	Mean square	F	p
Regression	1455.333	19	76.596	8.488	
Residual	252.667	28	9.024		

Table 5.22 ANOVA summary table for the mixed factorial experimental design GLM omitting the effect of subjects nested within Factor A

R: 0.882   R squared: 0.778   Adjusted R squared: 0.751

Source	SS	df	Mean square	F	p
Regression	1328.000	5	265.600	29.356	
Residual	380.000	42	9.048		

Table 5.23 ANOVA summary table for the reduced GLM which omits the Factor A experimental conditions

R: 0.774   R squared: 0.599   Adjusted R squared: 0.350

Source	SS	df	Mean square	F	p
Regression	1023.333	18	56.852	2.408	0.017
Residual	684.667	29	23.609		

			dfs
Factor A reduced GLM residual SS	=	684.667	29
Full GLM residual SS	=	252.667	28
SS attributable to Factor A	=	432.000	1

Next, the Factor B reduced GLM is applied by omitting only the predictor variables representing the Factor B experimental conditions (X_2 and X_3). The summary of this ANOVA presented in Table 5.24 provides the Factor B reduced GLM residual SS.

Table 5.24   ANOVA summary table for the reduced GLM which omits the Factor B experimental conditions

	R: 0.677	R squared: 0.459	Adjusted R squared: 0.152		
Source	SS	df	Mean square	F	p
Regression	783.333	17	46.078	1.495	0.163
Residual	924.667	30	30.822		

Therefore,

			dfs
Factor B reduced GLM residual SS	=	924.667	30
Full GLM residual SS	=	252.667	28
SS attributable to Factor B	=	672.000	2

Next, the Factor $A \times$ Factor B interaction reduced GLM is applied by omitting only the predictor variables representing the Factor $A \times$ Factor B interaction (X_4 and X_5). The summary of this ANOVA presented in Table 5.25, provides the Factor $A \times$ Factor B reduced GLM residual SS. Therefore,

			dfs
Factors $A \times B$ interaction reduced GLM residual SS	=	476.667	30
Full GLM residual SS	=	252.667	28
SS attributable to Factor $A \times$ Factor B interaction	=	224.000	2

Using the SS and dfs calculated for each effect by comparing full and reduced GLMs, the ANOVA summary table (Table 5.18) can be reconstructed.

Table 5.25   ANOVA summary table for the reduced GLM which omits the Factor A × Factor B interaction

	R: 0.849	R squared: 0.721	Adjusted R squared: 0.563		
Source	SS	df	Mean square	F	p
Regression	1231.333	17	72.431	4.559	< 0.001
Residual	476.667	30	15.889		

6 THE GLM APPROACH TO ANCOVA

6.1 The nature of ANCOVA

Consider the *story and imagery* experimental conditions described in Chapter 3. Different subjects are likely to have different story and imagery abilities. Although not a guarantee, random sampling of the population and random allocation to the three study time experimental conditions makes it most likely that across the three groups of subjects the average story and imagery abilities will be equivalent. Nevertheless, even when this is so, within each of the groups there will be subjects with greater story and imagery abilities and subjects with lesser story and imagery abilities, and this variation in story and imagery ability will have consequence for the subjects' memory recall scores. However, in most conventional experimental studies, subjects' story and imagery abilities will not have been measured prior to the experiment. Moreover, because there is no term in the ANOVA GLM to accommodate any systematic variation of subjects' story and imagery abilities with their memory recall scores, this variation increments the ANOVA error term. All else being equal, the consequence of a larger error term is a less powerful analysis (see Chapter 9) and so, a greater chance that any influence of study time on memory recall will not be detected. Obviously, a clearer picture of the influence of study time on memory recall when story and imagery encoding strategies are used would be obtained if all of the subjects had the same ability to construct stories and images.

ANCOVA offers a way to deal with such situations. As well as recording the independent and dependent variables, one or more other variables are measured for ANCOVA. These variables (variously known as covariates, predictor variables, concomitant variables or control variables) represent sources of variation that are thought to influence the dependent variable, but have not been controlled by the experimental procedures. In the present example, the covariates would be measures of the subjects' story and imagery abilities. The rationale underlying ANCOVA is that the effect of the independent variable(s) on the dependent variable is revealed more accurately when the influence on the dependent variable represented by the covariate(s) is equal across the experimental conditions. In psychology, when the GLM includes a quantitative variable in addition to the categorical coding of experimental conditions, but experimental effects remain the major concern, the analysis is termed ANCOVA (cf. Cox & McCullagh, 1982).

6.2   Single factor independent measures ANCOVA designs

In the following example, the story and imagery conditions of the memory experiment described in Chapter 3 will be regarded as a separate experiment. Further, it will be assumed that the subjects in this experiment completed a test which provided a single measure of their story and imagery abilities. Table 6.1 presents the subjects' story and imagery task (covariate) scores and the subjects' memory recall scores after story and imagery encoding in the three study time conditions.

The equation

$$Y_{ij} = \mu + \alpha_j + \beta Z_{ij} + \varepsilon_{ij} \tag{6.1}$$

describes an experimental design GLM for the single factor independent measures ANCOVA with one covariate applicable to the data presented in Table 6.1. Y_{ij} is the ith score in the jth treatment, μ is a constant common to all Y scores, α_j is the effect of the jth treatment level and the error term, ε_{ij}, reflects random variation due to any uncontrolled source. The new term βZ_{ij} represents the influence of the covariate on the dependent variable. It comprises the regression coefficient parameter β, which represents the degree of linear relationship between the covariate and the dependent variable and Z_{ij}, the particular covariate score corresponding to the Y_{ij}. It is important to appreciate that the degree of the linear relationship between the covariate and the dependent variable is determined empirically from the data. The ANCOVA GLM combines features of an ANOVA GLM and a regression GLM. The (categorical) experimental condition effects are specified as in ANOVA, while the relationship between the (quantitative) covariate and the dependent variable are specified as in regression.

Table 6.1   Story and imagery test scores and recall scores after story and imagery encoding

Study time (s)	30		60		180	
	Z	Y	Z	Y	Z	Y
	9	16	8	16	5	24
	5	7	5	10	8	29
	6	11	6	13	3	10
	4	9	5	10	4	22
	6	10	3	10	6	25
	8	11	6	14	9	28
	3	8	4	11	4	22
	5	8	6	12	5	24
$\sum Z/Y$	46	80	43	96	44	184
$\overline{Z}/\overline{Y}$	5.750	10.000	5.375	12.000	5.500	23.000
$(\sum Z/Y)^2$	292	856	247	1186	272	4470
$\sum Z^2/Y^2$	2116	6400	1849	9216	1936	33856

In Figure 6.1, the regression lines of subjects' dependent variable memory recall scores on their story and imagery ability test scores are plotted for each study time experimental condition (b_1, b_2 and b_3). Also shown is ($\hat{\beta}$), the slope of the regression line employed in the ANCOVA GLM, which is given by

$$\hat{\beta} = \frac{\sum_{j=1}^{P}\sum_{i=1}^{N}(Z_{ij} - \overline{Z}_j)(Y_{ij} - \overline{Y}_j)}{\sum_{j=1}^{P}\sum_{i=1}^{N}(Z_{ij} - \overline{Z}_j)^2} \qquad (6.2)$$

$\hat{\beta}$ also may be calculated from

$$\hat{\beta} = \frac{\sum_{i=1}^{N}(Z_{i1} - \overline{Z}_1)^2 b_1 + \sum_{i=1}^{N}(Z_{i2} - \overline{Z}_2)^2 b_2 + \sum_{i=1}^{N}(Z_{i3} - \overline{Z}_3)^2 b_3}{\sum_{i=1}^{N}(Z_{i1} - \overline{Z}_1)^2 + \sum_{i=1}^{N}(Z_{i2} - \overline{Z}_2)^2 + \sum_{i=1}^{N}(Z_{i3} - \overline{Z}_3)^2} \qquad (6.3)$$

Equation (6.3) reveals $\hat{\beta}$ as the weighted average of the separate (within group) regression lines, b_1, b_2 and b_3, where each experimental condition regression coefficient (b_1, b_2 and b_3) is weighted by the variation of the covariate scores in that experimental condition. Consequently, $\hat{\beta}$ may be called the within groups regression coefficient ($\hat{\beta}_w = b_w$). An important point to appreciate is that equations (6.2) and (6.3) provide a regression coefficient which is free of the

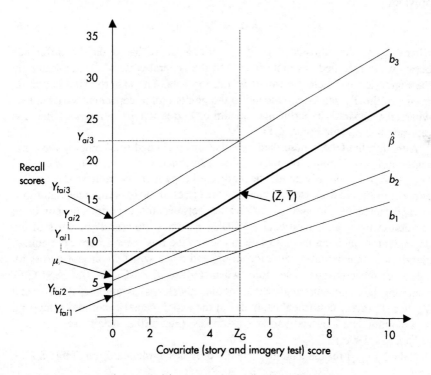

Figure 6.1 Dependent variable memory recall scores plotted on their story and imagery ability test scores for each study time experimental condition

influence exerted on the dependent variable scores by the experimental conditions.

A little algebra applied to equation (6.1) reveals

$$Y_{faij} = Y_{ij} - \beta Z_{ij} = \mu + \alpha_j + \varepsilon_{ij} \qquad (6.4)$$

where Y_{faij} is the fundamental adjusted dependent variable score observed if all influence of the covariate is removed from the dependent variable score. The Y_{faij} correspond to the points on the dependent variable axis intersected by each of the experimental condition regression lines (see Figure 6.1). This is where the value of the covariate equals zero. Traditionally in ANCOVA however, the dependent variable scores are not adjusted to remove all influence of the covariate. Instead, adjustment is made as though all subjects had obtained a covariate score equal to the general covariate mean ($Z_G = 5.542$). Replacing βZ_{ij} in equation (6.1) with $\beta(Z_{ij} - Z_G)$ provides the single factor independent measures experimental design GLM for traditional ANCOVA with one covariate,

$$Y_{ij} = \mu + \alpha_j + \beta(Z_{ij} - Z_G) + \varepsilon_{ij} \qquad (6.5)$$

Applying the same algebra to equation (6.5) as was applied to equation (6.1) provides

$$Y_{aij} = Y_{ij} - \beta(Z_{ij} - Z_G) = \mu + \alpha_j + \varepsilon_{ij} \qquad (6.6)$$

where Y_{aij} is the adjusted dependent variable score based on the difference between the recorded covariate score and the general covariate mean scaled by the regression coefficient estimated from the data. The experimental condition means of the Y_{aij} scores correspond to the points on the dependent variable axis where the separate experimental condition regression lines intersect the line representing Z_G (see Figure 6.1).

Although the GLMs described by equations (6.1) and (6.5) employ the same regression coefficient, obviously the adjustments provided by βZ_{ij} and $\beta(Z_{ij} - Z_G)$ do not provide identical adjusted dependent variable scores (cf. Y_{aij} and Y_{faij} in Figure 6.1). Nevertheless, as the effect of the experimental conditions is represented by the vertical differences between the experimental condition regression lines, and traditional ANCOVA assumes the regression lines of the dependent variable on the covariate in each of the treatment groups are parallel, clearly the experimental condition effect estimates will be constant across all values of the covariate. Therefore, when traditional ANCOVA (i.e. ANCOVA assuming homogeneous regression coefficients/slopes) is applied, the Y_{faij} and Y_{aij} terms provide equivalent estimates of the experimental conditions effect and so accommodate identical variance estimates. (For further details, see Maxwell & Delaney, 1990.)

Calculating $\hat{\beta}$ for the data in Table 6.1 provides Table 6.2. From Table 6.2 we find

$$\hat{\beta} = \frac{33 + 20 + 68}{27.500 + 15.875 + 30.000} = 1.649$$

Table 6.2 Calculations based on Table 6.1

b_1 30		b_2 60		b_3 180	
$Z_{ij} - \bar{Z}_i$	$Y_{ij} - \bar{Y}_i$	$Z_{ij} - \bar{Z}_i$	$Y_{ij} - \bar{Y}_i$	$Z_{ij} - \bar{Z}_i$	$Y_{ij} - \bar{Y}_i$
9 − 5.750 = 3.250	16 − 10 = 6	8 − 5.375 = 2.625	16 − 12 = 4	5 − 5.500 = −0.500	24 − 23 = 1
5 − 5.750 = −0.750	7 − 10 = −3	5 − 5.375 = −0.375	10 − 12 = −2	8 − 5.500 = 2.500	29 − 23 = 6
6 − 5.750 = 0.250	11 − 10 = 1	6 − 5.375 = 0.625	13 − 12 = 1	3 − 5.500 = −2.500	10 − 23 = −13
4 − 5.750 = −1.750	9 − 10 = −1	5 − 5.375 = −0.375	10 − 12 = −2	4 − 5.500 = −1.500	22 − 23 = −1
6 − 5.750 = 0.250	10 − 10 = 0	3 − 5.375 = −2.375	10 − 12 = −2	6 − 5.500 = 0.500	25 − 23 = 2
8 − 5.750 = 2.250	11 − 10 = 1	6 − 5.375 = 0.625	14 − 12 = 2	9 − 5.500 = 3.500	28 − 23 = 5
3 − 5.750 = −2.750	8 − 10 = −2	4 − 5.375 = −1.375	11 − 12 = −1	4 − 5.500 = −1.500	22 − 23 = −1
5 − 5.750 = −0.750	8 − 10 = −2	6 − 5.375 = 0.625	12 − 12 = 0	5 − 5.500 = −0.500	24 − 23 = 1

$\sum(Z_{ij} - \bar{Z}_i)^2 = 27.500$ $\qquad$ $\sum(Z_{ij} - \bar{Z}_i)^2 = 15.875$ $\qquad$ $\sum(Z_{ij} - \bar{Z}_i)^2 = 30.000$

b_1 30	b_2 60	b_3 180
$(Z_{ij} - \bar{Z}_i)(Y_{ij} - \bar{Y}_i)$	$(Z_{ij} - \bar{Z}_i)(Y_{ij} - \bar{Y}_i)$	$(Z_{ij} - \bar{Z}_i)(Y_{ij} - \bar{Y}_i)$
3.250(6) = 19.500	2.625(4.00) = 10.500	−0.500(1.00) = −0.500
−0.750(−3) = 2.250	−0.375(−2.00) = 0.750	2.500(6.00) = 15.000
0.250(1) = 0.250	0.625(1.00) = 0.625	−2.500(−13.00) = 32.500
−1.750(−1) = 1.750	−0.375(−2.00) = 0.750	−1.500(−1.00) = 1.500
0.250(0) = 0.000	−2.375(−2.00) = 4.750	0.500(2.00) = 1.000
2.250(1) = 2.250	0.625(2.00) = 1.250	3.500(5.00) = 17.500
−2.750(−2) = 5.500	−1.375(−1.00) = 1.375	−1.500(−1.00) = 1.500
−0.750(−2) = 1.500	0.625(0.00) = 0.000	−0.500(1.00) = −0.500

$\sum = 33.000$ $\qquad$ $\sum = 20.000$ $\qquad$ $\sum = 68.000$

One consequence of including the dependent variable on the covariate regression component in the ANCOVA GLM is that the definition of the parameter μ changes slightly. For balanced ANOVA, μ was defined as the mean of the experimental condition means, but this is not the case even for balanced ANCOVA. Nevertheless, as in ANOVA, μ remains the intercept on the Y-axis (cf. Figures 2.2 and 6.1) of the $\hat{\beta}$ regression line, which passes through the general covariate and dependent variable means and may be calculated simply by estimating the reduction from the dependent variable mean on the basis of the general mean of the covariate. In Figure 6.1, the $\hat{\beta}$ regression line intercepts the Y-axis at a point below the dependent variable general mean. This point is determined by the distance from the general mean of the covariate to the origin, scaled by the $\hat{\beta}$ regression coefficient. Therefore,

$$\hat{\mu} = Y_G - \hat{\beta}(Z_G) \tag{6.7}$$

Applying this to the data in Table 6.1 provides

$$\hat{\mu} = 15 - 1.649(5.542) = 5.861$$

The adjusted experimental condition means are given by

$$\overline{Y}_{aj} = \overline{Y}_j - \beta(\overline{Z}_j - \overline{Z}_G) \tag{6.8}$$

Therefore,

$$\overline{Y}_{a1} = \overline{Y}_1 - \beta(\overline{Z}_1 - Z_G) = 10 - 1.649(5.750 - 5.542) = 9.657$$

$$\overline{Y}_{a2} = \overline{Y}_2 - \beta(\overline{Z}_2 - Z_G) = 12 - 1.649(5.375 - 5.542) = 12.275$$

$$\overline{Y}_{a3} = \overline{Y}_3 - \beta(\overline{Z}_3 - Z_G) = 23 - 1.649(5.500 - 5.542) = 23.069$$

Moreover, just as experimental condition means in ANOVA comprise the constant μ plus the effect of the experimental condition, so ANCOVA adjusted means comprise the constant μ plus the effect of the experimental condition:

$$\overline{Y}_{aj} = \hat{\mu} + \hat{\alpha}_j \tag{6.9}$$

and so it follows that

$$\hat{\alpha}_j = \overline{Y}_{aj} - \hat{\mu} \tag{6.10}$$

For the data in Table 6.1 this provides

$$\hat{\alpha}_1 = 9.657 - 5.861 = 3.796$$

$$\alpha_2 = 12.275 - 5.861 = 6.414$$

$$\alpha_3 = 23.069 - 5.861 = 17.208$$

6.3   Estimating effects by comparing full and reduced ANCOVA GLMs

Although μ and the experimental condition effects just described are not needed to calculate the error terms for full and reduced GLMs, the calculation methods are provided for completeness. In fact, these experimental condition effect estimates should not be used to obtain the experimental condition SS, in the manner described for ANOVA GLMs, as this provides an inaccurate estimate (Cochran, 1957; Maxwell, Delaney & Manheimer, 1985; Rutherford, 1992).

The traditional full GLM for the single factor single covariate ANCOVA design was described in equation (6.5). The reduced GLM for this design omits the variable representing experimental conditions and is described by the equation

$$Y_{ij} = \mu + \beta_T(Z_{ij} - \overline{Z}_G) + \varepsilon_{ij} \qquad (6.11)$$

Equation (6.11) describes a simple linear regression, where the difference between each subjects' covariate score and the general covariate mean is used to predict the subjects' dependent variable scores. This GLM may be compared with the reduced GLM that employs Z_{ij} as the predictor:

$$Y_{ij} = \mu + \beta_T(Z_{ij}) + \varepsilon_{ij} \qquad (6.12)$$

This would be the reduced GLM for the ANCOVA model described by equation (6.1). As with the GLMs described by equations (6.1) and (6.5), the GLMs described by equations (6.11) and (6.12) accommodate the same amount of dependent variable variation and employ the same regression coefficient, (β_T). The T subscript is applied to this regression coefficient to identify it as the regression coefficient for the total set of scores, where all scores are treated as one large group: no distinctions are made on the basis of experimental condition.

The application of a little algebra to the full GLM for the single factor, single covariate ANCOVA defines the error term in the following way. If

$$Y_{aij} = Y_{ij} - \beta(Z_{ij} - \overline{Z}_G) = \mu + \alpha_j + \varepsilon_{ij} \qquad (6.6, \text{rptd})$$

then clearly

$$Y_{ij} - \beta(Z_{ij} - \overline{Z}_G) = Y_{aij} = \mu + \alpha_j + \varepsilon_{ij}$$

Omitting the terms to the left of the first equals sign and employing equation (6.9) provides

$$Y_{aij} = \overline{Y}_{aj} + \varepsilon_{ij}$$

Therefore,

$$\varepsilon_{ij} = Y_{aij} - \overline{Y}_{aj} \qquad (6.13)$$

In other words, the full GLM errors are equal to each subject's adjusted score minus the adjusted mean for the experimental condition. Equation (6.6) defines subjects' adjusted scores as

$$Y_{aij} = Y_{ij} - \beta(Z_{ij} - \overline{Z}_G) \qquad \text{(6.6, rptd)}$$

and these are calculated in Table 6.3.

As a check on the accuracy of the adjusted scores, they can be used to calculate group means for comparison with those calculated from equation (6.8). Error terms are calculated using the adjusted scores and adjusted experimental condition means according to equation (6.13). As always, the sum of the errors per experimental condition and across conditions equals zero (given rounding error). The sum of the squared errors across experimental conditions is the (reduced) error term for the full GLM (Table 6.4).

The reduced GLM errors for this ANCOVA design may be found in the same way as above. First, reordering the terms in equation (6.11) allows the subjects' adjusted scores to be specified. As

$$Y_{ij} = \mu + \beta_T(Z_{ij} - \overline{Z}_G) + \varepsilon_{ij} \qquad \text{(6.11, rptd)}$$

so,

$$Y_{ij} - \beta_T(Z_{ij} - \overline{Z}_G) = Y_{aij} = \mu + \varepsilon_{ij} \qquad \text{(6.14)}$$

As experimental conditions are ignored, μ is equal to the general mean of the adjusted scores (Y_{aG}). It follows that for the reduced GLM,

$$\varepsilon_{ij} = Y_{aij} - \overline{Y}_{aG} \qquad \text{(6.15)}$$

A first requirement to calculate the reduced GLM errors is the regression coefficient β_T,

$$\hat{\beta}_T = \frac{\sum_{j=1}^{P}\sum_{i=1}^{N}(Z_{ij} - \overline{Z}_G)(Y_{ij} - Y_G)}{\sum_{j=1}^{P}\sum_{i=1}^{N}(Z_{ij} - \overline{Z}_G)^2} \qquad \text{(6.16)}$$

Applying this to the data in Table 6.1 provides Table 6.5. From Table 6.5,

$$\hat{\beta}_T = \frac{114.000}{73.958} = 1.541$$

This regression coefficient estimate is used to calculate each subjects' adjusted score, according to equation (6.14) (Table 6.6).

With the reduced GLM, the mean of the adjusted scores equals the mean of the unadjusted scores, 15. Given rounding error, this is the value obtained from the adjusted scores. As specified by equation (6.15), the discrepancy between this mean and the subjects' adjusted scores provide the error term estimates.

Given rounding error, 0.012 is not too bad an estimate of the correct value of zero. The sum of the squared errors provides the estimate of the reduced GLM error SS. Therefore, the error reduction as a consequence of taking account of the experimental conditions is

reduced GLM SS$_{error}$ – full GLM SS$_{error}$ = 936.279 – 128.463 = 807.816

Again the Full GLM SS error is employed as the error term, but an additional degree of freedom is lost due to the use of the dependent variable on covariate regression line: for every regression line, or equivalently, covariate, employed,

Table 6.3 Calculation of adjusted scores

b_1 30 $Y_{i1} - \beta(Z_{i1} - Z_G) = Y_{a,1}$	b_2 60 $Y_{i2} - \beta(Z_{i2} - Z_G) = Y_{a,2}$	b_3 180 $Y_{i3} - \beta(Z_{i3} - Z_G) = Y_{a,3}$
$16 - 1.649(9 - 5.542) = 10.298$	$16 - 1.649(8 - 5.542) = 11.947$	$24 - 1.649(5 - 5.542) = 24.894$
$7 - 1.649(5 - 5.542) = 7.894$	$10 - 1.649(5 - 5.542) = 10.894$	$29 - 1.649(8 - 5.542) = 24.947$
$11 - 1.649(6 - 5.542) = 10.245$	$13 - 1.649(6 - 5.542) = 12.245$	$10 - 1.649(3 - 5.542) = 14.192$
$9 - 1.649(4 - 5.542) = 11.543$	$10 - 1.649(5 - 5.542) = 10.894$	$22 - 1.649(4 - 5.542) = 24.543$
$10 - 1.649(6 - 5.542) = 9.245$	$10 - 1.649(3 - 5.542) = 14.192$	$25 - 1.649(6 - 5.542) = 24.245$
$11 - 1.649(8 - 5.542) = 6.947$	$14 - 1.649(6 - 5.542) = 13.245$	$28 - 1.649(9 - 5.542) = 22.298$
$8 - 1.649(3 - 5.542) = 12.192$	$11 - 1.649(4 - 5.542) = 13.543$	$22 - 1.649(4 - 5.542) = 24.543$
$8 - 1.649(5 - 5.542) = 8.894$	$12 - 1.649(6 - 5.542) = 11.245$	$24 - 1.649(5 - 5.542) = 24.894$
$\bar{Y}_{a,1} = 9.657$	$\bar{Y}_{a,2} = 12.275$	$\bar{Y}_{a,3} = 23.069$

Table 6.4 Calculation of the error sum of squares

b_1 30 $Y_{ai1} - \overline{Y}_{a1} = \varepsilon_{i1}$	b_2 60 $Y_{ai2} - \overline{Y}_{a2} = \varepsilon_{i2}$	b_3 180 $Y_{ai3} - \overline{Y}_{a3} = \varepsilon_{i3}$
$10.298 - 9.657 = 0.641$	$11.947 - 12.275 = -0.328$	$24.894 - 23.069 = 1.825$
$7.894 - 9.657 = -1.763$	$10.894 - 12.275 = -1.381$	$24.947 - 23.069 = 1.878$
$10.245 - 9.657 = 0.588$	$12.245 - 12.275 = -0.030$	$14.192 - 23.069 = -8.877$
$11.543 - 9.657 = 1.886$	$10.894 - 12.275 = -1.381$	$24.543 - 23.069 = 1.474$
$9.245 - 9.657 = -0.412$	$14.192 - 12.275 = 1.917$	$24.245 - 23.069 = 1.176$
$6.947 - 9.657 = -2.710$	$13.245 - 12.275 = 0.970$	$22.298 - 23.069 = -0.771$
$12.192 - 9.657 = 2.535$	$13.543 - 12.275 = 1.268$	$24.543 - 23.069 = 1.474$
$8.894 - 9.657 = -0.763$	$11.245 - 12.275 = -1.030$	$24.894 - 23.069 = 1.825$

$$\sum_{i=1}^{N} \varepsilon_{i1} = 0.002 \qquad \sum_{i=1}^{N} \varepsilon_{i2} = 0.005 \qquad \sum_{i=1}^{N} \varepsilon_{i3} = 0.004$$

$$\sum_{i=1}^{N} \varepsilon_{i1}^2 = 21.944 \qquad \sum_{i=1}^{N} \varepsilon_{i2}^2 = 11.207 \qquad \sum_{i=1}^{N} \varepsilon_{i3}^2 = 95.312$$

$$\sum_{j=1}^{P} \sum_{i=1}^{N} \varepsilon_{ij}^2 = 128.463$$

an error df is lost. If desired, the SS accommodated by the covariate, may be determined by comparing the error SS from the Full ANCOVA with the error SS from an equivalent Full ANOVA GLM. As before, all of this information can be presented conveniently in an ANCOVA summary table (Table 6.8).

6.4 Regression GLMs for the single factor independent measures ANCOVA

The experimental design GLM equation (6.1) may be compared with the equivalent regression equation,

$$Y_{ij} = \beta_0 + \beta_1 X_{i,1} + \beta_2 X_{i,2} + \beta_3 Z_{ij} + \varepsilon_{ij} \qquad (6.17)$$

Similarly, the experimental design GLM equation (6.5) may be compared with the equivalent regression equation,

$$Y_{ij} = \beta_0 + \beta_1 X_{i,1} + \beta_2 X_{i,2} + \beta_3 (Z_{ij} - Z_G) + \varepsilon_{ij} \qquad (6.18)$$

In both equations (6.17) and (6.18), β_0 represents a constant common to all Y scores, β_1 is the regression coefficient for the predictor variable X_1 and β_2 is the regression coefficient for the predictor variable X_2, where the variables X_1 and X_2 code the differences between the three experimental conditions, β_3 is the regression coefficient for the covariate, Z_{ij} is the covariate score for the ith subject in the jth condition and as always, the random variable, e_{ij}, represents error. Table 6.9 presents effect coding for the single factor, single covariate

Table 6.5 Calculation of the regression coefficient β_T

$\dfrac{b_1}{30}$ $(Z_{ij} - \bar{Z}_G)(Y_{ij} - \bar{Y}_G)$	$\dfrac{b_2}{60}$ $(Z_{ij} - \bar{Z}_G)(Y_{ij} - \bar{Y}_G)$	$\dfrac{b_3}{180}$ $(Z_{ij} - \bar{Z}_G)(Y_{ij} - \bar{Y}_G)$
$(9 - 5.542)(16 - 15) = 3.458$	$(8 - 5.542)(16 - 15) = 2.458$	$(5 - 5.542)(24 - 15) = -4.878$
$(5 - 5.542)(7 - 15) = 4.336$	$(5 - 5.542)(10 - 15) = 2.710$	$(8 - 5.542)(29 - 15) = 34.412$
$(6 - 5.542)(11 - 15) = -1.832$	$(6 - 5.542)(13 - 15) = -0.916$	$(3 - 5.542)(10 - 15) = 12.710$
$(4 - 5.542)(9 - 15) = 9.252$	$(5 - 5.542)(10 - 15) = 2.710$	$(4 - 5.542)(22 - 15) = -10.794$
$(6 - 5.542)(10 - 15) = -2.290$	$(3 - 5.542)(10 - 15) = 12.710$	$(6 - 5.542)(25 - 15) = 4.580$
$(8 - 5.542)(11 - 15) = -9.832$	$(6 - 5.542)(14 - 15) = -0.458$	$(9 - 5.542)(28 - 15) = 44.954$
$(3 - 5.542)(8 - 15) = 17.794$	$(4 - 5.542)(11 - 15) = 6.168$	$(4 - 5.542)(22 - 15) = -10.794$
$(5 - 5.542)(8 - 15) = 3.794$	$(6 - 5.542)(12 - 15) = -1.374$	$(5 - 5.542)(24 - 15) = -4.878$
$\sum = 24.680$	$\sum = 24.008$	$\sum = 65.312$
	$\sum_{j=1}^{p}\sum_{i=1}^{N} = 73.958$	

$\dfrac{b_1}{30}$ $(Z_{ij} - \bar{Z}_G)$	$\dfrac{b_2}{60}$ $(Z_{ij} - \bar{Z}_G)$	$\dfrac{b_3}{180}$ $(Z_{ij} - \bar{Z}_G)$
$(9 - 5.458) = 3.458$	$(8 - 5.542) = 2.458$	$(5 - 5.542) = -0.542$
$(5 - 5.542) = -0.542$	$(5 - 5.542) = -0.542$	$(8 - 5.542) = 2.458$
$(6 - 5.542) = 0.458$	$(6 - 5.542) = 0.458$	$(3 - 5.542) = -2.542$
$(4 - 5.542) = -1.542$	$(5 - 5.542) = -0.542$	$(4 - 5.542) = -1.542$
$(6 - 5.542) = 0.458$	$(3 - 5.542) = -2.542$	$(6 - 5.542) = 0.458$
$(8 - 5.542) = 2.458$	$(6 - 5.542) = 0.458$	$(9 - 5.542) = 3.458$
$(3 - 5.542) = -2.542$	$(4 - 5.542) = -1.542$	$(4 - 5.542) = -1.542$
$(5 - 5.542) = -0.542$	$(6 - 5.542) = 0.458$	$(5 - 5.542) = -0.542$
$\sum (Z_{ij} - \bar{Z}_G)^2 = 27.846$	$\sum (Z_{ij} - \bar{Z}_G)^2 = 16.098$	$\sum (Z_{ij} - \bar{Z}_G)^2 = 30.014$
	$\sum_{j=1}^{p}\sum_{i=1}^{N} = 114.000$	

Table 6.6 Calculation of adjusted scores

b_1 30 $Y_{ij} - \beta_T(Z_{ij} - \overline{Z}_G) = Y_{aij}$	b_2 60 $Y_{ij} - \beta_T(Z_{ij} - \overline{Z}_G) = Y_{aij}$	b_3 180 $Y_{ij} - \beta_T(Z_{ij} - \overline{Z}_G) = Y_{aij}$
$16 - 1.541\ (3.548) = 10.671$	$16 - 1.541\ (2.458) = 12.212$	$24 - 1.541(-0.542) = 24.835$
$7 - 1.541(-0.542) = 7.835$	$10 - 1.541(-0.542) = 10.835$	$29 - 1.541\ (2.458) = 25.212$
$11 - 1.541\ (0.458) = 10.294$	$13 - 1.541\ (0.458) = 12.294$	$10 - 1.541(-2.542) = 13.917$
$9 - 1.541(-1.542) = 11.376$	$10 - 1.541(-0.542) = 10.835$	$22 - 1.541(-1.542) = 24.376$
$10 - 1.541\ (0.458) = 9.294$	$10 - 1.541(-2.542) = 13.917$	$25 - 1.541\ (0.458) = 24.294$
$11 - 1.541\ (2.458) = 7.212$	$14 - 1.541\ (0.458) = 13.294$	$28 - 1.541\ (3.458) = 22.671$
$8 - 1.541(-2.542) = 11.917$	$11 - 1.541(-1.542) = 13.376$	$22 - 1.541(-1.542) = 24.376$
$8 - 1.541(-0.542) = 8.835$	$12 - 1.541\ (0.458) = 11.294$	$24 - 1.541(-0.542) = 24.835$

$$\overline{Y}_i = 15.001$$

Table 6.7 Estimation of error terms

b_1 30 $Y_{ai1} - \bar{Y}_{a1} = \varepsilon_{i1}$	b_2 60 $Y_{ai2} - \bar{Y}_{a2} = \varepsilon_{i2}$	b_3 180 $Y_{ai3} - \bar{Y}_{a3} = \varepsilon_{i3}$
$10.671 - 15 = -4.329$	$12.212 - 15 = -2.788$	$24.835 - 15 = \ \ 9.835$
$7.835 - 15 = -7.165$	$10.835 - 15 = -4.165$	$25.212 - 15 = \ 10.212$
$10.294 - 15 = -4.706$	$12.294 - 15 = -2.706$	$13.917 - 15 = -1.083$
$11.376 - 15 = -3.624$	$10.835 - 15 = -4.165$	$24.376 - 15 = \ \ 9.376$
$9.294 - 15 = -5.706$	$13.917 - 15 = -1.083$	$24.294 - 15 = \ \ 9.294$
$7.212 - 15 = -7.788$	$13.294 - 15 = -1.706$	$22.671 - 15 = \ \ 7.671$
$11.917 - 15 = -3.083$	$13.376 - 15 = -1.624$	$24.376 - 15 = \ \ 9.376$
$8.835 - 15 = -6.165$	$11.294 - 15 = -3.706$	$24.835 - 15 = \ \ 9.835$

$$\sum_{j=1}^{P}\sum_{i=1}^{N} \varepsilon_{ij} = 0.012$$

$$\sum_{j=1}^{P}\sum_{i=1}^{N} \varepsilon_{i2}^{2} = 936.279$$

Table 6.8 Single factor, single covariate ANCOVA summary table

Source	SS	df	MS	F	p
Error reduction due to experimental conditions	807.816	2	403.908	62.883	< 0.001
Error reduction due to covariate	199.537	1	199.537	31.065	< 0.001
Full GLM error	128.463	20	6.423		

regression GLM. It can be seen that apart from the addition of the Z covariate, the set up is identical to the effect coding for a single factor ANOVA with three levels.

As with other design analyses, implementing a single factor, single covariate ANCOVA is a two stage procedure if only the variance attributable to the experimental conditions is to be assessed, and a three stage procedure if the variance attributable to the covariate regression is to be assessed. Consistent with estimating effects by comparing full and reduced GLMs, the first regression carried out is for the full single factor, single covariate experimental design GLM, when all experimental condition predictor variables (X_1 and X_2) and the covariate are included. The results of this analysis are presented in Tables 6.10 and 6.11.

Table 6.10 presents the predictor variable regression coefficients and standard deviations, the standardized regression coefficients, and significance tests (t-

Table 6.9   Effect coding and covariate for a single factor ANCOVA with one covariate. Subject number and the dependent variable score also are shown

Subject	Z	X_1	X_2	Y
1	9	1	0	16
2	5	1	0	7
3	6	1	0	11
4	4	1	0	9
5	6	1	0	10
6	8	1	0	11
7	3	1	0	8
8	5	1	0	8
9	8	0	1	16
10	5	0	1	10
11	6	0	1	13
12	5	0	1	10
13	3	0	1	10
14	6	0	1	14
15	4	0	1	11
16	6	0	1	12
17	5	−1	−1	24
18	8	−1	−1	29
19	3	−1	−1	10
20	4	−1	−1	22
21	6	−1	−1	25
22	9	−1	−1	28
23	4	−1	−1	22
24	5	−1	−1	24

Table 6.10   Results for the full single factor, single covariate ANCOVA regression GLM

Variable	Coefficient	Std error	Std coef	t	p (2 tail)
Constant	5.861	1.719	0.000	3.409	0.003
B_1	−5.344	0.734	−0.641	−7.278	< 0.001
B_2	−2.725	0.733	−0.327	−3.716	0.001
Z	1.649	0.296	0.425	5.574	< 0.001

and p-values) of the regression coefficient. As can be seen, the constant (coefficient) is equivalent to μ. Another useful value from this table is the estimate of the full ANCOVA GLM covariate regression coefficient, $\hat{\beta}$ or b_w. A t-test of this regression coefficient also is provided.

Table 6.11 presents the ANOVA summary table for the regression GLM describing the complete single factor, single covariate ANCOVA. As the residual SS is that obtained when both covariate and experimental conditions are

Table 6.11 ANOVA summary table for covariate and experimental conditions regression

	R: 0.940	R squared: 0.884		Adjusted R squared: 0.867	
Source	SS	df	Mean square	F	p
Regression	983.537	3	327.846	51.041	< 0.001
Residual	128.463	20	6.423		

included in the regression, this is the error term obtained when the single factor, single covariate ANCOVA GLM is applied.

The second stage of the procedure to implement a single factor, single covariate ANCOVA via regression is to carry out a regression where the experimental conditions are omitted and the only regression predictor is the covariate (Z). This regression GLM is equivalent to the reduced GLM for the single factor, single covariate ANCOVA. The results of this analysis are presented in Tables 6.12 and 6.13, although the former are rather redundant, as they pertain to a GLM in which there is virtually no interest. Of most concern is the regression error SS provided in Table 6.13.

The difference between the residual/error SS in Table 6.11 and that in Table 6.13 is equivalent to the SS attributable to experimental conditions. (This SS is presented in Table 6.15.) However, the SS attributed to the covariate in Table 6.13 is not the covariate SS calculated when the full ANCOVA GLM is applied. As mentioned in Section 6.3, the SS for the covariate in the full ANCOVA GLM

Table 6.12 Results for the reduced single factor, single covariate ANCOVA regression GLM

Variable	Coefficient	Std error	Std coef	t	p (2 tail)
Constant	6.458	4.410	0.000	1.465	0.157
Z	1.541	0.759	0.398	2.032	0.054

Table 6.13 ANOVA summary table for covariate regression

	R: 0.398	R squared: 0.158		Adjusted R squared: 0.120	
Source	SS	df	Mean square	F	p
Regression	175.721	1	175.721	4.129	0.054
Residual	936.279	22	42.558		

Table 6.14   ANOVA summary table for experimental conditions regression

R: 0.840	R squared: 0.705		Adjusted R squared: 0.677		
Source	SS	df	Mean square	F	p
Experimental condition regression predictors	784.000	2	392.000	25.098	< 0.001
Residual	328.000	21	15.619		

Table 6.15   ANOVA summary table for covariate and experimental conditions regression

R: 0.940	R squared: 0.884		Adjusted R squared: 0.867		
Source	SS	df	Mean square	F	p
Error reduction due to experimental conditions	807.816	2	403.908	62.883	<0.001
Error reduction due to covariate	199.537	1	199.537	31.065	<0.001
Full ANCOVA GLM residual	128.463	20	6.423		

may be obtained by comparing the error SS from the full ANCOVA with the error SS from an equivalent full ANOVA GLM. A full ANOVA GLM is implemented by a regression that uses only the predictors representing the experimental conditions (X_1 and X_2). Table 6.14 presents the ANOVA summary of this analysis.

Armed with the error term from the regression GLM implementation of the single factor ANOVA, the error reduction attributable to the covariate can be calculated. This information is summarized in Table 6.15.

6.5   Other ANCOVA designs

Many texts on experimental design and statistical analysis are vague about any form of ANCOVA other than single factor independent measures ANCOVA. Although there is insufficient space here to consider other ANCOVA designs in a detailed fashion, the following discussion is presented to provide some appreciation of the different types of ANCOVA designs and analyses available.

6.5.1   Related measures ANCOVA designs

Single factor repeated measures designs and indeed, all fully related factorial designs derive no benefit from ANCOVA. In these designs, as all subjects experience and provide a dependent variable score in all of the experimental conditions, there are no group differences to adjust and so no role for ANCOVA. (See Keppel & Zedeck, 1989, for a similar account.)

6.5.2   Mixed measures factorial ANCOVA

In contrast to fully related factorial designs, there may be advantages in applying ANCOVA to mixed designs. There are two sorts of mixed ANCOVA design. In the simplest of these designs (Table 6.16(a)), each subject provides a single score on the covariate(s). In the more complicated design (in Table 6.16(b)), each subject provides covariate scores in each experimental condition, and so provides covariate scores for each dependent variable score.

Table 6.16   Mixed factorial ANCOVA designs

(a) Mixed factorial ANCOVA design with one covariate measure per subject

Factor A	Subject	Z	Factor B b_1 Y	b_2 Y	b_3 Y
a1	1				
	2				
	3				
a2	4				
	5				
	6				

(b) Mixed factorial ANCOVA design with one covariate measure per repeated measure

Factor A	Subject	Factor B b_1 Z	Y	b_2 Z	Y	b_3 Z	Y
a1	1						
	2						
	3						
a2	4						
	5						
	6						

For the simpler mixed measures factorial ANCOVA design, the covariate(s) will have consequences for the independent measures factor (Factor A in Table 6.16(a)) and, for the same reasons as described for single factor repeated measures designs, the covariate will have no effect on the related factor effect (Factor B in Table 6.16(a)), nor will the covariate exert any influence on the interaction between the related and the independent factor. Therefore, the simpler mixed measures factorial ANCOVA design may be analysed by carrying out two separate analyses: one a single independent measures factor ANCOVA and the other a mixed measures factorial ANOVA. The effect of the independent measures factor is assessed by a single factor ANCOVA applied to the subjects' covariate score(s) and the mean of their repeated measures scores. The related factor main effect and the independent factor and related factor interaction effect are assessed by a mixed measures factorial ANOVA. Huitema (1980) describes the regression GLM for this form of factorial ANCOVA.

In the more complicated mixed measures factorial ANCOVA design (Table 6.16(b)), the covariate(s) have consequence for both independent and related factor effects. Consequently and in contrast to the simpler mixed measures factorial ANCOVA design, there are no convenient short-cuts or checks. The traditional ANOVA approach to both mixed factorial ANCOVA designs is presented by Winer et al. (1991), although beware errors in some of the numerical examples. Considerable care also should be taken when using statistical software to implement this sort of ANCOVA. Indeed, there is sufficient ambiguity over the form of ANCOVA implemented by some statistical software packages, despite the apparent set-up, that initially testing the package by having it analyse example data (as provided in statistics texts) and inspecting the results output to see if they match with the expected results is a wise strategy.

7 ASSUMPTIONS UNDERLYING ANOVA, TRADITIONAL ANCOVA AND GLMS

7.1 ANOVA and GLM assumptions

7.1.1 Independent measures

It has been said a number of times that ANOVA, the special case of multivariate regression with the side condition that effects sum to zero, is subsumed by the GLM. Therefore, it should come as no surprise that an identical set of assumptions underly both ANOVA and any GLM. This would be obvious if it was not for the separate histories of these approaches leading to the same assumptions being expressed in slightly different terms.

The assumptions typically described as underlying fixed effect independent measures ANOVA and GLMs are those presented in Table 7.1. Whereas ANOVA assumptions are described in terms of the dependent variable scores, GLM assumptions are described mainly in terms of errors. This is because there are actually two parts to any GLM. The first part, which has been presented frequently, is the GLM equation describing the data in terms of model parameters and error terms. The second part is a set of assumptions that specify both restrictions on the model parameters and the error terms.

For fixed effect independent measures GLMs, each dependent variable score

Table 7.1   Fixed effect independent measures ANOVA and GLM assumptions

	ANOVA assumptions	GLM assumptions
(a)	Each condition contains a random sample of the population of such scores	Each condition contains a random sample of the population of such scores
(b)	The scores in each condition are distributed normally	Errors are distributed normally
(c)	The scores in each condition are independent of each other	Errors are independent
(d)	The variances of the scores in each experimental condition are homogeneous	Errors are homoscedastic (errors exhibit common variance across all values of the predictor variables)

is conceived as being constituted of fixed and random parts. The fixed part comprises the model components, while the random part comprises just the error component. As only the error component is taken to be random, the remaining GLM assumptions apply only to the errors. As might be expected, this conception also applies to ANOVA. The mean of each experimental condition is taken by ANOVA to be the score for that condition and the deviation between the subjects' actual scores and the condition mean is taken to represent sampling error. This is manifest in the way the variance per condition is calculated: this variance is based on the discrepancy between each score and its condition mean. As the variation in scores can arise only from this discrepancy, which is the GLM error, clearly the same division of fixed and random components arises in ANOVA, but it tends not to be expressed as such.

Obviously, the ANOVA and GLM assumptions labelled (a) in Table 7.1 are equivalent. For the reasons described in the previous paragraph, the (b) assumptions are equivalent, as are the (c) assumptions of independent scores and independent GLM errors. However, the relationship between the (d) assumptions of homogeneous treatment group variances and homoscedastic errors is slightly more complicated. In fact, the homoscedasticity assumption is a more general statement about variance homogeneity, which subsumes the ANOVA assumption. The homoscedasticity assumption states that the error variance at any combination of predictor variable values will be equivalent, whereas the ANOVA assumption refers only to homogeneous variance across experimental conditions. For ANOVA, the experimental conditions constitute all of the predictors, but GLMs, as in ANCOVA, may also include predictors that are not experimental conditions.

Valid significance tests require normally and independently distributed (NID) errors. Therefore, the assumptions of NID errors are made for the purpose of carrying out significance tests (e.g. Draper & Smith, 1998; Kirk, 1995; Pedhazur, 1997; Snedecor & Cochran, 1980). Although these assumptions are not necessary when a GLM is used only to describe data, as most GLMs are applied with the intent to test the significance of parameter estimates, in most cases NID errors are necessary assumptions.

The level of measurement appropriate for the GLM dependent variable is not presented as an ANOVA or GLM assumption. Some authors consider the level of measurement of the dependent variable as determining which statistical analyses are and are not appropriate (e.g. Stevens, 1951; Suppes & Zinnes, 1963). Typically, such authors would consider ANOVA as assuming an interval level of dependent variable measurement. However, there are also authors who consider the level of the dependent variable measurement to be largely irrelevant as far as choosing a statistical technique is concerned (e.g. Townsend & Ashby, 1984; Mitchell, 1986). Recent texts covering ANOVA have tended, either implicitly (Kirk, 1995) or explicitly (e.g. Winer et al., 1991; Howell, 1997) to accord with the latter view. Currently, the general opinion seems to be that the measurement issue falls within the realm of methodology rather than statistics, and it is more important that the numbers representing the dependent variable accurately reflect the entity in which there is interest, than they comply with the requirements of a particular measurement scale. After all, it may be that the entity in which we are interested does not increment in an orderly fashion.

7.1.2   Related measures

When scores through their error components are related, both the F-ratio mean square numerator and denominator are biased (e.g. Kenny & Judd, 1986). Nevertheless, if the data relations manifest a spherical or circular variance–covariance matrix and group effects are accommodated by additional terms in the GLM, the biases in the F-ratio mean squares cancel out and a valid F-test is obtained.

In related measures ANOVAs and GLMs, a spherical variance–covariance matrix is obtained when the variances of the differences between the experimental condition scores are homogeneous. For example, given a related ANOVA with three experimental conditions, A, B and C, the variance of the differences between the subjects scores in conditions A and B should be the same as the variance of the differences between the subjects scores in conditions A and C, or B and C. For psychological data, the need to assume a spherical variance–covariance matrix tends to be a significant restriction.

The consequences of the violation of the spherical variance–covariance matrix assumption can be accommodated by modifying the F-value numerator and denominator dfs, which provides an adjusted omnibus F-test: modifying numerator and denominator dfs has consequence for the p-values associated with the F-value. A number of different modifications have been suggested. Box (1954) described a parameter that indexes the extent of the sphericity assumption violation. (Unfortunately, the Greek letter epsilon, ε, is used to denote this parameter, which sets up potential confusion as epsilon also is used to denote the error term parameter.) Box's ε varies between 0 and 1, with lower values indicating greater violation of sphericity, but tends to underestimate the parameter ε. However, due to the laborious calculation required to obtain an estimate of ε ($\hat{\varepsilon}$), most workers used Geisser and Greenhouse's lower bound adjustment instead. Geisser and Greenhouse (1958) demonstrated that the lowest possible value for the parameter ε in a single factor ANOVA design with p levels provides a numerator df of 1 and denominator dfs of $(p-1)$. Of course this is a very conservative adjustment, as for most data the true value of ε would be much larger than that which would provide the lowest bound adjustment. In an attempt to compensate for the underestimate bias of $\hat{\varepsilon}$, Huynh and Feldt (1976) suggested the estimate $\tilde{\varepsilon}$. However, $\tilde{\varepsilon}$ tends to overstimate ε. Laborious calculations are required to obtain $\hat{\varepsilon}$ and $\tilde{\varepsilon}$, but from the late 1970s, these estimates were provided by many statistical packages and began to be used in preference to Geisser and Greenhouse's lowest bound adjustment. Confusingly however, the statistical packages usually label $\hat{\varepsilon}$ as the Geisser and Greenhouse adjustment. This is because these programs follow Geisser and Greenhouse's (1958) generalization of $\hat{\varepsilon}$ to more complicated designs.

Greater access to statistical computing resources also has supported the application of a multivariate approach to the analysis of related measures data (e.g. Hand & Taylor, 1987; Maxwell & Delaney, 1990; O'Brien & Kaiser, 1985). Although empirical evidence indicates that with balanced designs, both the corrected df and multivariate approaches provide valid and effective control of Type 1 error (Keselman, Lix & Keselman, 1996), generally the univariate approach is more powerful (see Davidson, 1972, or the summary provided by Maxwell & Delaney, 1990). Therefore, this text concentrates on the univariate GLM approach to related measures.

7.1.3 Traditional ANCOVA

Amongst the standard descriptions of ANCOVA assumptions and tests are some ambiguous and even some misleading accounts. Clearly it is important to distinguish genuine statistical assumptions from those made to simplify ANCO-VA interpretation, to test the appropriate statistical assumptions, and to employ pertinent techniques to assess the tenability of these assumptions.

In addition to all of the ANOVA assumptions, most psychology statistical texts present ANCOVA as making the assumptions listed in Table 7.2. However, these three assumptions have no counterparts in GLM terms because all are made to simplify the interpretation and/or calculation of the ANCOVA.

GLMs can accommodate nonlinear regression of the dependent variable on the covariate (see polynomial regression, e.g. Draper & Smith, 1998; Neter et al., 1990), heterogeneous regressions (e.g. Rutherford, 1992; Searle, 1979, 1987) and correlations between the covariate and treatments. Although covariate-treatment correlations may cause particular interpretation problems, they do not preclude accurate and informative analysis (Cohen & Cohen, 1983; Rutherford, 1992).

The form of ANCOVA incorporating the assumptions listed in Table 7.2 may be termed traditional ANCOVA to distinguish it from less constrained forms of ANCOVA. Traditional ANCOVA is still the most common form of ANCOVA applied in psychological research and the programs labelled ANCOVA in most commercial statistical packages implement traditional ANCOVA. Beyond the benefits accrued from simplifying ANCOVA interpretation and/or calculation, there are other reasons for choosing traditional ANCOVA. First, the good ANCOVA design practice of measuring the covariate before administering the

Table 7.2   Specific ANCOVA assumptions

(a)	The covariate is independent of the treatments
(b)	In each treatment group the relationship between the covariate and the dependent variable is linear (the covariate and dependent variable are expressed at the first power only)
(c)	The regression coefficients of the dependent variable on the covariate in each treatment group are homogeneous

experimental manipulation(s) usually ensures the experimental conditions do not influence the covariate (to do so would require their effect to be exerted backwards through time). Second, most relationships between covariates and dependent variables in psychology appear to be linear, or are approximately linear. Therefore, it is very likely that two of the three traditional assumptions will be tenable for most ANCOVAs. Unfortunately, however, the third assumption of homogeneous regressions within each of the experimental conditions becomes more tenuous as the number of experimental conditions increases, as in factorial experimental designs (Winer et al.,1991).

7.2   A strategy for checking ANOVA and traditional ANCOVA assumptions

A general strategy for checking the ANOVA and traditional ANCOVA assumptions is presented. Although lack of space prevents the detailed description of measures to remedy data that fail to meet ANOVA or ANCOVA assumptions, these may be found in Daniel and Wood (1980), Kirk (1995), Mosteller and Tukey (1977), Neter et al. (1990) and Weisberg (1985), while alternatives to traditional ANCOVA are described in the next chapter.

The GLM assumptions provide the fundamental criteria by which the statistical validity of any GLM is judged. Even violations of specific traditional ANCOVA assumptions manifest as violations of one or more GLM assumptions (when an inappropriate GLM is applied). However, compliance with the specific assumptions made by traditional ANCOVA does not mean compliance with the GLM assumptions. Therefore, assessing the extent to which a model complies with the GLM assumptions provides the best criteria to judge the statistical validity of any traditional ANCOVA model.

The general strategy advocated to check ANOVA and ANCOVA assumptions employs a stepwise, and, when necessary, iterative, approach. A basic outline of this strategy is presented in Figure 7.1, with the boxes labelled for easy reference. First, the analysis is implemented and the GLM residuals are obtained (B_1 and B_2). These residuals are analysed in terms of their conformity to GLM assumptions (B_3). At this point the first branch in the assessment path is reached. If the GLM assumptions are judged to be tenable, nothing more need be done and the analysis results can be interpreted (B_4). However, if any of the GLM assumptions are judged to be untenable after an ANOVA was implemented (B_5), then remedial action(s) must be undertaken with respect to the model or data (B_6). If any of the GLM assumptions are judged untenable after an ANCOVA was implemented (B_7), then it is possible that the cause of the GLM assumption violation(s) is a failure of one or more of the specific traditional ANCOVA assumptions (B_8). If violations of any specific traditional ANCOVA assumptions are detected, then appropriate remedial action on the model or data should be undertaken (B_6). If there are no specific traditional ANCOVA assumption violations, then a failure of one or more of the GLM assumptions is indicated

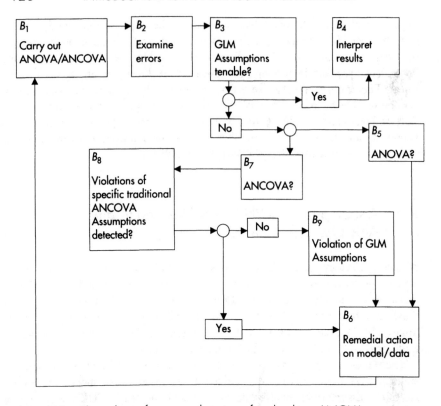

Figure 7.1   Flow chart of a general strategy for checking ANOVA and ANCOVA assumptions

(B_9). In such circumstances, remedial actions with respect to the model or data should be undertaken (B_6) and the analysis repeated (B_1). Nevertheless, after the second analysis, it is again necessary to ensure the underlying assumptions are tenable before interpreting the results.

7.3   Assumption checks and some assumption violation consequences

There are both graphical and significance test methods for assessing assumption conformity. Although the former approach seems more popular (e.g. Cohen & Cohen, 1983; Cook & Weisberg, 1982; Draper & Smith, 1998; Lovie, 1991; Montgomery & Peck, 1982; Neter et al., 1990; Norusis, 1985, 1990; Pedhazur, 1997), it may be difficult for the less experienced to determine assumption violations in this way. With graphical approaches there may be a tendency to ignore or fail to appreciate the spread of scores in relation to the specific aspect of the data considered. In contrast, it is exactly these relations that most significance tests formalize. Nevertheless, as sample size increases, test power increases and with large enough samples, virtually all tests will have sufficient power to reject the null hypothesis. This is a problem because the influence of random processes makes exact conformity with assumptions extremely unlikely and so the issue always is the extent to which assumptions are met. With large data sets, the ability to reject the null hypothesis may not be the best assessment criterion. As well as determining the significance level, the extent of the assumption violation should be considered, perhaps by comparing the size of the test statistic obtained with its expected value under the null hypothesis.

To illustrate graphical and significance test methods, some of the assessment techniques described are applied to the single factor independent measures ANCOVA with one covariate data presented in Chapter 6. Most commercially available statistical packages are able to describe ANCOVA in terms of the experimental design GLM and can provide ANCOVA model errors/residuals as part of the output. Once obtained, the residuals, the error term estimators, can be input to other programs in the statistical package for examination. However, implementing ANOVA and ANCOVA as regression models does offer an advantage with respect to the analysis of errors. As most good quality regression software provides a range of techniques for examining errors, ANOVAs and ANCOVAs as regression models can make use of these (frequently automatic) regression diagnostics programs.

7.3.1   ANOVA and ANCOVA

Random sampling

Ideally, assumption (a) in Table 7.1 should be satisfied by implementing two randomization procedures, one after the other. First, subjects are sampled randomly from the population of interest. The manner of this sampling determines the validity of the inferences from the sample to the population of interest. However, very few experiments in psychology invest great effort to ensure a random sample of the population to which inferences will be generalized. Most research conducted in European and American unversities employs convenience samples of the undergraduate population. Usually results are generalized to the western, if not world, populations on the presumption that with respect to the psychological processes examined in the experiment, there are no real differences between the participating undergraduates, the rest of the undergraduate population, and the western and world populations (see Maxwell & Delaney, 1990; Wright, 1998).

Second, the subjects constituting the sample are assigned randomly to the experimental conditions. After such random assignment, it is most likely that any subject characteristics such as academic ability, friendliness, etc. will be distributed equally across all conditions. In other words, it is most unlikely that differences in subjects' dependent variable scores will be due to differences in subject characteristics across experimental conditions. Consequently, random assignation of subjects to experimental conditions is the basis for attributing any differences observed between the experimental conditions to these experimental conditions. The validity of any ANOVA is severely questioned whenever these sampling procedures are compromised.

Normality

Recently, Wilcox (e.g. 1998a) has raised the profile of the normality assumption. Wilcox argues strongly that even slight deviations from the normal distribution can have substantial consequences for analysis power. Wilcox's view is considered further in Chapter 9. However, most psychology statistical texts report ANOVA (and so ANCOVA) as being robust with respect to violations of the normality assumption (e.g. Hays, 1994; Kirk, 1995; Winer et al., 1991), especially when the experimental condition sample distributions are symmetrical and the sample sizes are equal and greater than 12 (Clinch & Keselman, 1982; Tan, 1982). Indeed, Hays (1994) describes the robustness of ANOVA to non-normal distributions to be in proportion to the sample size; greater non-normality exerts less influence on the F-test as the sample size increases. Although data which mildly violates the normality assumption is not uncommon, severe departures from normality are quite rare (but see the differing views of Bradley, 1978 and Glass, Peckham & Sanders, 1972). Nevertheless, robustness is a matter of degree and greater departures from normality will affect the F-test Type 1 error rate (also see Chapter 9). Therefore, screening data to ensure there is no gross departure from normality or to determine the extent of the departure from normality is prudent.

Note that the ANOVA assumption concerns the dependent variable scores and assumes a normal distribution within each experimental condition. In contrast, the GLM assumption simply is that all of the errors are distributed normally. The difference between the two assumptions is the dependent variable scores contain the fixed component, which is responsible for any differerences between the experimental conditions. With this component in the scores, any experimental differences can interfere with a proper assessment of the data normality, hence the requirement to examine the data from the experimental conditions separately. However, with errors, the fixed component is absent, so the normality assessment can afford to ignore experimental conditions.

Conformity to a normal distribution can be assessed in a number of ways. Hays (1994) suggests the use of the Kolmogorov–Smirnov test, which assess the discrepancy between hypothetical and sample distributions. This appears to be more powerful than the alternative chi-square test (Siegel & Castellan, 1988). However, the Shapiro–Wilk (1965) test is another popular means of assessing normality, as is the Lilliefors test (Lilliefors, 1967), which is a modification of the Kolmogorov–Smirnov test, specifically for sample data. The Shapiro–Wilk is a more conservative test than the Lilliefors, but as ANOVA and ANCOVA are robust with respect to violations of the normality assumption and the aim is to screen for large deviations, very powerful tests are unnecessary (but again see Wilcox's views reported in Chapter 9).

Several statistical packages provide skew and kurtosis statistics and also the standard errors of these statistics. (Karl Pearson originally labelled the skew index g_1 and the kurtosis index g_2. Skew and kurtosis are also known, respectively, as the 3rd and 4th moments of the normal distribution.) Dividing the skew and kurtosis statistics by their standard errors provides an approximation to a Z-score that can be used as a significance test. However, standard error is a function of sample size (all else being equal, larger samples have smaller standard errors) and so larger samples tend to provide greater Z-scores. Consequently, although Z-tables have no obvious markers of sample size, such as dfs, it should be appreciated that the power of these Z-score tests also increases with sample size.

Popular graphical methods for assessing normality include normal and half-normal (i.e. unsigned) probability plots of residuals (Draper & Smith, 1998). The benefit of such normal probability plots is that deviation from a normal distribution is represented by deviation from a straight line. With computer output, usually the data points should fall approximately along the straight diagonal line from bottom left to top right. However, when the sample size tends towards the small, expect this line not to be smooth, perhaps with smaller approximately straight line components. Generally, normal probability plots are easier to appreciate than alternatives, such as plots of residual distributions, as these have to be compared with the normal distribution *per se*.

Often half-normal probability plots of residuals (obtained by plotting absolute residual values) are suggested when there are few data points (e.g. Lovie, 1991). Unfortunately however, half-normal probability plots of residuals often suggest greater deviation from linearity than the equivalent "full-normal" probability plots and greater experience may be required to interpret these plots accurately (Draper & Smith, 1998; also see Judd & McClelland, 1989). A normal probability plot of the Chapter 6 ANCOVA errors and the results of the Lilliefors tests are presented in Figure 7.2. Both the normal probability plot and the significance test indicate some deviation from a normal distribution, but, given the robustness of ANOVA and the size and balanced nature of the sample, insufficient to affect the F-test interpretation.

Independence

The value of one GLM error is assumed not to affect the value of another. However, while error terms are conceived as independent, when h GLM parameters are estimated from n observations, there are only $n - h$ degrees of freedom, so the residuals, the error term estimators, will covary (Draper & Smith, 1998). Residuals related only in this way are of little concern. However, residuals may be related in additional ways and relatively few statistical texts point out that ANOVA and ANCOVA are not robust with respect to violation of the independent errors assumption (e.g. Maxwell & Delaney, 1990).

As well as being part of the basis for attributing experimental effects to the experimental manipulation, randomization procedures also increase the likelihood of independent scores: there is no reason to believe that scores from subjects randomly selected from the population of interest and randomly allocated to experimental conditions will be related. Generally, appropriate

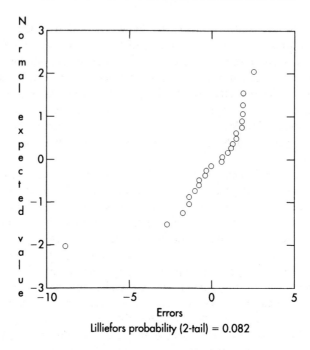

Lilliefors probability (2-tail) = 0.082

Figure 7.2   Normal probability plot of ANCOVA errors and the Lilliefors significance test result

randomization procedures, and the application of a pertinent type of analysis, provide independent errors. However, contrary to some claims (e.g. Winer et al. 1991), randomization procedures cannot assure error independence. Sometimes, despite random sampling and assignment, relations between scores can arise. In particular, the way in which the dependent variable scores are collected may produce related scores. For example, scores from subjects tested as a group, or scores obtained using a certain piece of equipment, or questionnaire, etc. may be related. Consequently, consideration of the full study methodology, ideally before its implementation, is necessary to ensure independent errors.

Kenny and Judd (1986) describe means of assessing the nonindependence of ANOVA errors due to groups, sequence and space, as well as methods, to eliminate the F-ratio numerator and denominator mean square biases caused by non-independent errors. Of these three sources, non-independence due to groups is most frequently encountered in psychological research. Groups may be defined in a variety of different ways (e.g. blocking, see Hays 1994; Kirk, 1995; Winer et al., 1991). Most familiar and obvious is the situation where groups and experimental conditions are equivalent. However, data sharing any common feature can be grouped. Ideally, groups should be crossed with experimental conditions. Repeated measures designs are examples of grouping on the basis that all scores are provided by the same subject.

Kenny and Judd (1986) provide a formula for estimating the non-independence of errors due to groupings when a spherical variance–covariance matrix is assumed. In a single factor ANOVA design, where data is arranged on the basis of the grouping criteria, this is given by the within groups correlation

$$\text{WGC} = \frac{MS_b - MS_w}{MS_b + MS_w(N_j - 1)} \tag{7.1}$$

where MS_b and MS_w are the mean squares between and within groups, and N_j is the number of scores in each group. The WGC calculated can be treated as an F-ratio with $(N - 1)$ numerator and $(N - 1)$ denominator degrees of freedom (Donner & Koval, 1980). Negative group linkage is indicated by significant WGC values below 1 and positive group linkage is indicated by significant WGC values above 1. Positive values indicate greater similarity of residuals within groups than between, while negative values indicate the converse. Preliminary application of this formula may indicate non-independence that should be accommodated in the experimental design GLM.

Once the related scores are identified, they are treated just as scores from the same subject (or block) would be treated. In other words, the statistical procedures used to analyse repeated measures (or blocked) designs are applied. Nevertheless, prevention of non-independence is far preferable to cure, not least because, unlike the use of blocks in a planned experiment, *post hoc* groupings may not be conveniently nested or crossed.

Graphical assessment of errors related through groups is also possible. When errors are plotted against the suspected groupings, dependence should be revealed by errors bunching within groups. This is a graphical analogue of (7.1). In addition to non-independence due to grouping, Kenny and Judd (1986) also discuss significance test methods of assessing error dependence due to sequence and space, while Draper and Smith (1998), Montgomery and Peck (1982), and Neter et al. (1990) present graphical methods of assessing error dependence due to sequence.

Homoscedasticity: homogeneity of variance

Homoscedasticity can be defined as constant error variance (estimated by the GLM residuals) at every value of the predictor variable, and/or every combination of the predictors (e.g. Kirby, 1993). Alternatively, some authors define homoscedasticity as constant error variance across all of the predicted values of the dependent variable (e.g. Cohen & Cohen, 1983; Judd & McClelland, 1989). However, the most detailed set of predictor value combinations available from any data set are provided by the predictor combinations associated with each data point. As each data point has a corresponding predicted value, examining variance by predicted values is equivalent to variance examination at every combination of predictor values.

The F-test denominator, the MSe, is the average of all the deviations between the predicted and actual values of the dependent variable. With heteroscedasticity, the averaging procedure introduces error into the MSe, making it a poor estimate of error variation for all of the predicted values so compromising the accuracy of the F-test. Most psychology statistical texts report ANOVA as being robust with respect to moderate violations of variance homogeneity, provided the experimental condition sample sizes are equal and greater than five. However, the argument made with regard to the normality assumption also applies here. Moreover, to appreciate the adequacy of the GLM for the data, it is important to know if heteroscedasticity is present.

Errors plotted on the ANOVA or ANCOVA experimental conditions, as in Figure 7.3, should take the shape of a horizontal band. Discrepancies in the length of the vertical error "stripes" over the experimental conditions indicate heterogeneous error variance as a function of the experimental conditions. However, errors also should be plotted on the predicted values, as in Figure 7.4. Indeed, this may be the easier method of graphical assessment, particularly if more than two experimental conditions have been coded for a regression model implementation of ANOVA or ANCOVA. Ideally, the errors should take the shape of a horizontal band. Other shapes most likely indicate error variance increasing with the size of the GLM estimate. Although in theory error variance may decrease as the predicted values increase, this is seen rarely in practice.

Also presented in Figures 7.3 and 7.4 are the results from Cook and Weisberg's (1983) score test. The score statistic is the regression of U, the standardized residual squared, on the predicted values (or any independent variable), divided by 2. The score statistic has an approximate chi-square distribution with one df, which provides a very useful significance test of homoscedasticity. Step by step accounts of how to calculate the score test are

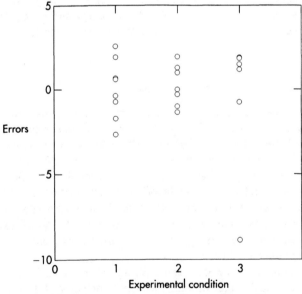

Cook and Weisberg's score test: experimental conditions, $\chi^2_{(1)} = 5.871, p = 0.015$.

Figure 7.3 Errors plotted on experimental conditions

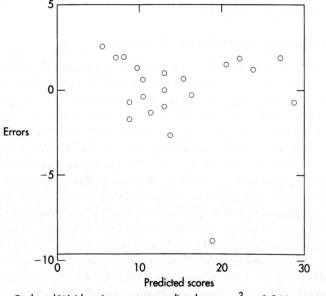

Cook and Weisberg's score test: predicted scores, $\chi^2_{(1)} = 1.246, p = 0.264$.

Figure 7.4   Errors on predicted scores and Cook and Weisberg's score test for predicted scores

presented by Weisberg (1985) and Kirby (1993). This test also is incorporated into the BMDP regression program P2R. Unfortunately however, the score test is very poorly documented and easily could be missed. The score test result appears as a single line directly below the diagnostic error variance plot to which it refers. Moreover, there is no account in the BMDP manuals of the fact that separate score test statistics are calculated for each predictor and for the predicted values, but only the plot and score test for the variable associated with the largest score test and so, greatest heteroscedasticity, is provided. Indeed, nowhere in the BMDP manuals is there mention of this extremely useful significance test of homoscedasticity (see *BMDP Communications*, 1983, Vol 16, No. 2, p. 2).

Whereas the graphical and significance test assessments of errors by predicted scores suggest conformity to the homoscedasticity assumption (Figure 7.4), this is not the case when the graphical and significance test assessments examine errors by experimental condition (Figure 7.3). This difference emphasises the value of examining errors as a function of a variety of GLM components. The error attributable to an outlier (the data point nearest the X-axis in both graphs) also is very noticeable. The most appropriate way to deal with outliers is a topic beyond the scope of this text, but a good introduction is provided by Pedhazur (1997).

7.3.2 Traditional ANCOVA

Covariate independent of experimental conditions

Although it is inevitable that the covariate(s) and experimental conditions will have some sort of conceptual link, traditional ANCOVA assumes the covariate(s) and experimental conditions are statistically independent: experimental conditions should not affect the distribution of covariate scores, nor should the covariate(s) influence the nature of the experimental conditions. When the covariate(s) and experimental conditions are related, traditional ANCOVA adjustments on the basis of the general covariate mean(s) are equivalent to modifying the experimental conditions, so that adjustments to the dependent variable can remove part of the experimental effect or produce an artefactual experimental effect (Cochran, 1957; Elashoff, 1969; Keppel, 1991; Kirk, 1995; Smith, 1957). Good design practice in ANCOVA involves measuring the covariate(s) before the experimental manipulation. Logically, this makes it impossible for the experimental conditions to influence the covariate (e.g. Howell, 1997; Keppel, 1991; Kirk, 1995; Winer et al., 1991). Measuring the covariate(s) after the experimental manipulation affords the opportunity for the experimental conditions to exert an influence on the covariate(s) and is one way in which a relation between covariate(s) and experimental conditions can arise. However in ANCOVA, a relation between covariate(s) and experimental conditions also can arise as a consequence of the procedures employed to assign subjects to experimental conditions.

The least serious relation between covariate(s) and experimental conditions has been termed fluke assignment (Maxwell & Delaney, 1990). Fluke assignment is when, despite random assignment, different experimental condition covariate distributions are obtained. With fluke assignment, the differences between experimental condition covariate distributions that produce the relation between covariate(s) and experimental conditions reflect a Type 1 error. However, in these circumstances, ANCOVA is the appropriate analysis to control any resulting bias (Permutt, 1990; Senn, 1989; Shirley & Newnham, 1984).

A more serious relation between covariate(s) and experimental conditions caused by assignment procedures is known as biased assignment. Here, the covariate scores are used as an assignment criterion. Two types of assignment may be used. In one, only subjects with particular covariate scores (e.g. below the mean of all covariate scores recorded) are assigned to the experimental conditions. With the other type of assignment, subjects scoring high on the covariate are placed in one experimental condition and low scoring subjects are placed in another experimental condition (Huitema, 1980). Even when biased assignment has been used, traditional ANCOVA will adjust for the differences between the covariate distributions and will provide an unbiased test of the experimental effects (Rubin, 1977). Nevertheless, as experimental condition covariate distributions become more distinct, so the tenability of the traditional model assumptions becomes more important for the interpretation of the analysis (see Cochran, 1957; Huitema, 1980; Maxwell & Delaney, 1990). Taylor and

Innocenti (1993) also refer to this issue, when they assert that if the general covariate mean is not logical for a variable, then it should not be used as a covariate. They state this is most often true for dichotomous (i.e. categorical) covariates, but it is difficult to think of a situation where it would be appropriate to use a categorical variable as a covaricate.

The most serious covariate–experimental condition relation caused by assignment procedures occurs when intact groups serve as the subjects in each of the experimental conditions. A typical example is the use of two classes of school children to compare two types of teaching method. When intact groups constitute the experimental conditions, interpretation of the ANCOVA results should proceed with considerable caution. With biased assignment, the basis for the difference between experimental conditions is known. In contrast, intact groups may be distinguished on the basis of a whole range of unknown variables. If the covariate scores of the intact experimental conditions differ, this can be conceived as an effect of the experimental conditions on the covariate(s). However, as the relationship between the covariate(s) and any set of (unknown) variables distinguishing the experimental conditions cannot be determined, there is a model specification error and the nature and consequences of the ANCOVA adjustment cannot be known (e.g. Overall & Woodward, 1977).

The issue of covariate measurement error is also pertinent here. Strictly, the covariate (in common with all of the independent variables) is assumed to be measured without error. However, provided random assignment or even biased assignment to experimental conditions is employed and all other assumptions are tenable, the consequence of covariate measurement error (cf. no covariate measurement error) is only a slight reduction in the power of the ANCOVA. However, when intact experimental conditions are used, covariate measurement error is expected to provide biased ANCOVA experimental effects. (For further discussion of assignment to experimental conditions procedures, and the consequences of covariate measurement errors and methods of repair, see Maxwell & Delaney, 1990; Huitema 1980 and Bollen, 1989.)

In the GLM context, correlations amongst predictor variables, such as the covariate and experimental conditions, is termed multicollinearity (e.g. Cohen & Cohen, 1983; Pedhazur, 1997; Neter et al., 1990). Previously, this term was used to describe predictors that were exact linear combinations of other model predictors (e.g. Draper & Smith, 1998), but now it tends to be applied more generally. Data exhibiting multicollinearity can be analysed, but this should be done in a structured manner (e.g. Cohen & Cohen, 1983; also see Rutherford, 1992, regarding the use of heterogeneous regression ANCOVA to attenuate the problems caused by covariate–experimental conditions dependence). Multicollinearity also may arise through correlations between two or more covariates. However, because there is seldom concern about the relative composition of the extraneous variance removed by covariates, this is much less problematic than a relation between the covariate(s) and the experimental conditions.

One symptom of a covariate–experimental conditions relation is that the ANCOVA regression homogeneity assumption may not be tenable (Evans & Anastasio, 1968). Elashoff (1969), Maxwell & Delaney (1990) and Winer et al.

(1991) claim that carrying out an ANOVA on the treatment group covariate scores can be a useful indicator of experimental conditions influencing the covariate. However, as said, with random assignment, the expectation is equal covariate treatment means. Similarly, the null hypothesis of an ANOVA applied to the covariate scores is equal experimental condition means. Given that the covariate was measured before any experimental manipulation, what is to be made of a significant F-test? In such circumstances, covariate imbalance should reflect just less likely covariate distributions and, as argued by Senn (1989) and Permutt (1990), ANCOVA is the appropriate analysis to control any resulting bias. Consequently, an ANOVA on the treatment group covariate scores is appropriate only when there are theoretical or empirical reasons to believe that something more serious than fluke assignment has occurred. Adopting good ANCOVA design practice and applying all knowledge about the relationships between the study variables seem the only ways to avoid violating this assumption.

Linear regression

When a linear regression is applied to describe a nonlinear relationship between two variables, the regression line will not only provide a poorer overall fit to the data, but also it will fit the data better at some points than at others. At the well fitting points there will be smaller deviations between the actual and adjusted scores than at the ill fitting points. Consequently, the residual variance is likely to be heterogeneous and it is possible that the residuals may not be distributed normally (Elashoff, 1969). Moreover, as the points through which the regression line passes provide the predicted scores, a regression line that does not track the data properly provides predicted scores of questionable meaning.

Atiqullah (1964) examined in purely mathematical terms the traditional ANCOVA F-test when the real relationship was quadratic. With just two experimental conditions Atiqullah found that the F-test was biased unless there was random assignment of subjects to experimental conditions. The other situation considered by Atiqullah was a single factor ANCOVA where the number of experimental conditions approached infinity. In such circumstances, despite random assignment, the traditional ANCOVA F-test was gravely biased, with the amount of bias depending upon the size of the quadratic component. However, precisely because the number of experimental conditions approached infinity, there is considerable dubiety concerning the relevance of these conclusions for any real ANCOVA study (Glass et al., 1972). Moreover, because Atiqullah's examination was in purely mathematical terms, dealing with expectations over many, many experiments, these reservations may extend to the whole study.

Huitema (1980) states that the assumption of linear regression is less important than the traditional ANCOVA assumptions of random assignment, covariate–experimental conditions independence and homogeneity of regression. This claim is made on the grounds that linear regression provides an approximate fit to most behavioural data and that nonlinearity reduces the power of the ANCOVA F-test by only a small amount. Nevertheless, as Huitema illustrates, in the face of substantial nonlinearity, ANOVA can provide a more powerful analysis than traditional ANCOVA. Moreover, with nonlinearity, as experimental conditions covariate distribution imbalance increases, ANCOVA adjustments become extremely dubious.

Although it may interfere with the smooth execution of the planned data analysis, nonlinearity should not be considered as a statistical nuisance preventing proper analysis of the data. Not only is nonlinearity a pertinent finding in its own right, but also it is a feature of the data that must be accommodated in the model in order to allow its proper analysis.

Many psychology statistical texts deliver a rather enigmatic presentation of regression linearity assessment. Most psychology statistics texts merely state the regression linearity assumption (e.g. Hays, 1994), or like Keppel (e.g. 1991), they refer readers to Kirk (e.g. 1995, who cites Kendall, 1948), or Winer (e.g. Winer et al., 1991). Winer et al. (1991) distinguish between ANCOVA assumption tests and tests of other properties of the data. However, Winer (1962, 1971) includes tests of the regression linearity of the dependent variable experimental condition means on the covariate experimental condition means ($\hat{\beta}_{ECM}$) and the linearity of the regression line based on the total set of scores ($\hat{\beta}_T$), plus a test of $\hat{\beta}_T = \hat{\beta}_W$ (see Chapter 6). Winer (1962) states,

If this regression ... ($\hat{\beta}_{ECM}$) ... does not prove to be linear, interpretation of the adjusted treatment means becomes difficult. (Winer, 1962, p. 588)

Winer (1971) omits this sentence, but as the presentation is identical otherwise, the same meaning is conveyed. Similarly, in his section on ANCOVA assumptions, Kirk (1968; 1982; 1995) includes tests of the regression linearity of $\hat{\beta}_{ECM}$, and the linearity of $\hat{\beta}_T$, but no distinction is made in the text between these tests and those which assess the specific ANCOVA assumptions. Unfortunately, considerable misunderstanding and confusion about the nature of the traditional ANCOVA regression linearity assumption and how it should be tested can be caused by these accounts.

The traditional ANCOVA linearity assumption is that the regression of the dependent variable on the covariate(s) in each of the experimental conditions is linear (i.e. the $\hat{\beta}_{Wj}$ are linear). No other tests of regression linearity are pertinent. Linearity of $\hat{\beta}_T$ and $\hat{\beta}_{ECM}$ is expected only when there are no experimental effects. Given that regression linearity should be determined prior to the assessment and in the presence of experimental effects, the indirect tests of $\hat{\beta}_{Wj}$ linearity are not satisfactory.

Probably the most obvious way to assess the linearity of the separate groups regressions is to plot the dependent variable against the covariate (or each covariate) for each experimental condition. Another popular, but much less direct approach is to ignore experimental conditions and to plot residuals against the predicted scores. This approach has the advantage of generalizing over covariates. However, nonlinearity within one condition may be masked by the linearity within the other conditions, particularly when there are many conditions. Moreover, when any nonlinearity is detected, it will need to be traced to source and so, eventually, checks per covariate per condition will be required. Further discussion of graphic checks of regression linearity is provided by Draper and Smith (1998) Montgomery and Peck (1982) and Neter et al. (1990).

Assessing linearity by inspecting data plots may be more difficult than the graphic assessments of normality and homoscedasticity, particularly when the linearity assessments are carried out per experimental condition, where there are fewer data upon which to form an opinion. Consequently, significance test methods may have a larger role to play, particularly for those less experienced in graphical assessment.

One way of checking regression linearity is to carry out a significance test for the reduction in errors due to the inclusion of nonlinear components (e.g. Maxwell & Delaney, 1990). A nonlinear relationship between the dependent variable and a covariate can be modelled by including the covariate raised above the first power as a predictor. For example, the ANCOVA GLM equation,

$$Y_{ij} = \mu + \alpha_j + \beta(Z_{ij} - Z_G) + \beta(Z_{ij} - Z_G)^2 + \varepsilon_{ij} \qquad (7.2)$$

is termed a second order polynomial model and describes a quadratic curve. The ANCOVA GLM equation,

$$Y_{ij} = \mu + \alpha_j + \beta(Z_{ij} - Z_G) + \beta(Z_{ij} - Z_G)^2 + \beta(Z_{ij} - Z_G)^3 + \varepsilon_{ij} \qquad (7.3)$$

is termed a third order polynomial model and describes a cubic curve. Further components (e.g. quartic, quintic, etc.) can be added to increase the order of a GLM, but the highest order any equation may take is equal to the number of experimental conditions minus 1 (here, $p - 1$). However, it is exceptional for more than a third order polynomial model to be needed to describe psychological data.

To apply a polynomial model as described by equation (7.3), two new predictor variables must be created: Z^2 and Z^3. However, these variables will be correlated with Z, so the problem of multicollinearity arises. To deal with this, the data should be analysed in a structured manner (e.g. Cohen & Cohen, 1983). For example, the traditional ANCOVA model,

$$Y_{ij} = \mu + \alpha_j + \beta(Z_{ij} - Z_G) + \varepsilon_{ij} \qquad (6.5, \text{ rptd})$$

should be compared with the traditional ANCOVA model described by (7.2). Any decrement in the error estimate of GLM (7.2) in comparison to the same estimate in (6.5) can be attributed to the $\beta(Z_{ij} - Z_G)^2$ component. The component is retained if an F-test of the variance attributed to the component is significant. However, if error examination suggests that further curvilinearity exists, a third order GLM may be compared with the second order GLM. (For further information on curvilinear ANCOVA, see Cohen & Cohen, 1983; Huitema, 1980; Maxwell & Delaney, 1990. For further information on polynomial models, see Cohen & Cohen, 1983; Draper & Smith, 1998; Neter et al., 1990; Pedhazur, 1997). One advantage of this approach is that when all significant curvilinear components are included, the description of the curvilinear ANCOVA GLM is complete and the ANCOVA results can be interpreted.

Figure 7.5 contains a plot of the dependent variable on the covariate, with the

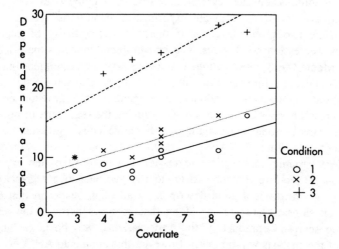

Figure 7.5   A plot of the dependent variable on the covariate per experimental condition

linear regression lines depicted, for each experimental condition. The ANCOVA summary for the GLM described by equation (6.5) is presented in Chapter 6, while the ANCOVA summaries of the second and third order ANCOVA GLMs are presented in Table 7.3. As can be seen, graphically assessing linearity per experimental condition with few data can be a difficult task. However, the insignificant reduction in error variance attributable to the inclusion of the quadratic and cubic components suggests that the assumption of linearity for the dependent variable–covariate regression is tenable.

Homogeneous regression

The final traditional ANCOVA assumption is that the regression slopes, described by the regression coefficients, are homogeneous across the experi-

Table 7.3   Summaries of error reduction due to the second and third order ANCOVA GLMs

	R: 0.941	R squared: 0.886		Adjusted R squared: 0.862	
Source	SS increment	df	Mean square	F	p
Covariate (Z_2) GLM equation (7.2)	2.086	1	2.086	0.308	0.586
Covariate (Z_3) GLM equation (7.3)	4.464	1	4.464	0.659	0.428
Error from GLM equation (7.3)	121.913	18	6.773		

mental conditions. As the regression coefficient employed in ANCOVA is a weighted average of the separate experimental conditions' regression coefficients ($\hat{\beta}_w$), two problems occur if there is heterogeneity of experimental condition regression coefficients. The first problem concerns the effect on the F-test. Monte Carlo investigations employing random assignment (e.g. Hamilton, 1976; also see Huitema, 1980) indicate that provided sample sizes are equal and exhibit homogeneous variance, heterogeneity of regression coefficients tends to result in conservative F-values, reducing the sensitivity or power of the analysis. This is because averaging over heterogeneous regression coefficients introduces error into $\hat{\beta}_w$, with the result that it is a poor estimate of the dependent variable on covariate regression slopes in all of the experimental conditions. Therefore, in comparison to the homogeneous regression slopes situation, where $\hat{\beta}_w$ is a good descriptor of all of the experimental condition regression slopes, there will be larger discrepancies between the actual and predicted scores. Consequently, the error variance will be larger and so the power of the analysis will be lower. However, this applies to ANCOVA employing random assignment, where the differences between experimental condition covariate means are expected to be zero. Hollingsworth (1976, cited by Huitema, 1980) found Type 1 error increased with regression heterogeneity when nonzero differences between experimental condition covariate means were provided by nonrandom assignment.

The second problem posed by heterogeneous regression ANCOVA is that treatment effects vary as a function of the covariate. As a result, and in contrast to the homogeneous regression situation, an assessment of experimental effects at any one measure of the covariate cannot be taken to reflect experimental effects at any other measures of the covariate. (This is discussed further in Chapter 8.)

As with the regression linearity of the dependent variable on the covariate, heterogeneous regression coefficients across experimental conditions should not be considered a statistical nuisance interfering with the proper analysis of the data. Heterogeneous regression across experimental conditions is an important finding. Regression heterogeneity indicates that the dependent variable on covariate relationship differs between experimental conditions. This is a result that should be considered on a par with differences observed between experimental condition dependent variable means and it must be accommodated in the GLM to allow proper analysis of the data. However, it is worth repeating that heterogeneous regression coefficients may be symptomatic of a relationship between the covariate and the experimental conditions (Evans & Anastasio, 1968).

Regression homogeneity may be assessed graphically by judging the relative slopes of experimental condition regression lines (see Figure 7.5). Alternatively, a significance test approach can be applied by examining the reduction in errors due to the inclusion in the GLM of a term representing the interaction between the covariate and the experimental conditions. The predictor variables representing the interaction between the covariate and the experimental conditions is constructed in exactly the same manner as those variables representing factor interactions were constructed (see Chapters 3 & 5. For further details see Cohen

& Cohen, 1983; Howell, 1997; Pedhazur, 1997; Neter et al., 1990). However, as with the tests of regression linearity, the problem of multicollinearity arises: the predictor variables representing the interaction between the covariate and the experimental conditions will be correlated with Z. Therefore, the data analysis should proceed in a structured manner (e.g. Cohen & Cohen, 1983). This emphasizes the point that the significance test approach examines the (further) reduction in errors due to the inclusion in the GLM of a term representing the interaction between the covariate and the experimental conditions, after those terms representing experimental conditions and the single regression line have been included in the GLM. A significant reduction in error (i.e. a significant interaction term) indicates regression heterogeneity. This means the model fit to data can be improved by employing a different regression coefficient in at least one of the experimental conditions.

The ANCOVA table summarizing the error reduction when separate regression slopes are employed in the different experimental conditions is presented in Table 7.4. As can be seen, no significant improvement is observed and so the tenability of the assumption of homogeneous regression coefficients is accepted.

If a significant interaction between the covariate and the experimental conditions had been detected, the next question should be, which of the experimental conditions require distinct regression coefficients? It may be that only one or two of the experimental conditions requires a unique regression slope. As a degree of freedom is lost from the error variance estimate with every distinct regression line employed, for this and other reasons (e.g. Draper & Smith, 1998), applying only the minimum number of terms required is a guiding principle of linear modelling.

Which experimental conditions require distinct regression lines can be determined by comparing different models which employ a common regression line for all but one of the experimental conditions. Rather than obtaining an estimate of the error when all experimental conditions employ distinct regression lines, an error estimate is obtained when only one experimental condition employs a distinct regression line. The reduction in residuals due to this one distinct regression line then can be assessed in comparison to the residual estimate obtained when a common regression line is applied in all treatment groups. Successive estimations can be made and each time a distinct regression

Table 7.4   Summary of additional error reduction due to heterogeneous regression ANCOVA

R: 0.941	R squared: 0.886		Adjusted R squared: 0.862		
Source	SS Increment	df	Mean square	F	p
Additional error reduction due to covariate x experimental conditions	19.394	2	9.697	1.600	0.229
Full GLM error	109.070	18	6.059		

line is employed in a different experimental condition, any significant reduction in errors indicates a significant improvement in the fit of the model to the data.

The significance test method described above is equivalent to the standard test of regression homogeneity presented by Kendall (1948), reproduced by Hays (1994), Keppel (1991), Kirk (1995) and Winer et al. (1991). For the single factor, single covariate independent sample design, this is

$$F[(p-1),\ p(N-2)] = \frac{S_2/(p-1)}{S_1/p(N-2)} \tag{7.4}$$

where S_1 is the residual variation when separate group regressions have been employed and S_2 is the variation of the separate experimental condition regressions about the weighted average regression line (see texts above for computational formulae). The sum of squares S_2 estimates the variation not accommodated when the weighted average regression line, rather than separate experimental condition regression lines, are used and is equivalent to the estimate of the interaction effect, or the reduction in residuals due to the separate experimental condition regression lines. For all of the significance test methods, the same F-test denominator estimate is employed and a significant F-value indicates that the homogeneity of regression coefficients assumption is untenable. In order to avoid Type 2 errors, Kirk (1995) and Hays (1994) recommend the use of a liberal level of significance (about 0.25) with the regression homogeneity test. However, test power increases with large data sets, so more conservative significance levels should be set when the test is applied to large data sets.

Regression homogeneity also must be checked after polynomial components have been added to the traditional ANCOVA model to accommodate curvilinear regression. This is achieved most easily by applying a significance test in a manner similar to that described above. Another set of predictors is created to represent the interaction between the polynomial components (added to accommodate the curvilinearity) and the experimental conditions. For example, had it been decided that the GLM described by equation (7.2) was most appropriate for the data, incorporating an additional term to represent an experimental conditions–curvilinear interaction would result in the model

$$Y_{ij} = \mu + \alpha_j + \beta(Z_{ij} - Z_G) + \beta(Z_{ij} - Z_G)^2$$

$$+ [(\alpha_j)(\beta(Z_{ij} - Z_G) + \beta(Z_{ij} - Z_G)^2)] + \varepsilon_{ij} \tag{7.5}$$

An F-test is applied to the reduction in error variance attributed to the interaction term. A significant F-test indicates that better prediction is provided when at least one of the experimental conditions employs a different curvilinear regression line. Therefore, the next step is to determine which experimental conditions actually require distinct regression lines. As always, when any new GLM is considered, it is necessary to check that it conforms to the set of GLM assumptions. As with curvilinear regression, an advantage of this approach is that when all significant heterogeneous regression components are included, the description of the heterogeneous regression ANCOVA GLM is complete and the ANCOVA results can be interpreted.

8 SOME ALTERNATIVES TO TRADITIONAL ANCOVA

8.1 Alternatives to traditional ANCOVA

Most alternatives to traditional ANCOVA address the problem caused by heterogeneous regression coefficients across experimental conditions. There are a number of good reasons for this focus. First, regression homogeneity probably is the most frequently violated traditional ANCOVA assumption. Second, most regression of dependent variables on covariates are at least approximately linear. Third, homogeneous curvilinear regression does not complicate the interpretation of the ANCOVA as much as heterogeneous regression. Fourth, although not generally appreciated, one of the benefits of applying heterogeneous regression ANCOVA is amelioration of the problems caused by a relation between the covariate(s) and experimental conditions.

An implicit assumption is that relaxing restrictions by developing more sophisticated GLMs allows greater accuracy in representing the influence and relations of the recorded variables. By dispensing with the homogeneous regression requirement, heterogeneous regression ANCOVA can provide more realistic models of a far greater number of situations. A variety of approaches have been suggested to cope with the violation of the assumption of homogeneous regression coefficients across experimental conditions (Rutherford, 1992). However, here three alternatives to traditional ANCOVA are presented. Although all employ the GLM in one way or another, they are sufficiently distinct to merit separate discussion.

8.2 The heterogeneous regression problem

As the term ANCOVA is applied, the main concern is the determination of experimental effects. However, the basic problem posed by heterogeneous regression ANCOVA is that experimental effects vary as a function of the covariate. This is illustrated in Figure 8.1, where a simple independent measures, single covariate, single factor (with just two levels) experimental design is depicted.

From Figure 8.1, it can be appreciated that the experimental effect, represented by the vertical distance between the regression lines, is not constant across the range of the covariate values, as is the case in traditional ANCOVA, but instead varies as a function of the covariate values. As a result and in contrast to the homogeneous regression situation, an assessment of experimental

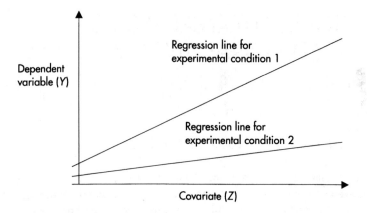

Figure 8.1   Heterogeneous regression across two experimental conditions

effect at any one measure of the covariate cannot be taken to reflect the experimental effect at any other measures of the covariate. In essence therefore, heterogeneous regression ANCOVA presents a problem of experimental effect determination and description.

If the process of model selection determines that distinct regressions (in graphical terms, lines which pass through all fitted values) are required to accommodate the data, then there seems little reason to consider the null hypothesis that the separate regressions predict the same dependent variable values. Yet by definition, non-parallel regression lines intersect at some point. Here, the same values will be predicted by the two distinct regression lines and importantly, the experimental effect observed below this covariate value will be the converse of the experimental effect observed above this value. (A plot of the regression lines is the most obvious way to determine if regressions intersect within the range of observed covariate values.) Depending upon the location of this intersection point, it may be necessary to determine the covariate values at which significant experimental effects are exerted and to specify the nature of these experimental effects. As the the intersection point in Figure 8.1 is below $Z = 0$, although the effect size may vary, the nature of the experimental effect is consistent across the range of positive covariate values.

8.3   The heterogeneous regression ANCOVA GLM

In Chapter 6, two versions of the ANCOVA GLM were described. The typical traditional ANCOVA GLM expresses the covariate scores in terms of their deviation from the overall covariate mean, while the more general ANCOVA GLM simply expresses the covariate score. The latter version of the independent measures, single factor, single covariate experimental design GLM is

$$Y_{ij} = \mu + \alpha_j + \beta Z_{ij} + \varepsilon_{ij}$$ (6.1, rptd)

As described in Chapter 6, subtracting the term BZ from the dependent variable score removes all influence of the covariate, leaving the fundamental adjusted score (Y_{faij}). This is the predicted dependent variable score when $Z = 0$.

$$Y_{faij} = Y_{ij} - \beta Z_{ij} = \mu + \alpha_j + \varepsilon_{ij} \qquad (6.4, \text{rptd})$$

If the general covariate mean ($\overline{Z}_G$) is substituted for Z_{ij}, then the predicted dependent variable scores are the values Y_{aij}, as in traditional ANCOVA. Both of these predictions are specific instances of the general prediction on the basis of Z, where Z is any measure of the covariate.

To accommodate the heterogeneous regressions depicted in Figure 8.1, equation (6.1) may be re-written as

$$Y_{ij} = \mu + \alpha_j + \beta_j Z_{ij} + \varepsilon_{ij} \qquad (8.1)$$

where the regression coefficient β of equation (6.1) is replaced by β_j, which, by virtue of the j subscript, denotes a different regression coefficient per experimental condition. An important point to appreciate about the separate regression lines is that they are statistically independent (e.g. Searle, 1987).

As heterogeneous regression ANCOVA GLMs simply incorporate terms to accommodate the different slopes, they are able to provide tests comparable with the traditional ANCOVA hypotheses, as well as tests of the covariate effect and factor interactions. In traditional ANCOVA, the omnibus F-test of experimental conditions compares adjusted means, which are those scores predicted on the basis of the general covariate mean ($\overline{Z}_G$). However, when heterogeneous regression ANCOVA is applied, the omnibus F-test of experimental conditions compares the predicted scores when $Z = 0$ (e.g. Searle, 1987): the Y-intercepts of the separate regression lines are compared (see Figure 8.1). Nevertheless, it is unlikely there will be much interest in comparing treatment groups at the zero value of the covariate, not least because it may be impossible to observe a zero covariate score in the real world.

Of course, once the heterogeneous regression ANCOVA GLM is selected and parameter estimates obtained, it is possible to predict a dependent variable score based on any covariate value for each experimental condition. Moreover, as the standard errors associated with these predicted scores also are determinable, it is possible to carry out F-tests of the effect of experimental conditions at any covariate value(s). For example, F-tests of the experimental effects might be carried out at $\overline{Z}_G$, or at the separate experimental condition covariate means ($\overline{Z}_j$).

In ANCOVA, the accuracy of the predicted dependent variable scores and so the power of the F-test of experimental effects is greatest when the covariate value employed is that which lies at the centre of the covariate distribution. This is known as the centre of accuracy (C_a). Interestingly, Rogosa (1980) revealed that the heterogeneous regression ANCOVA experimental effect at C_a is identical to the traditional homogeneous regression ANCOVA experimental effect at C_a. Moreover, with balanced designs, estimating experimental effects on the basis of the separate $\overline{Z}_j$ values provides an F-test at C_a (because $\sum \overline{Z}_j / p = \overline{Z}_G$). Paradoxically, therefore, estimating experimental effects at $\overline{Z}_j$

provides a simple heterogeneous regression alternative to the traditional ANCO-
VA experimental effect estimate, which is also identical to the traditional
ANCOVA experimental effect estimate. There may be theoretical reasons for
comparing all subjects across the experimental conditions at the same covariate
value, but as prediction accuracy drops with distance from the experimental
condition covariate means, the power cost inherent in these comparisons
depends on the difference between $\overline{Z}_G$ and each of the $\overline{Z}_j$.

It is important to appreciate that most statistical packages able to implement
heterogeneous regressions will apply GLMs in the form of equation (8.1), and
so the ANCOVA summary table will present experimental effects assessed when
all influence of the covariate has been removed (i.e. at $Z = 0$). If experimental
effects are to be assessed at any other covariate values, further analysis beyond
that presented in the ANCOVA summary table is necessary. Moreover, when
statistical software is used to implement heterogeneous regression ANCOVA, it
is advisable to check (empirically) which covariate value(s) are the basis for any
adjusted experimental condition means presented.

8.4   Single factor independent measures heterogeneous regression ANCOVA

In the following example, two of the conditions reported in Chapter 6 will be
presented as if they constituted a separate experiment. Table 8.1 presents the
subjects' story and imagery task (covariate) scores and the subjects' memory
recall scores after story and imagery encoding in two study time conditions.

Table 8.1   Story and imagery test scores and recall
scores after story and imagery encoding

Study time (s)	b_1 30		b_3 180	
	Z	Y	Z	Y
	9	16	5	24
	5	7	8	29
	6	11	3	10
	4	9	4	22
	6	10	6	25
	8	11	9	28
	3	8	4	22
	5	8	5	24
$\sum Z/Y$	46	80	44	184
$\overline{Z}/\overline{Y}$	5.750	10.000	5.500	23.000
$(\sum Z/Y)^2$	292	856	272	4470
$\sum Z^2/Y^2$	2116	6400	1936	33856

Maxwell and Delaney (1990) argue for a bias in applying heterogeneous regression ANCOVA as the only disadvantage is a slight loss of power if the experimental condition regressions are completely homogeneous. In line with this view, heterogeneous regression ANCOVA is applied to the data presented in Table 8.1 (also see Figure 7.5).

The slope of the regression lines $(\hat{\beta}_j)$ for each of the experimental conditions employed in the ANCOVA GLM are given by

$$\hat{\beta}_j = \frac{\sum_{i=1}^{N}(Z_{ij} - \overline{Z}_j)(Y_{ij} - \overline{Y}_j)}{\sum_{i=1}^{N}(Z_{ij} - \overline{Z}_j)^2} \tag{8.2}$$

For $\hat{\beta}_1$ this provides Table 8.2, which gives

$$\hat{\beta}_1 = \frac{33.000}{27.500} = 1.200$$

for $\hat{\beta}_3$ Table 8.3 is obtained, which provides

$$\hat{\beta}_3 = \frac{68.000}{30.000} = 2.267$$

Table 8.2   Calculation of $\hat{\beta}_1$

$(Z_{ij} - \overline{Z}_j)^2$	$Y_{ij} - \overline{Y}_j$	$(Z_{ij} - \overline{Z}_j)(Y_{ij} - \overline{Y}_j)$
$9 - 5.750 = 3.250$	$16 - 10 = 6$	19.500
$5 - 5.750 = -0.750$	$7 - 10 = -3$	2.250
$6 - 5.750 = 0.250$	$11 - 10 = 1$	0.250
$4 - 5.750 = -1.750$	$9 - 10 = -1$	1.750
$6 - 5.750 = 0.250$	$10 - 10 = 0$	0.000
$8 - 5.750 = 2.250$	$11 - 10 = 1$	2.250
$3 - 5.750 = -2.750$	$8 - 10 = -2$	5.500
$5 - 5.750 = -0.750$	$8 - 10 = -2$	1.500
$\sum(Z_{ij} - \overline{Z}_j)^2 = 27.500$		$\sum = 33.000$

Table 8.3   Calculation of $\hat{\beta}_3$

$(Z_{ij} - \overline{Z}_j)^2$	$Y_{ij} - \overline{Y}_j$	$(Z_{ij} - \overline{Y}_j)(Y_{ij} - \overline{Y}_j)$
$5 - 5.500 = -0.500$	$24 - 23 = 1$	-0.500
$8 - 5.500 = 2.500$	$29 - 23 = 6$	15.000
$3 - 5.500 = -2.500$	$10 - 23 = -13$	32.500
$4 - 5.500 = -1.500$	$22 - 23 = -1$	1.500
$6 - 5.500 = 0.500$	$25 - 23 = 2$	1.000
$9 - 5.500 = 3.500$	$28 - 23 = 5$	17.500
$4 - 5.500 = -1.500$	$22 - 23 = -1$	1.500
$5 - 5.500 = -0.500$	$24 - 23 = 1$	-0.500
$\sum(Z_{ij} - \overline{Z}_j)^2 = 30.000$		$\sum = 68.000$

The formula for calculating adjusted means used in Chapter 6 is repeated below:

$$\overline{Y}_{aj} = \overline{Y}_j - \beta(\overline{Z}_j - \overline{Z}_G) \qquad \text{(6.8, rptd)}$$

Applying this to the heterogeneous regression situation where each experimental condition has a distinct regression line and employs the experimental condition covariate mean as a predictor reveals the adjusted experimental condition means to be equal to the unadjusted experimental means:

$$\overline{Y}_{aj} = \overline{Y}_j - \beta(\overline{Z}_j - \overline{Z}_j)$$

$$\overline{Y}_{aj} = \overline{Y}_j - \beta(0)$$

$$\overline{Y}_{aj} = \overline{Y}_j \qquad \text{(8.3)}$$

However, it is worth noting that the equivalence of adjusted and unadjusted means is a consequence of employing distinct regression lines in each experimental condition and employing the respective experimental condition covariate means as predictors. Consequently, when heterogeneous regression ANCOVA which does not fit a distinct regression line per experimental condition or does not employ experimental condition covariate means as predictors is applied, adjusted and unadjusted means may not be equivalent.

8.5   Estimating heterogeneous regression ANCOVA effects

The Full GLM for the single factor single covariate heterogeneous regression ANCOVA design was described in equation (8.1). The reduced GLM for this design omits the variable representing experimental conditions and is described by the equation

$$Y_{ij} = \mu + \beta_j Z_{ij} + \varepsilon_{ij} \qquad \text{(8.4)}$$

The GLM equation (8.4) describes p dependent variable on covariate regression lines all with a common Y-intercept (μ). However, the estimates of the $\hat{\beta}_j$ in equation (8.4) and those estimated for equation (8.1) are not equal (see Searle, 1987). Therefore, to minimize the amount of calculation required, an alternative approach to estimating heterogeneous regression ANCOVA effects will be described. This approach simply applies and extends the check of the regression homogeneity assumption.

First, the full traditional ANCOVA error term is required. As these calculations were described in Chapter 6, albeit for all three experimental conditions, the traditional ANCOVA error SS will be accepted as, 116.591, with dfs = 13.

Next, the full heterogeneous regression ANCOVA GLM predicted scores must be calculated. A little algebra applied to equation (8.1) reveals

$$Y_{ij} - \beta_j Z_{ij} = \mu + \alpha_j + \varepsilon_{ij} \qquad \text{(8.5)}$$

Simply re-writing this equation in terms of the parameter estimates provides

$$\hat{Y}_{ij} - \hat{\beta}_j Z_{ij} = \hat{\mu} + \hat{\alpha}_j \qquad (8.6)$$

which states that when all influence of the covariate has been removed, the predicted dependent variable score is equivalent to the constant plus the effect of the particular experimental condition. Of course, when all influence of the covariate is removed, $Z = 0$. Therefore, $(\hat{\mu} + \hat{\alpha}_j)$ must be equivalent to the Y-intercept of each experimental condition regression line (see Figure 8.1). Indeed, with balanced data,

$$\mu = \frac{\sum_{j=1}^{p}(\mu + \alpha_j)}{p} \qquad (8.7)$$

As well as passing through the $(\hat{\mu} + \hat{\alpha}_j)$ intercepts, each of the regression lines passes through the point defined by the experimental condition dependent variable mean and the experimental condition covariate mean $(\overline{Z}_j \overline{Y}_j)$. Substituting these mean values into equation (8.6), along with the pertinent regression coefficient estimates, allows calculation of the regression line intercepts. For experimental condition 1,

$$(\hat{\mu} + \hat{\alpha}_1) = 10.000 - 1.200(5.750) = 3.100$$

and for experimental condition 3

$$(\hat{\mu} + \hat{\alpha}_3) = 23.000 - 2.267(5.500) = 10.532$$

In fact, the $(\hat{\mu} + \hat{\alpha}_j)$ values are actually the means of the distribution of predicted scores, as can be seen by adding the Y_{faij} term to equation (8.5):

$$Y_{faij} = Y_{ij} - \beta_j Z_{ij} = \mu + \alpha_j + \varepsilon_{ij} \qquad (8.8)$$

Therefore, substituting each subjects' dependent variable and covariate scores into the first half of equation (8.8),

$$Y_{faij} = Y_{ij} - \beta_j Z_{ij} \qquad (8.9)$$

provides the $\hat{Y}_{faij}$ scores (Table 8.4).

As said, the $\hat{Y}_{faij}$ are the scores distributed about the $(\hat{\mu} + \hat{\alpha}_j)$ means. There-

Table 8.4

b_1 30 $Y_{ij} - \hat{\beta}_1(Z_{ij}) = \hat{Y}_{faij}$	b_3 180 $Y_{ij} - \hat{\beta}_3(Z_{ij}) = \hat{Y}_{faij}$
$16 - 1.200(9) = 5.200$	$24 - 2.267(5) = 12.665$
$7 - 1.200(5) = 1.000$	$29 - 2.267(8) = 10.864$
$11 - 1.200(6) = 3.800$	$10 - 2.267(3) = 3.199$
$9 - 1.200(4) = 4.200$	$22 - 2.267(4) = 12.932$
$10 - 1.200(6) = 2.800$	$25 - 2.267(6) = 11.398$
$11 - 1.200(8) = 1.400$	$28 - 2.267(9) = 7.597$
$8 - 1.200(3) = 4.400$	$22 - 2.267(4) = 12.932$
$8 - 1.200(5) = 2.000$	$24 - 2.267(5) = 12.665$

fore, the discrepancy between the $\hat{Y}_{faij}$ scores and the $(\hat{\mu} + \hat{a}_j)$ intercepts provide the error term estimates, $\hat{\varepsilon}_{ij}$. This may be appreciated through the application of a little algebra to equation (8.8):

$$Y_{faij} = Y_{ij} - \beta_j Z_{ij} = \mu + a_j + \varepsilon_{ij} \qquad \text{(8.8, rptd)}$$

so,

$$Y_{faij} = (\mu + a_j) + \varepsilon_{ij}$$

and

$$Y_{faij} - (\mu + a_j) = \varepsilon_{ij} \qquad \text{(8.10)}$$

Table 8.5 shows calculation of the error estimates, and Table 8.6 summarizes the SS error and its df obtained when homogeneous and heterogeneous regression ANCOVA GLMs are applied to the data.

As before, an F-test of the reduction in the error SS, attributed to heterogeneous regressions, is given by

$$F = \frac{\text{SSerror reduction/dfs reduction}}{\text{SSHeterogeneous regression/dfHeterogeneous regression}}$$

$$F = \frac{16.338/1}{100.253/12} = 1.956$$

Table 8.5   Error term estimates

b_1 30 $\hat{Y}_{fai1} - (\hat{\mu} + \hat{a}_1) = \hat{\varepsilon}_{i1}$	b_3 180 $\hat{Y}_{fai3} - (\hat{\mu} + \hat{a}_3) = \hat{\varepsilon}_{i3}$
$5.200 - 3.100 = 2.100$	$12.665 - 10.532 = 2.133$
$1.000 - 3.100 = -2.100$	$10.864 - 10.532 = 0.334$
$3.800 - 3.100 = 0.699$	$3.199 - 10.532 = -7.333$
$4.200 - 3.100 = 1.100$	$12.932 - 10.532 = 2.400$
$2.800 - 3.100 = -0.300$	$11.398 - 10.532 = 0.867$
$1.400 - 3.100 = -1.699$	$7.597 - 10.532 = -2.933$
$4.400 - 3.100 = 1.300$	$12.932 - 10.532 = 2.400$
$2.000 - 3.100 = -1.100$	$12.665 - 10.532 = 2.133$
$\sum \varepsilon_{i1}^2 = 16.395$	$\sum \varepsilon_{i1}^2 = 83.858$
$\sum_{i=1}^{N} \sum_{j=1}^{P} \varepsilon_{ij}^2 = 100.253$	

Table 8.6   SS error and dfs with homogeneous and heterogeneous regression ANCOVA GLMs

	Homogeneous regression ANCOVA GLM	Heterogeneous regression ANCOVA GLM	Reduction
SS	116.591	100.253	16.338
df	13	12	1

As $F(1, 12) = 1.956$ is not significant at the 0.05 level, the traditional ANCOVA homogeneity of regression assumption is tenable. Nevertheless, following Maxwell and Delaney's (1990) recommendation, analysis of the data presented in Table 8.1 will continue on the basis of the heterogeneous regression ANCOVA GLM, despite the tenability of the homogeneity assumption. Later in this chapter (8.7), another benefit of applying heterogeneous regression ANCOVA will be discussed.

Earlier it was said that the omnibus F-test of the effect of experimental conditions when a heterogeneous regression ANCOVA GLM is applied compares the separate experimental condition regression line Y-intercepts – the predicted differences between the experimental conditions when $Z = 0$. Therefore, a simple comparison of these Y-intercepts provides the same test of the effect of the experimental conditions.

In general, the experimental effect is denoted by the vertical difference between the experimental condition regression lines at any experimental condition covariate value, i.e. the experimental effect can be predicted using different covariate values in the different experimental conditions. Equation (8.11) provides a formula for calculating such experimental effects when there are two experimental conditions:

$$ F = \frac{(\hat{Y}_{Zpj} - \hat{Y}_{Zpj})^2}{MSe\left[1/N_j + 1/N_j + \dfrac{(Z_{pj} - \overline{Z}_j)^2}{\sum_{i=1}^{N}(Z_{ij} - \overline{Z}_j)^2} + \dfrac{(Z_{pj} - \overline{Z}_j)^2}{\sum_{i=1}^{N}(Z_{ij} - \overline{Z}_j)^2}\right]^2} \tag{8.11}$$

where MSe is the heterogeneous regression ANCOVA mean square error, the $\hat{Y}_{Zpj}$ are the predicted means given the covariate values for the particular experimental condition, the N_j are the number of subjects per experimental condition, the Z_{pj} are the experimental condition covariate values upon which the dependent variable means are predicted and the $\overline{Z}_j$ are the experimental condition covariate means. Substituting the values for the current example provides

$$ F = \frac{(3.100 - 10.532)^2}{8.354\left[1/8 + 1/8 + \dfrac{(0 - 5.750)^2}{27.500} + \dfrac{(0 - 5.500)^2}{30.000}\right]} $$

$$ = \frac{55.235}{20.552} $$

$$ = 2.688 $$

As $F(1, 12) = 2.688$ is not significant at the 0.05 level, the null hypothesis that the two experimental condition regression line Y-intercepts are equivalent cannot be rejected. However, examination of Figure 8.1 shows that the difference between the regression lines is at its minimum (ignoring negative covariate values) when $Z = 0$. For theoretical reasons, there may be relatively little interest in comparing the predicted experimental condition means when the covariate is zero. Probably of much more interest is the predicted effect of experimental conditions when subjects obtain covariate scores equal to the experimental condition covariate means. Given balanced data, the convenient fact that the predicted experimental effect at the respective experimental condition covariate means obtained with heterogeneous regression ANCOVA is equal to that obtained with traditional homogeneous regression ANCOVA may be employed. If the strategy outlined here, of fitting a traditional homogeneous regression ANCOVA GLM and then testing for error reduction after fitting heterogeneous regressions, has been applied, then both the traditional ANCOVA experimental effect and the heterogeneous regression ANCOVA experimental effect will have been calculated already. Table 8.7 summarizes the traditional ANCOVA GLM applied to the data presented in Table 8.1.

Clearly Table 8.7 reveals a significant effect of experimental conditions predicted on the basis of the experimental condition covariate means. Equation (8.10) may be used to check the F-value reported.

8.6   Regression GLMs for heterogeneous ANCOVA

The experimental design GLM equation (8.1) may be compared with the equivalent regression equation,

$$Y_{ij} = \beta_0 + \beta_1 X_{i,1} + \beta_2 Z_{ij} + \beta_3(XZ) + \varepsilon_{ij} \tag{8.12}$$

As always, β_0 represents a constant common to all Y scores, β_1 is the regression coefficient for the predictor variable X_1, which distinguishes between the two experimental conditions, and β_2 is the regression coefficient for the covariate, Z_{ij} is the covariate score for the ith subject in the jth condition, β_3 is the regression coefficient for the (XZ) interaction, which represents the heterogeneous regression, and as always, the random variable, e_{ij}, represents error. Table 8.8 presents effect coding for the single factor, single covariate heterogeneous regression ANCOVA GLM.

As with other design analyses, implementing a single factor, single covariate heterogeneous regression ANCOVA is a two stage procedure if only the variance attributable to the experimental conditions is to be assessed, and a three stage procedure if the variance attributable to the covariate regression is to be

Table 8.7   Summary of the traditional ANCOVA of the data in Table 8.1

Source	SS	df	MS	F	P
Error reduction due to experimental conditions	719.313	1	719.313	80.204	<0.001
Error reduction due to covariate	177.409	1	177.409	19.781	0.001
Full GLM error	116.591	13	8.969		

Table 8.8 Effect coding and covariate for a
single factor single covariate heterogeneous
regression ANCOVA. Subject number and the
dependent variable score also are shown

Subject	Z	X_1	XZ	Y
1	9	1	9	16
2	5	1	5	7
3	6	1	6	11
4	4	1	4	9
5	6	1	6	10
6	8	1	8	11
7	3	1	3	8
8	5	1	5	8
17	5	−1	−5	24
18	8	−1	−8	29
19	3	−1	−3	10
20	4	−1	−4	22
21	6	−1	−6	25
22	9	−1	−9	28
23	4	−1	−4	22
24	5	−1	−5	24

assessed. Consistent with estimating effects by comparing full and reduced
GLMs, the first regression carried out is for the full single factor, single
covariate heterogeneous regression experimental design GLM, when all experimental condition predictor variables (X_1), the covariate (Z) and the experimental condition–covariate interaction (XZ) are included. The results of this
analysis are presented in Tables 8.9 and 8.10.

Table 8.9 presents the predictor variable regression coefficients and standard
deviations, the standardized regression coefficients, and significance tests (t-
and p-values) of the regression coefficients. Table 8.5 is also interesting in that
the Constant is the value of μ free of α_j. This confirms

$$\mu = \frac{\sum_{j=1}^{p}(\mu + \alpha_j)}{p}$$

(8.7, rptd)

Table 8.9 Results for the full single factor, single covariate
heterogeneous regression ANCOVA regression GLM

Variable	Coefficient	Std error	Std coef	t	p (2 tail)
Constant	6.817	2.267	0.000	3.007	0.011
X_1	−3.717	2.267	0.477	−1.639	0.127
Z	1.733	0.382	0.423	4.543	0.001
XZ	−0.533	0.382	−0.407	−1.398	0.187

Table 8.10   ANOVA summary table for experimental conditions and heterogeneous regressions

	R: 0.947	R squared: 0.897		Adjusted R squared: 0.871	
Source	SS	df	Mean square	F	p
Regression	869.733	3	289.911	34.697	<0.001
Residual	100.267	12	8.356		

Table 8.10 presents the ANOVA summary table for the regression GLM describing the complete single factor, single covariate ANCOVA.

As the residual SS is that obtained when both covariate and experimental conditions are included in the regression, this is the error term obtained when the single factor, single covariate ANCOVA GLM is applied.

The second stage is to carry out a regression where the experimental conditions are omitted, but all other regression predictors are included. This regression GLM is equivalent to the reduced GLM for the single factor, single covariate heterogeneous regression ANCOVA. The results of this analysis are presented in Tables 8.11 and 8.12.

The results presented in Table 8.11 are of little interest, but they do demonstrate that the reduced GLM estimates of the constant (μ) and the dependent variable on covariate regressions per experimental condition differ from those of the full GLM estimate, the additional calculation of which was the reason given earlier for taking an alternative approach to calculating the effects of the experimental conditions. Of most interest is the residual/error term from the heterogeneous regression presented in Table 8.12.

Table 8.11   Results for the heterogeneous regression ANCOVA GLM omitting experimental conditions

Variable	Coefficient	Std error	Std coef	t	p (2 tail)
Constant	7.110	2.402	0.000	2.959	0.011
Z	1.694	0.405	0.413	4.186	0.001
XZ	−1.126	0.130	−0.858	−8.692	<0.001

Table 8.12   ANOVA summary table for the heterogeneous regression GLM omitting experimental conditions

	R: 0.935	R squared: 0.873		Adjusted R squared: 0.854	
Source	SS	df	Mean square	F	p
Regression	847.278	2	423.639	44.876	<0.001
Residual	122.722	13	9.440		

The difference between the residual/error SS in Table 8.10 and that in Table 8.12 is equivalent to the SS attributable to experimental conditions. However, the SS attributed to the regressions in Table 8.12 is not equivalent to the covariate SS calculated when the full ANCOVA GLM is applied. The SS for the covariate in the full ANCOVA GLM may be obtained by comparing the error SS from the full ANCOVA with the error SS from an equivalent full ANOVA GLM. A full ANOVA GLM is implemented by a regression that uses only the predictors representing the experimental conditions (X_1). Table 8.13 presents the ANOVA Summary of this analysis.

Armed with the error term from the regression GLM implementation of the single factor ANOVA, the error reduction attributable to the covariate can be calculated. This information is summarized in Table 8.14. Of course, like the full experimental design heterogeneous regression ANCOVA, this regression ANCOVA GLM assess the experimental effect when $Z = 0$.

8.7 Covariate–experimental condition relations

A particularly useful consequence of heterogeneous regression is that it allows a relaxation of the traditional requirement that the covariate is unaffected by the

Table 8.13 ANOVA summary table for experimental conditions regression

	R: 0.835	R squared: 0.697	Adjusted R squared: 0.675		
Source	SS	df	Mean square	F	p
Experimental condition regression predictors	676.000	1	676.000	32.190	< 0.001
Residual	294.000	14	21.000		

Table 8.14 ANOVA summary Table for experimental conditions regression and heterogeneous covariate regressions

	R: 0.940	R squared: 0.884	Adjusted R squared: 0.867		
Source	SS	df	Mean square	F	p
Error reduction due to experimental conditions	22.456	1	22.456	2.688	0.127
Error reduction due to covariate	188.754	2	94.377	20.636	< 0.001
Full ANCOVA GLM residual	100.267	12	8.356	1.954	

experimental conditions. A traditional ANCOVA where covariate and treatment(s) are related will be correct in terms of its statistical validity and accuracy, but it is unlikely to pertain easily or usefully to the real world (see Huitema, 1980, for the traditional ANCOVA approach to this issue).

In what probably remains the most detailed consideration of covariate and treatment covariation in traditional ANCOVA, Smith (1957) identified three situations that result in such an association (also see Huitema, 1980; Maxwell & Delaney, 1990). The first situation is when a variable not included in the GLM exerts an effect on the dependent variable and also influences the covariate. The best way of dealing with this source of systematic bias is to include the pertinent variable in the GLM. The two other situations identified by Smith are when the covariate is affected by the experimental conditions, and when the covariate and dependent variable are both measures of the one entity.

Just as separate experimental condition means may better describe a dependent variable, in situations where covariate and experimental conditions are related, so separate group means may better describe the covariate scores also. In such circumstances, a general covariate mean may lie between the group covariate score distributions. Estimation of the experimental effects at such a general covariate mean value is comparable to estimating experimental effects given a new experimental condition, which may have no counterpart in reality (Huitema, 1980; Smith, 1957).

In contrast, heterogeneous regression allows separate and independent regression lines to be fitted to groups with different covariate score distributions (Searle, 1987). Therefore, heterogeneous regression maintains any differences between the covariate distributions of these groups and obviates any spurious adjustments based on fictitious covariate values (see Urquhart, 1982, for a similar assessment and conclusion).

Although heterogeneous regression ANCOVA maintains the integrity of the separate covariate score distributions, the correlation between the experimental conditions and the covariate continues to exert an effect. Specifically, variation removed from the dependent variable on the basis of its regressions on the covariate would have been part of the experimental effect, with the amount of common variance extracted determined by the size of the correlation between the covariate and the experimental conditions. Although this can be problematic, by avoiding conflated covariate distributions, the relation between the experimental conditions and the covariate in heterogeneous regression ANCOVA reduces from a condition that seriously questions the validity and complicates the interpretation of adjusted experimental effects to the familiar regression topic of multicollinearity.

8.7.1 Multicollinearity

As described in Chapter 1, multicollinearity creates three problems that affect the processes of model selection and parameter estimation: the substantive interpretation of partial coefficients (if calculated simultaneously, correlated predictors' partial coefficients are reduced), the sampling stability of partial coefficients and the accuracy of their calculation (Cohen & Cohen, 1983). When multicollinearity exists and there is interest in the contribution of each of the predictors, a hierarchical analysis can be adopted (Cohen & Cohen, 1983). This approach also concords with Nelder's (1977; McCullagh & Nelder, 1989) linear model approach to ANOVA and ANCOVA, which attributes variance to factors in an ordered manner that accommodates the marginality of factors and their interactions (also see Bingham & Fienberg, 1982).

In situations of multicollinearity, the reduction of partial coefficient estimates is due to correlated predictor variables accounting for similar parts of the dependent variable variance. As a result, in a hierarchical analysis, the common variance will be attributed to the first correlated predictor to be included in the linear model. Therefore, different perspectives on the amount of variance accounted for by the correlated predictors can be obtained by changing their order of entry into the linear model.

To illustrate a hierarchical analysis, consider a simple hypothetical experiment that compares memory performance for differently encoded words. A single factor independent measures design with just two levels might be implemented. The two levels should be defined by the different encoding strategies. In a semantic encoding condition, subjects should be presented with a stimulus word and should have to decide whether it is a member of a specific semantic category. In the phonetic encoding condition, subjects should have to decide if a stimulus word rhymes with a comparison word. 30 minutes after presentation, memory is tested by cued recall. Subjects in the phonetic encoding condition are presented with phonetic cues and subjects in the semantic encoding condition are presented with semantic cues. The dependent variable measure could be the number of words correctly remembered.

Although a controlled experiment should take care to standardize the stimulus materials used and the instructions delivered, still there is likely to be variation in subjects' performance. This variation could arise from at least two aspects of performance. First, there may be variation in the extent of appropriate processing in encoding conditions across stimulus words: for any subject not all words may receive the appropriate processing and some words may not receive any processing. Second, there may be variation between subjects in terms of the efficiency of any mode of processing when engaged. An assessment of these aspects of subjects' performance should be a very useful covariate for an ANCOVA of the experimental data. Although the form of assessment should be determined by the theoretical issues of pertinence to the particular study, tests that could provide scores related to these performance aspects range from a score based on subjects' performance on earlier and similar tasks, through subjects' scores on a standard recognition task on a small proportion of the current experimental stimulus items, to a self-assessment rating of how well all of the stimulus words had been learned.

Conventional design practice presumes that if the covariate is measured before the experimental manipulation then the covariate cannot be influenced by the treatment and the treatment and covariate will be independent (e.g. Keppel, 1991; Kirk, 1995; Winer et al., 1991). However, in itself, this does not guarantee independence. For example, if a covariate is obtained on the basis of earlier and similar tasks, precisely because these tasks are similar to the tasks that define the experimental conditions, it is highly likely that both the covariate and the experimental conditions will measure the same entity. Consequently, the covariate will be related to the treatment, despite the fact that the covariate is obtained before the experimental manipulation. The other covariate measures suggested also should be related to the covariate, but as they are measured after the experimental manipulation and violate conventional design practice, perhaps this is more obvious.

Nevertheless, even with a relation between the covariate and the experimental conditions, if heterogeneous regression across the two groups is employed, the integrity of the separate covariate distributions is maintained and dependent variable adjustments across the two groups are independent. A heterogeneous regression ANCOVA could be applied to the data obtained from the experiment on the basis of the experimental design GLM equation (8.1), where $\beta_j Z_{ij}$ represents the heterogeneous regression across the p levels of Factor A, the types of encoding processing.

As the covariate and experimental conditions are not orthogonal, and because covariation of encoding conditions and covariate in this hypothetical experiment results in multicollinearity, the ANCOVA should be implemented by a hierarchical analysis, i.e. there should be a specific order of extraction of variance attributable to terms in the linear model.

In hierarchical analysis 1, the dependent variable variance due to the encoding manipulation (α_j) is extracted first. When this is done, the estimate of the effect of the experimental conditions will equal that which would be obtained with a conventional ANOVA. If the variance due to the covariate is extracted next, using heterogeneous regression, only that variance which is uniquely attributable to the covariate will be extracted. As all of the dependent variable variance associated with α_j has been extracted already, only variance independent of the experimental conditions remains. Therefore, any part of the remaining dependent variable variance attributed to the covariate will be independent of the experimental conditions.

However, in hierarchical analysis 2, if the dependent variable variance attributable to the covariate on the basis of a heterogeneous regression is extracted first, variance that could have been attributed to the experimental conditions will be removed. Therefore, the variance subsequently attributed to the experimental conditions will be found to be less than that obtained when the experimental condition variance is extracted first, the difference being a function of the degree of relationship between the experimental conditions and the covariate. In most experiments this form of analysis would not be implemented, due to a primary interest in the effect of the experimental conditions. However, it does suggest another way of analysing the experimental data (see Section 8.8.2).

8.8 Other alternatives

8.8.1 Stratification (blocking)

Rather than a statistical operation, stratification is a modification to the design of the study, which necessitates a change in the experimental design GLM. The strategy employed is to allocate subjects to groups defined by certain ranges of the covariate scores. This creates another factor in the study design, with the same number of levels as the number of newly defined groups. This modification also changes the ANCOVA into an ANOVA: the dependent variable scores are input to a conventional ANOVA on the basis of the new experimental design GLM. For example, the GLM equation for the independent measures, single covariate, single factor design, described by equation (8.1), after stratification would be described by equation (8.13),

$$Y_{ijk} = \mu + \alpha_j + \beta_k + (\alpha\beta)_{jk} + \varepsilon_{ijk} \qquad (8.13)$$

where β_k is the new factor with q levels, from 1 to k. The q levels of β_k represent the defined ranges of the covariate values (see Cochran, 1957; Elashoff, 1969; Kirk, 1995; Maxwell & Delaney, 1990; Winer et al., 1991).

Ideally, the decision to employ this sort of analysis would be taken before subjects are recruited to the experiment. This would enable the appropriate allocation procedures to be implemented (Maxwell & Delaney, 1990). The major advantage conferred by stratification is that no assumptions are made about the form of the relationship between the treatments and the covariate. Consequently, all of the problems unique to ANCOVA are avoided.

Nevertheless, as Maxwell and Delaney (1990) describe, when ANCOVA assumptions are tenable, there are disadvantages of stratification compared with ANCOVA. First, information is lost in the change from the covariate measurement scale to the categorical stratification measurement scale.

The consequence is that variance accommodated by the covariate in ANCOVA cannot be accommodated by the stratified covariate. Second, while ANCOVA typically accommodates only linear trend, with stratification all possible trends, such as linear, quadratic, cubic, etc., are accommodated: another trend component with each level of the new factor. The consequence is that where ANCOVA devotes only one df to the covariate, stratification devotes $(q - 1)$ dfs. Unfortunately, this is not economical, as the linear trend component accommodates the vast majority of the variance in most psychological data. Both of these stratification features result in a loss of analysis power in comparison with ANCOVA. Third, the increase in the number of experimental conditions reduces considerably the dfs associated with the error term. The largest reduction is due to the dfs associated with the most complex or highest order interaction involving the covariate stratification factor. This interaction provides the approximation to the ANCOVA capability of assessing experimental effects at any value of the covariate. Generally, the reduction in error term dfs results in higher error term estimates and so again, less powerful F-tests in comparison with ANCOVA.

Given the preceding points, a stratified analysis is most likely to be applied when one or more ANCOVA assumptions are untenable. As the untenability of ANCOVA assumptions is likely to be determined only after the experiment has been completed and the data analysed, a major difficulty with stratification is that the distribution of subjects' covariate scores may not allow convenient allocation to useful covariate range groups to conform to conventional ANOVA design requirements. In other words, without discarding data, which itself raises problematic issues, it is likely that this approach will require analysis of unbalanced designs. Therefore, when an ANCOVA design is in the planning stage, it would seem wise to consider that all assumptions may not be tenable and carry out the experiment such that the data obtained are compatible with the requirements of a stratification analysis.

8.8.2   Replacing the experimental conditions with the covariate

In some situations of multicollinearity caused by covariate and treatment covariation, as when both variables measure the same entity, it may be beneficial to modify the experimental conception by dropping the terms representing the correlated experimental conditions (factors) from the experimental design GLM and employ only the covariate (and any non-correlated factors) to predict dependent variable scores. Certainly, one advantage enjoyed by the covariate is measurement on a ratio or interval scale (although sometimes this is stretched to an ordinal scale), in contrast to the categorical scale on which the factor levels are measured. An analysis based on a new linear model may be carried out by dropping the correlated factor and its interactions, and introducing terms to represent covariate interactions with other variables. Naturally, with a different GLM fitted to the data, consideration would need to be given to the suitability of the new hypotheses tested and the conclusions that could be drawn from their rejection or support. (See Cohen & Cohen, 1983; Pedhazur, 1997, and McCullagh & Nelder, 1989, regarding the interpretation of categorical and quantitative variable interactions.)

8.9   The role of ANCOVA

Although heterogeneous regression ANCOVA is only an extension of traditional ANCOVA, its application to real problems pushes to the foreground a particularly important issue: the nature of the relationship between the covariate and the dependent variable. Smith (1957) pointed out that a direct causal link between covariate and dependent variable is not a necessary requirement in traditional ANCOVA, but without knowledge of the causal effects, the interpretation of adjusted means is hazardous. In heterogeneous regression this state of affairs would appear to be even more pronounced, due to the potential increase in causal routes provided by the separate regressions. Therefore, the price of achieving an accurate interpretation of effects in heterogeneous regression ANCOVA is a more extensive theoretical consideration of the relationship between the covariate and the dependent variable under the different experimental conditions than needs to be undertaken when traditional ANCOVA is employed.

With the emphasis on a GLM approach to heterogeneous ANCOVA, the similarities between the theoretical description of causality required of the linear model and the causality which is examined usually with structural equation models (Bentler, 1980), such as LISREL (e.g. Joreskog & Sorbom, 1993) becomes more apparent (also see Cohen & Cohen, 1983; Pedhazur, 1997). It is for these reasons that heterogeneous regression should be regarded as a means by which the validity of theoretical accounts can be further assessed and not as a cheap way to circumvent research effort or repair faulty research designs.

9 FURTHER ISSUES IN ANOVA AND ANCOVA

9.1 Power

When all assumptions are valid, ANOVA provides the most powerful test of the omnibus null hypothesis. When all the additional assumptions of ANCOVA are valid and the covariates employed are correlated with the dependent variable (e.g. Cochran, 1957), ANCOVA provides an even more powerful test of the omnibus null hypothesis concerning the experimental conditions.

The credit for making clear the importance of power analysis is due to Cohen (e.g. 1969, 1988). However, Welkowitz, Ewen and Cohen (1991) have presented a slightly simpler account that employs a very accurate approximation technique to determine analysis power (also see Howell, 1997). The discussion of power presented here is based on the latter account.

Power can be defined in a variety of equivalent ways. For example, the power of an analysis is the probability that it will detect an effect in the sample data, at the chosen significance level, when this effect exists in the population(s). Alternatively, power is the probability of rejecting a false null hypothesis. As a Type 2 error (β) is the probability of not detecting an effect, power also may be defined as $1 - \beta$.

ANOVA power is increased by increases in the probability of a Type 1 error, the size of the effect to be detected and the sample size. In related measures designs, the degree of correlation between the related measures also influences power.

Type 1 error is equal to the significance level chosen: a less rigorous significance level will increase analysis power – the likelihood of detecting an effect. The size of the effect is the difference between the means of the different experimental condition sample distributions divided by the (homogeneous) standard deviation. Effect size increases with greater differences between the experimental condition means (provided the standard deviation does not increase), or with a smaller standard deviation (provided the differences between the experimental condition means do not decrease). Of course, the (homogeneous) standard deviation is the square root of the ANOVA MSe, so two aspects of the experimental data are encompassed by effect size: the differences between experimental condition means and the error variance.

Differences between experimental condition means and error variance are set by nature and not the experimenter, although error variance may be constrained by the implementation of appropriate experimental controls. The Type 1 error tolerated in an experiment is bound by the significance level convention and the undesirability of increasing Type 1 error beyond 0.05. Therefore, of the three variables affecting ANOVA power, the most easily manipulated is sample size, and so most attempts to increase ANOVA power have involved increasing the size of the sample.

9.1.1 Optimal experimental designs

Rather than just include more and more subjects in experiments to increase analysis power, McClelland (1997) argues that psychologists should follow the lead of researchers in other disciplines by optimizing experimental designs to increase the power of the important experimental comparisons. McClelland describes how reducing the variance of parameter estimates increases analysis power. Increasing the sample size, decreasing the error variance, or increasing the variance of the independent variables all reduce parameter estimate variance and increment the power of analysis. As the variance of the independent variables is affected by varying the number of subjects allocated to the different experimental conditions, McClelland advocates this as a method of optimizing the experimental design to increase the power of the important experimental comparisons. Although different numbers of subjects would need to be allocated to different experimental conditions to obtain the maximum power for each comparison, it is also possible to obtain slightly less powerful optimal solutions for one or more comparisons.

McClelland also discusses some of the reasons why researchers have persevered with non-optimal designs that employ equal numbers of subjects per experimental condition (i.e. balanced data). One reason for balanced data is to minimize the affect of statistical assumption violations. However, in contrast to the research presented in Chapter 7, McClelland claims that balanced data makes little difference to the robustness of ANOVA and has a high power cost in comparison to applying an unbalanced optimum design. Instead, McClelland suggests checks for assumption violations and remedy by data transformation, or the adoption of modern robust comparison methods (see below) when assumption violations are detected. The other two reasons for employing balanced data dismissed by McClelland are: the ease of calculation with balanced data and the interpretation of parameter estimates. As these two matters are related, they will be considered together. McClelland claims that computer based statistical calculation has made the ease of calculation with balanced data largely irrelevant. Nevertheless, there are a number of different ways to implement ANOVA. With balanced data in factorial experiments, factors and their interactions are orthogonal, and so the same variance estimates are obtained irrespective of the order in which the variance is attributed. However, with unbalanced data, factors and their interactions are not necessarily orthogonal, and so appropriate analysis techniques must be employed to obtain accurate estimates of the variance due to the factors and their interactions. Essentially, with unbalanced data, reparameterization and estimable function techniques can provide parameter estimates that are ambiguous and so provide ambiguous hypothesis tests, and this problem is compounded by the opacity of much statistical software (Searle, 1987). Therefore, while statistical software may ease calculation with unbalanced data, it also may exacerbate the serious problem of accurately interpreting the parameter estimates.

Optimizing experimental designs by allocating different numbers of subjects to different experimental conditions to increase the power of the comparisons is certainly a very useful approach. However, even from the brief presentation above, it is obvious this approach is not without its drawbacks. Clearly, considerable thought needs to be given to the pros and cons of this type of experimental design, particularly in the light of the typical data obtained in the area under study.

9.1.2 Normality violations

Although most sources report ANOVA (and so ANCOVA) as being robust with respect to violations of the normality assumption (see Chapter 7), Wilcox (e.g. 1995; 1998a) has argued strongly that even small deviations from normality can result in ANOVA with low power. Wilcox identifies skewed or leptokurtic distributions as being responsible for low analysis power. (A distribution exhibiting positive kurtosis may be labelled a leptokurtic distribution, i.e. it possesses longer or thicker tails than the normal distribution: see De Carlo, 1997 for discussion of kurtosis.) The reason for lower power is that skewed and/ or leptokurtic distributions are more likely to contain outliers (extreme scores) than normal distributions and these outliers can increase the sample variance estimates substantially. Wilcox also argues that large reductions in analysis power can occur even when the deviation of the skewed and/or leptokurtic distribution from normal is small enough to go undetected by distribution normality checks such as the Kolmogorov–Smirnov test or the Lilliefors test (see Chapter 7). Consequently, Wilcox promotes the application of modern robust analysis techniques (e.g. Wilcox, 1997, 1998b) as a way of maintaining high analysis power.

Beyond simple single df t-test like comparisons, regression (of which ANOVA and ANCOVA are special instances) presents a number of problems for modern robust methods. Unfortunately, for regression and other types of analysis, there is no single best robust method. There are a variety of robust methods, all of which perform differently under different conditions. Therefore, selecting a robust method is not necessarily simple and the use of different robust methods across laboratories, studies or experiments reduces the comparability of results.

Wilcox's examples demonstrate that small skewed and/or leptokurtic deviations from a normal distribution can substantially reduce analysis power. However, Wilcox is at odds with the results of the majority of studies investigating the consequences of normality violations for ANOVA F-tests reported in Chapter 7. Ideally, some resolution of these differences, which also provides account of the circumstances under which ANOVA F-tests are robust in the face of deviations from normality, will be forthcoming.

9.1.3   Main effects and interactions

In a two factor experiment, at least three ANOVA F-tests are carried out. An F-test is carried out to assess each factor main effect and another assesses the interaction between the two factors.

In fully independent factorial designs, a single error term is employed in all three F-tests. Therefore, if the same differences between pertinent means are assumed for the three F-test comparisons, then the effect sizes across each of the three F-tests will be equal. Similarly, if all F-tests are assessed at the same significance level, then the Type 2 error for each of the three F-tests will be equal too. However, a major feature of the experimental data that always affects F-test power is the size of the sample involved in each F-test. Table 9.1 outlines a fully independent two factor (2×3) design, with 8 subjects in each of the 6 conditions.

When the main effect of Factor A is assessed, the dependent variable measures of 24 subjects (i.e. $a_1 - 8 + 8 + 8$) are compared with the dependent variable measures of the other 24 subjects (i.e. $a_2 - 8 + 8 + 8$). When the main effect of Factor B is assessed, the dependent variable measures of three groups of 16 subjects are compared (i.e. $b_1 - 8 + 8$, $b_2 - 8 + 8$, $b_3 - 8 + 8$). When the Factor $A \times$ Factor B interaction effect is assessed, the dependent variable measures of six groups of 8 subjects are compared. Given the assumptions made above, it is clear that the Factor A main effect F-test is most powerful, next most powerful is the Factor B main effect F-test and least powerful is the F-test of the $A \times B$ interaction.

The relative differences between the power of each of the F-tests varies with the number of levels of each factor and the total number of subjects allocated. Nevertheless, irrespective of whether the experimental design is fully independent, fully related or mixed, when all other influences on power are equal, the powers of the omnibus F-tests always follow the same rank order. First is the main effect of the factor with fewest levels, next is the main effect of the factor with most levels and last is the F-test of the interaction effect. Knowledge of this general pattern of factorial ANOVA F-test power should be used to combat the tendency to treat all omnibus ANOVA F-tests as if they operated at the same power and provide an appropriate basis for drawing conclusions about effect size.

Table 9.1   A fully independent two factor (2×3) design outline with eight subjects per condition

Level of Factor A	a_1			a_2		
Level of Factor B	b_1	b_2	b_3	b_1	b_2	b_3
N	8	8	8	8	8	8

9.2   Error rate and the omnibus F-tests

In Chapter 2, it was mentioned that the likelihood of obtaining a significant effect by chance increases as the number of statistical tests carried out on a data set increases. Whereas this Type 1 error increases with the number of t-tests carried out, ANOVA F-tests simultaneously examine for differences between any number of conditions while holding the Type 1 error at the chosen significance level. The probability of at least one Type 1 error occurring when a number of tests are carried out is given by

$$\text{Probability of at least one Type 1 error} = 1 - (1 - \alpha)^c \qquad (9.1)$$

where α is the significance level and c is the number of tests or comparisons carried out. However, equation (9.1) is based on the assumption that all of the tests carried out are orthogonal and the probability of at least one Type 1 error occurring will be overestimated when this condition is not met.

Nevertheless, in a two factor experiment, three (orthogonal) omnibus ANOVA F-tests are routinely carried out. This begs the question, why is the likelihood of obtaining a significant effect by chance not increased in these circumstances? The short answer to this is that in a two factor experiment where any three ANOVA F-tests are carried out, the likelihood of obtaining a significant effect by chance is increased. In fact, the probability of at least one Type 1 error occurring when three omnibus F-tests are carried out in a balanced two factor design is

$$= 1 - (1 - 0.05)^3$$

$$= 1 - (0.857)$$

$$= 0.143$$

Therefore, the true probability of a Type 1 error occurring when three omnibus F-tests are carried out (when Type 1 error rate is set at 0.05 for each test) is not 0.05, but 0.143. The true probability has to be calculated because the probabilities reported by statistical software or presented in tables assume only one test is carried out. In the same way that the true Type 1 error rate can be calculated from the nominal p-values, so, conversely, the nominal Type 1 error rate reflecting a true Type 1 error rate can be calculated. The nominal Type 1 error rate reflecting a true Type 1 error rate is given by

$$1 - \sqrt[c]{(1 - \alpha)} \qquad (9.2)$$

where again α is the significance level and c is the number of comparisons carried out. Applying equation (9.2) to the three omnibus F-test situation provides

$$1 - \sqrt[3]{(1 - 0.05)} = 1 - 0.983$$

$$= 0.017$$

Therefore, when three comparisons are applied, the nominal Type 1 error rate of 0.017 is required to achieve a true Type 1 error rate 0.05. As the significance level and the Type 1 error always are equivalent, this means setting the nominal significance level at 0.017 per test will provide tests operating at the 0.05 level of significance with a true Type 1 error rate of 0.05.

The fact that no such adjustments are made to the omnibus F-test p-values reported for each of the main and interaction effects indicates that a *familywise* error rate strategy is applied. Essentially, Type 1 error rate may be conceived as applying to each and every test (*testwise* Type 1 error rate) or to each family of tests (*familywise* Type 1 error rate), or to each experiment (*experimentwise* Type 1 error rate). If Type 1 error rate is controlled for each test separately, then for each test the unadjusted p-values apply. If Type 1 error rate is controlled for each family of tests, then each of the main and interaction effects is considered a family and control is exerted over the number of tests carried out per family. If Type 1 error rate is controlled for the whole experiment, then control is exerted over the total number of tests carried out in the analysis of the whole experiment. Of course, in single factor studies, *familywise* and *experimentwise* error rate are equivalent.

9.3 Error rate and multiple comparisons

The overview of multiple comparison tests presented here is best considered as a primer for further reading on this topic. The aim is to introduce the purpose of multiple comparison tests and to consider some of the issues that determine the type of multiple comparison tests employed. The approach is intentionally discussive and so, either the references or other sources must be consulted to obtain formulae and implementation procedures.

A significant omnibus ANOVA F-test indicates that of the experimental means compared, at least one differs significantly from another. Usually, the next step is to determine exactly where the significant difference or differences are located. In single factor studies, this amounts to determining which experimental condition means differ significantly from which other experimental condition means. For example, in a single factor study involving four experimental conditions, A, B, C and D, there may be interest in whether A and B differ significantly, whether B and C differ significantly and whether C and D differ significantly. Of course, other comparisons may be of interest and these may include comparisons of the average performance over two experimental conditions, e.g. $(A + B)/2$ cf. $(C + D)/2$. Clearly, for any experiment it is likely that comparisons between several pairs of experimental condition means or averages over experimental condition means will be necessary. Tests that accommodate comparisons of both experimental condition means and averages over experimental condition means are termed "multiple comparison tests". Tests which only compare pairs of experimental condition means are called "pairwise comparison tests".

As a main effect in a factorial study is similar to a significant effect in a single factor study, both sorts of effect can be analysed in a similar manner. Usually interaction effects are analysed in terms of simple effects (see Chapter 3). As simple effects analysis treats a factorial design as if it were a set of single factor analyses, a significant simple effect can be analysed as if it were a significant effect in a single factor study.

Although there are a number of excellent accounts of multiple comparisons tests (e.g. Hays, 1994; Howell, 1997; Keppel, 1991; Kirk, 1994, 1995; Toothaker, 1993), they can appear complicated. This is due to the discussion of such issues as comparison orthogonality, control of Type 1 error rate, whether comparisons were planned (*a priori*) or unplanned (*a posteriori*) and to the large number of multiple comparison tests available. A variety of different views on which multiple comparison test is appropriate in which circumstances also can complicate the choice of test.

Nevertheless, some simplification is provided by the fact that orthogonality should not influence which experimental condition means are compared, nor the choice of test. Orthogonality really need only come into consideration if the variance explained by the pertinent omnibus F-test and the variance explained by the multiple comparisons are tracked. As the omnibus F-test assesses the total variance due to any set of orthogonal contrasts, it is possible for non-orthogonal multiple comparisons to appear to accommodate more variance than the omnibus F-test. Of course, this is false and is due to variance involved in one non-orthogonal comparison also being involved in one or more other non-orthogonal comparisons.

Planned comparisons are those theoretically motivated and intended from the inception of the experiment. In fact, it is perfectly legitimate to carry out any planned comparisons directly, without the intercession of an ANOVA omnibus F-test. However, when the assumption of homogeneous error variance is tenable, the ANOVA MSe provides its best estimate. Therefore, the error variance estimate employed in the multiple comparison tests should be based on the ANOVA MSe. Not only is this the best estimate, but the extra dfs associated with the ANOVA MSe (cf. the dfs associated with the error estimate based on the specific experimental conditions being compared) also increases the power of the multiple comparison tests. When the assumption of homogeneous error variance is not tenable, the error variance estimated from the specific conditions being compared may be homogeneous, and consequently may provide more powerful multiple comparison tests than those based on the heterogeneous ANOVA MSe. As the experiment is designed specifically to test the hypotheses implicit in the planned comparisons, the current convention is to assess planned comparisons (of which there should be relatively few) at the nominal significance levels, i.e. without controlling Type 1 error rate.

Unplanned comparisons are data driven and are suggested by the experimental results. Data snooping, a slightly pejorative term, is applied when experimental data is investigated using a number of unplanned comparisons. In contrast to planned comparisons, current convention dictates that a pertinent significant omnibus F-test is required before embarking on unplanned comparisons. Again, provided the assumption of homogeneous error variance is tenable, the error variance estimate employed in the multiple comparison tests should be based on the ANOVA MSe, as this is the best estimate of error variance and provides more powerful multiple comparison tests. Whenever unplanned comparisons are applied, Type 1 error rate is controlled. Generally, unplanned multiple comparison tests control the *familywise* error rate and it is the way they try to control this Type 1 error rate that distinguishes the various multiple comparison tests.

9.4   The role of the omnibus *F*-test

It has been said already that planned comparisons can be applied directly, without reference to any omnibus *F*-test. This is not because a significant multiple comparison test guarantees a significant omnibus *F*-test, or vice versa. In fact, it is possible to obtain significance with a multiple comparison test, but not with the omnibus *F*-test. For example, consider an omnibus *F*-test that compares four experimental condition means (*A, B, C* and *D*) by assessing the three orthogonal contrasts. If mean *A* is greater than *B*, which equals *C* and *D*, then the omnibus *F*-test assesses the effect (i.e. the differences between means) averaged over the three orthogonal contrasts (dfs), and this may not be significant. However, with planned multiple comparisons, it is possible to draw comparisons only between particular experimental condition means. Therefore, if a particular comparison specifically compared the *A* experimental condition mean with another experimental condition mean (or even the average of the other experimental condition means) is more likely to be significant than the omnibus *F*-test. As (1) the hypotheses tested by omnibus *F*-tests are not equivalent to those tested by multiple comparison tests, there is no statistical reason why multiple comparison tests may not be applied irrespective of the omnibus *F*-tests, (2) significant differences may be missed by the omnibus *F*-test but detected by a multiple comparison test and (3) even when significant omnibus *F*-tests are obtained, usually multiple comparison tests still are required to disambiguate the results. These features of data analysis have caused some authors (e.g. Howell, 1997; O'Brien, 1983; Rosnow & Rosenthal, 1989) to ask the question, why carry out ANOVA omnibus *F*-tests?

A short and simple answer to this question is provided by (1) above – different hypotheses are tested by omnibus *F*-tests and multiple comparison tests. This is especially so with interactions. As O'Brien (1983) states, the procedures used to analyse experimental data should depend upon what the experimenter wants to know and the Type 1 error rate to be tolerated. An omnibus *F*-test is appropriate when the experimenter wants to know if there are any differences between the experimental condition means (the null hypothesis tested is that all experimental condition means are equal). However, if the experimenter only wants to know about specific differences between particular experimental condition means, then carrying out planned or unplanned comparisons directly may be an appropriate strategy. Nevertheless, if Type 1 error is to be controlled and the possibility of observing unpredicted differences is to be maintained, then applying an ANOVA omnibus F-test is a better strategy than conducting planned and unplanned comparisons directly to compare any/all differences between experimental condition means.

Another way to answer this question would be in terms of the data analysis perspective. From the GLM perspective, an overall F-test reveals if the complete GLM significantly predicts the dependent variable scores. In factorial studies, the omnibus F-tests reveal whether particular components of the GLM make significant contributions to this prediction. If the overall F-test and the omnibus F-tests in factorial studies indicate significant prediction, then further analyses are carried out to identify how the particular component elements manifest the prediction. In short, the GLM perspective employs overall and omnibus F-tests as part of a coherent data analysis strategy that accommodates ANOVA, ANCOVA and regression. If however, the data analysis perspective is solely in terms of where significant differences lie, then conducting planned and/or unplanned comparisons directly may be appropriate. This sort of strategy may seem simpler and easier at first, but its piecemeal approach also can be the source of a great deal of mistakes and confusion in the control of Type 1 error. As the coherent rationale underlying the application of planned and/or unplanned comparisons directly to experimental data actually is achieved by implicit reference to the GLM, it seems most sensible to make this explicit from the start.

REFERENCES

Atiqullah, M. (1964). The robustness of the covariance analysis of a one-way classification. *Biometrika, 49*, 83–92.

Bentler, P.M. (1980). Multivariate analysis with latent variables: causal modelling. *Annual Review of Psychology, 31*, 419–456.

Bingham, C. & Fienberg, S.E. (1982). Textbook analysis of covariance – is it correct? *Biometrics, 38*, 747–753.

Bollen, K.A. (1989). *Structural Equations with Latent Variables.* New York: Wiley.

Box, G.E.P. (1954). Some theorems on quadratic forms applied in the study of analysis of variance problems: II. Effects of inequality of variance and of correlation between errors in the two-way classification. *Annals of Mathematical Statistics, 25*, 484–498.

Box, G.E.P. & Jenkins, G.M. (1976). *Time Series Analysis: Forecasting and Control.* San Francisco, CA: Holden-Day.

Bradley, J.V. (1978). Robustness? *British Journal of Mathematical and Statistical Psychology, 31*, 144–152.

Clinch, J.J & Keselman, H.J. (1982). Parametric alternatives to the analysis of variance. *Journal of Educational Statistics, 7*, 207–214.

Cochran, W.G. (1957). Analysis of covariance: its nature and uses. *Biometrics 13*, 261–281.

Cohen, J. (1969). *Statistical power analysis for the behavioral sciences.* Hillsdale, NJ: LEA.

Cohen, J. (1988). *Statistical power analysis for the behavioral sciences.* 2nd edition. Hillsdale, NJ: LEA.

Cohen, J. & Cohen, P. (1983). *Applied Multiple Regression/Correlation Analysis for the Behavioural Sciences.* 2nd edition. Hillsdale, NJ: LEA.

Collier, R.O. and Hummel, T.J. (1977). *Experimental Design and Interpretation.* Berkeley, CA: McCutchan.

Cook, R.D. & Weisberg, S. (1982). *Residuals and Influence in Regression.* New York: Chapman & Hall.

Cook, R.D. & Weisberg, S. (1983). Diagnostics for heteroscedasticity in regression. *Biometrika, 70*, 1–10.

Cox, D.R. & McCullagh, P. (1982). Some aspects of analysis of covariance. *Biometrics 38*, 541–561.

Daniel, C. & Wood, F.S. (1980). *Fitting Equations to Data.* 2nd edition. New York: Chapman & Hall.

Darlington, R.B. (1968). Multiple regression in psychological research. *Psychological Bulletin, 69*, 161–182.

Davidson, M.L. (1972). Univariate versus multivariate tests in repeated measures experiments. *Psychological Bulletin 77*, 446–452.

De Carlo, L.T. (1997). On the meaning and use of kurtosis. *Psychological Methods, 2*, 292–307.

Donner, A. & Koval, J.J. (1980). The estimation of the intraclass correlation in the analysis of family data. *Biometrics, 36*, 19–25.

Draper, N.R. & Smith, H. (1998). *Applied Regression Analysis*. 3rd edition. New York: Wiley.

Edgeworth, F.Y. (1886). Progressive means. *Journal of the Royal Statistical Society, 49*, 469–475.

Elashoff, J.D. (1969). Analysis of covariance: a delicate instrument. *American Educational Research Journal, 6*, 383–401.

Evans, S.H. & Anastasio, E.J. (1968). Misuse of analysis of covariance when treatment effect and covariate are confounded. *Psychological Bulletin, 69*, 225–234.

Fisher, R.A. (1924). International Mathematical Conference. Toronto.

Fisher, R.A. (1932). *Statistical Methods for Research Workers*. Edinburgh: Oliver & Boyd.

Fisher, R.A. (1935). *The Design of Experiments*. Edinburgh: Oliver & Boyd.

Galton, F. (1886). Regression toward mediocrity in hereditary stature. *Journal of the Anthropological Institute, 15*, 246–263.

Galton, F. (1888). Co-relations and their measurement, chiefly from anthropometric data. *Proceedings of the Royal Society, 15*, 135–145.

Geisser, S. & Greenhouse, S.W. (1958). An extension of Box's results on the use of the *F* distribution in multivariate analysis. *Annals of Mathematical Statistics, 29*, 885–891.

Glass, G.V., Peckham, P.D. & Sanders, J.R. (1972). Consequences of failure to meet assumptions underlying the fixed effects analysis of variance and covariance. *Review of Educational Research, 42*, 237–288.

Gordon, R.A. (1968). Issues in multiple regression. *American Journal of Sociology, 73*, 592–616.

Gosset, W.S. (1908). The probable error of the mean. *Biometrika, 6*, 1–25.

Green, S.B., Marquis, J.G., Hershberger, S.L., Thompson, M.S. & McCollam, K.M. (1999). The overparameterized analysis of variance model. *Psychological Methods, 4*, 214–233.

Hamilton, B.L. (1976). A Monte Carlo test of the robustness of parametric and nonparametric analysis of covariance against unequal regression slopes. *Journal of the American Statistical Association, 71*, 864–869.

Hand, D.H. & Crowder, M. (1996). *Practical Longitudinal Data Analysis*. London: Chapman & Hall.

Hand, D.J. & Taylor, C.C. (1987). *Multivariate Analysis of Variance and Repeated Measures: A Practical Approach for Behavioural Scientists*. London: Chapman & Hall.

Hays, W.L. (1994). *Statistics*. 5th edition. Fort Worth, TX: Harcourt Brace.

Hollingsworth, H.H. (1976). An analytical investigation of the robustness and power of ANCOVA with the presence of heterogeneous regression slopes. Paper presented at the *Annual Meeting of the American Educational Research Association*, Washington, DC.

Howell, D.C. (1997). *Statistical Methods for Psychology*. 4th edition. Belmont, CA: Duxbury/Wadsworth.

Huitema, B.E. (1980). *The Analysis of Covariance and Alternatives*. New York: Wiley.

Huynh, H. & Feldt, L.S. (1976). Estimation of the Box correction for degrees of freedom from sample data in randomized block and split-plot designs. *Journal of Educational Statistics, 1*, 69–82.

Joreskog, K.G. and Sorbom, D. (1993). *LISREL 8: Structural Equation Modelling with the SIMPLIS command language*. Hillsdale, NJ: LEA.

Judd, C.M. & McClelland, G.H. (1989). *Data Analysis: A Model-comparison Approach*. San Diego, CA: Harcourt Brace Jovanovich.

Kempthorne, O. (1980). The term design matrix. *The American Statistician, 34*, 249.

Kenny, D.A. & Judd, C.M. (1986). Consequences of violating the independence assumption in analysis of variance. *Psychological Bulletin*, *99*, 422–431.

Kendall, M.G. (1948). *The Advanced Theory of Statistics*. Volume 2. London: Charles Griffin & Company.

Keppel, G. (1991). *Design and Analysis: A Researcher's Handbook*. 3rd edition. Englewood Cliffs, NJ: Prentice Hall.

Keppel, G. & Zedeck, S. (1989). *Data Analysis for Research Designs: Analysis of Variance and Multiple Regression/Correlation Approaches*. New York: Freeman.

Keselman, J.C., Lix, L.M. & Keselman, H.J. (1996). The analysis of repeated measurments: a quantitative research synthesis. *British Journal of Mathematical & Statistical Psychology*, *49*, 275–298.

Kirby, K.N. (1993). *Advanced Data Analysis with SYSTAT*. New York: Van Nostrand Reinhold.

Kirk, R.E. (1968). *Experimental Design: Procedures for the Behavioural Sciences*. Monterey, CA: Brookes/Cole.

Kirk, R.E. (1982). *Experimental Design: Procedures for the Behavioural Sciences*. 2nd edition. Monterey, CA: Brookes/Cole.

Kirk, R.E. (1994). Choosing a multiple comparison procedure. In B. Thompson (ed.), *Advances in Social Science Methodology*. New York: Marcel Dekker.

Kirk, R.E. (1995). *Experimental Design: Procedures for the Behavioural Sciences*. 3rd edition. Pacific Grove, CA: Brookes/Cole.

Kmenta, J. (1971). *Elements of Econometrics*. New York: Macmillan.

Lane, P.W. & Nelder, J.A. (1982). Analysis of covariance and standardization as instances of prediction. *Biometrics*, *38*, 613–621.

Lilliefors, H.W. (1967). On the Kolmogrov–Smirnov test for normality with mean and variance unknown. *Journal of the American Statistical Association*, *62*, 399–402.

Lovie, A.D. (1991). A short history of statistics in twentieth century psychology. In P. Lovie & A.D. Lovie (eds), *New Developments in Statistics for Psychology and the Social Sciences*. London: British Psychological Society and Routledge.

Lovie, P. (1991). Regression diagnostics: a rough guide to safer regression. In P. Lovie & A.D. Lovie (eds), *New Developments in Statistics for Psychology and the Social Sciences*. London: Routledge/BPS.

MacRae, A.W. (1995). Descriptive and inferential statistics. In A.M. Coleman (ed.), *Psychological Research Methods and Statistics*. London: Longman.

Maxwell, S.E. & Delaney, H.D. (1990). *Designing Experiments and Analysing Data*. Wadsworth: Belmont, CA.

Maxwell, S.E., Delaney, H.D. & Manheimer, J.M. (1985). ANOVA of residuals and ANCOVA: correcting an illusion by using model comparisons and graphs. *Journal of Educational Statistics*, *10*, 197–209.

McClelland, G.H. (1997). Optimal Design in Psychological Research. *Psychological Methods*, *2*, 3–19.

McCullagh, P. & Nelder, J.A. (1989). *Generalised Linear Models*. 2nd edition. London: Chapman & Hall.

Mitchell, J. (1986). Measurement scales and statistics: a clash of paradigms. *Psychological Bulletin*, *100*, 398–407.

Montgomery, D.C. & Peck, E.A. (1982). *Introduction to Linear Regression Analysis*. New York: Wiley.

Mosteller, F. & Tukey, J.W. (1977). *Data Analysis and Regression*. New York: Addison-Wesley.

Nelder, J.A. (1977). A reformulation of linear models. *Journal of the Royal Statistical Society, Series A 140*, 48–77.

Neter, J., Wasserman, W. & Kutner, M.H. (1990). *Applied Linear Statistical Models: Regression, Analysis of Variance and Experimental Designs.* 3rd edition. Homewood, IL: Irwin Inc.

Norusis, M.J. (1985). *SPSS^X Advanced Statistics Guide.* Chicago, IL: SPSS Inc.

Norusis, M.J. (1990). *SPSS/PC+ Statistics^{TM} 4.0.* Chicago, IL: SPSS Inc.

O'Brien, P.C. (1983). The appropriateness of analysis of variance and multiple comparison procedures. *Biometrika, 39,* 787–788.

O'Brien, R.G. & Kaiser, M.K. (1985). MANOVA method for analysing repeated measures designs: an extensive primer. *Psychological Bulletin, 97,* 316–333.

Overall, J.E. & Woodward, J.A. (1977). Nonrandom assignment and the analysis of covariance. *Psychological Bulletin, 84,* 588–594.

Pearson, K. (1896). Regression, heredity and panmixia. *Philosophical Transactions of the Royal Society,* Series A, *187,* 253–267.

Pedhazur, E.J. (1997). *Multiple Regression in Behavioural Research.* 3rd edition. Fort Worth, TX: Harcourt Brace.

Permutt, T. (1990). Testing for imbalance of covariates in controlled experiments. *Statistics in Medicine, 9,* 1455–1462.

Plackett, R.L. (1972). Studies in the history of probability and statistics. XXIX. The discovery of the method of least squares. *Biometrica, 59,* 239–251.

Rao, C.R. (1965). *Linear Statistical Inference and Its Applications.* New York: Wiley.

Rogosa, D.R. (1980). Comparing non-parallel regression lines. *Psychological Bulletin, 88,* 307–321.

Rose, S. (1992). *The Making of Memory.* London: Bantam Press.

Rosnow, R.L. & Rosenthal, R. (1989). Statistical procedures and the justification of knowledge in psychological science. *American Psychologist, 44,* 1276–1284.

Rubin, D.B. (1977). Assignment to treatment group on the basis of a covariate. *Journal of Educational Statistics, 2,* 1–26.

Rutherford, A. (1992). Alternatives to traditional analysis of covariance. *British Journal of Mathematical and Statistical Psychology, 45,* 197–223.

Searle, S.R. (1979). Alternative covariance models for the 2-way crossed classification. *Communications in Statistics, A8,* 799–818.

Searle, S.R. (1987). *Linear Models for Unbalanced Data.* New York: Wiley.

Searle, S.R. (1997). *Linear Models.* New York: Wiley.

Seber, G.A.F. (1977). *Linear Regression Analysis.* New York: Wiley.

Senn, S.J. (1989). Covariate imbalance and random allocation in clinical trials. *Statistics in Medicine, 8,* 467–475.

Shapiro, S.S. & Wilk, M.B. (1965). An analysis of variance test for normality (complete samples). *Biometrika, 52,* 591–611.

Shirley, E.A.C. & Newnham, P. (1984). The choice between analysis of variance and analysis of covariance with special reference to the analysis of organ weights in toxicology studies. *Statistics in Medicine, 3,* 85–91.

Siegel, S. & Castellan, N.J. (1988). *Non-parametric statistics for the Behavioural Sciences.* New York: McGraw-Hill.

Smith, H.F. (1957). Interpretation of adjusted treatment means and regressions in analysis of covariance. *Biometrics, 13,* 282–308.

Snedecor, G.W. (1934). *Analysis of Variance and Covariance.* Ames, Iowa: Iowa State University Press.

Snedecor, G.W. & Cochran, W.G. (1980). *Statistical Methods.* 7th edition. Ames, IA: Iowa State University.

Stevens, S.S. (1951). Mathematics, measurement and psychophysics. In S.S. Stevens (ed.), *Handbook of Experimental Psychology*. New York: Wiley.

Stigler, S.M. (1986). *The History of Statistics: The Measurement of Uncertainty Before 1900*. Cambridge, MA: Belknap Press.

Suppes, P. & Zinnes, J.L. (1963). Basic Measurement Theory. In R.D. Luce, R.R. Bush & E. Galanter (eds), *Handbook of Mathematical Psychology*. Volume 1. New York: Wiley.

Tan, W.Y. (1982). Sampling distributions and robustness of t, F and variance-ratio in two samples and ANOVA models with respect to departure from normality. *Communications in Statistics–Theory and Methods*, *11*, 486–511.

Taylor, M.J. & Innocenti, M.S. (1993). Why covariance? A rationale for using analysis of covariance procedures in randomized studies. *Journal of Early Intervention*, *17*, 455–466.

Toothaker, L.E. (1993). *Multiple Comparison Procedures*. Newbury Park, CA: Sage.

Townsend, J.T. & Ashby, F.G. (1984). Measurement scales and statistics: the misconception misconceived. *Psychological Bulletin*, *96*, 394–401.

Tukey, J.W. (1949). One degree of freedom for non-additivity. *Biometrics*, *5*, 232–249.

Tukey, J.W. (1955). Queries. *Biometrics*, *11*, 111–113.

Urquhart, N.S. (1982). Adjustment in covariance when one factor affects the covariate. *Biometrics*, *38*, 651–660.

Weisberg, S. (1985). *Applied Linear Regression*. 2nd edition. New York: Wiley.

Welkowitz, J., Ewen, R.B. & Cohen, J. (1991). *Introductory Statistics for the Behavioral Sciences*. 4th edition. New York: Academic Press.

Wilcox, R.R. (1995). ANOVA: a paradigm for low power and misleading measures of effect size. *Review of Educational Research*, *65*, 51–77.

Wilcox, R.R. (1997). *Introduction to Robust Estimation and Hypothesis Testing*. San Diego, CA: Academic Press.

Wilcox, R.R. (1998a). How many discoveries have been lost by ignoring modern statistical methods? *American Psychologist*, *53*, 300–314.

Wilcox, R.R. (1998b). The goals and strategies of robust methods. *British Journal of Mathematical and Statistical Psychology*, *51*, 1–39.

Wilkinson, G.N. & Rogers, C.E. (1973). Symbolic description of factorial models for analysis of variance. *Applied Statistics*, *22*, 392–399.

Winer, B.J. (1962). *Statistical Principles in Experimental Design*. New York: McGraw-Hill.

Winer, B.J. (1971). *Statistical Principles in Experimental Design*. 2nd edition. New York: McGraw-Hill.

Winer, B.J., Brown, D.R. & Michels, K.M. (1991). *Statistical Principles in Experimental Design*. 3rd edition. New York: McGraw-Hill.

Winer, B.J., Brown, D.R. & Michels, K.M. (1991). *Statistical Principles in Experimental Design*. 3rd edition. New York: McGraw-Hill.

Wonnacott, R.J. & Wonnacott, T.H. (1970). *Econometrics*. New York: Wiley.

Wright, D.B. (1998). People, materials and situations. In J. Nunn (ed.), *Laboratory Psychology*. Hove: Psychology Press.

Yule, G.U. (1907). On the theory of correlation for any number of variables treated by a new system of notation. *Proceedings of the Royal Society*, Series A, *79*, 182–193.

INDEX

Lightning Source UK Ltd.
Milton Keynes UK
UKOW04f0745210114

224943UK00002B/154/P